HONDA
& ACURA
PERFORMANCE HANDBOOK

Mike Ancas

MOTORBOOKS
INTERNATIONAL

This edition first published in1999 by Motorbooks International, an imprint of MBI Publishing Company, Galtier Plaza, Suite 200, 380 Jackson Street, St. Paul, MN 55101-3885 USA

© Mike Ancas, 1999

Motorbooks International titles are also available at discounts in bulk quantity for industrial or sales-promotional use. For details write to Special Sales Manager at Motorbooks International Wholesalers & Distributors, Galtier Plaza, Suite 200, 380 Jackson Street, St. Paul, MN 55101-3885 USA.

Information contained in these pages is true to the best of the author's knowledge. Always consult your owners and/or workshop manual, and take safety precautions when attempting to make any changes or repairs to your automobile. This book is not to be used as a repair manual. The buyer of the book must weigh the author's opinion along with his or her own common sense when making changes to an automobile. Neither the author nor the publisher assumes responsibility for any damages to automobiles as a result of modifications made based on information within these pages.

The tips contained in these pages were up-to-date as of the publication of this book. Much of the information contained in this book is intended for racing use only, and some performance modifications and engine transplants may not be legal for vehicles used on the street. Check with your local and state ordinances before undertaking any of these modifications.

The author and publisher are in no way associated with the American Honda Motor Company, Inc. The terms "Honda," "Acura," and model names such as "Civic," "Prelude," "Integra," etc., are used for reference purposes only.

Photos by Mike Ancas
Others credited individually

Comments/questions welcome at: MCA, PO Box 9, McDonald, PA 15057, Fax: (724) 926-0215, or visit the Honda/Acura Performance Handbook web page at www.hondabook.com.

Library of Congress Cataloging-in-Publication Data

Ancas, Mike
        Honda & Acura performance handbook / Mike Ancas.
        p. cm. — (MBI Publishing Company Power Pro series)
        Includes index.
        ISBN 0-7603-0669-9 (pbk. : alk. paper)
        1. Honda automobile—Motors—Modification. 2. Honda automobile—Performance. 3. Acura automobile—Motors—Modification. 4. Acura automobile—Performance. I. Title. II. Series.
        TL2.5.H58 A53 1999
        629.25'04—dc21

Printed in the United States of America

Contents

Sam Carson (shown spraying Jack and Cathy Wilson with a shaken can of soda) made a point of never taking life too seriously.

Dedication

This book is dedicated to the memory of Sam Carson,
who continues to enrich the lives of all who knew him.

Acknowledgments

I would like to thank my family, Brenda Ancas and Zac Tolan, as well as my parents, Ed and Millie Ancas. I also want to recognize the contribution of Dennis Witt, who wrote some of the text and put in countless hours serving as my technical editor. Two other people also provided both technical advice and friendship over the past several years: John Holzer and Gary Graf.

This book would also not have been possible without the support of my friends at *Grassroots Motorsports Magazine:* Tim and Margie Suddard, David Wallens, and J. G. Pasterjack.

Finally, over the past 10 years, I have received a great deal of support and advice from the following experts and companies: Javier Gutierrez of J. G. Engine Dynamics, Russ Collins of RC Engineering, Tim Marren of Marren Motorsports, Joe Pondo of MSD, Oscar Jackson of Jackson Racing, OPM, Carrera, Racetech, Stillen, Advanced Engine Management, Diamond Star Creative Group, Sway-a-way, as well as the helpful staff of American Honda Motor Company, Inc.

And I must not forget all the Honda/Acura fans who contributed photos of their cars for this project. You continue to give life to the Import Performance Movement.

Introduction

With the new millennium upon us, many people are searching for renewed meaning in their lives, and coming up empty. Science fiction writers of the past had depicted us living on the moon and exploring distant galaxies by the year 2000, but in reality, a large portion of our population still can't figure out how to set the clocks on their VCRs. But there is a lot we can be proud of. Even though we are not yet breaking bread with our Vulcan neighbors, from a scientific viewpoint the human race has done rather well.

Many of the advances we take for granted today can be traced back to the engineers from the 1960s. Their task was to figure out a way to blast our astronauts into space, and then bring them safely back to earth. As a result of this endeavor, current technology has progressed to the point where computer science is developing at the speed of light, the internet is changing the way many of us work and play, and physicists are struggling with mind-boggling issues such as the infinitely expanding universe.

So, what does all of this have to do with cars? Except for the fact that the internal combustion engine is still around, automobile technology has also evolved in terms of design, mechanics, and electronics. When the hop-up movement first took hold in the 1950s, cars were relatively simple creatures. The introduction of affordable aftermarket parts made it possible for the average guy to improve the performance of his American-made musclecar, and "working on the car" became a popular pastime.

In the 1960s, Detroit began to take notice of the public's increasing desire for performance and offered factory hopped-up versions of the more popular models: Corvette Sting Rays, Shelby Mustangs, Chevy Z28 Camaros, Plymouth Roadrunners, etc. Those who had a "need for speed" began flocking to the local drag strips for bragging rights about which of the "Big Three" built the better car.

But all that changed with the gas crisis of the 1970s. The economy also shifted, and many families found it increasingly difficult to make ends meet. As we became more environmentally and economically conscious, the cars we designed reflected this shift in priorities. Emission controls choked the horsepower from even the high performance models. The

The 1992–1995 Civic is one of the most popular bodies to choose for a hop-up project. This hatchback once lived the life of a typical street car, but now it is a purpose-built, fire-breathing, 10-second drag car—one of the many cars that now come out of the shop that Javier Gutierrez founded 10 years ago: J. G. Engine Dynamics. *Turbo Magazine*

outlandish was gradually replaced by the practical, speed and excitement gave way to sensibility and efficiency. This was the environment in which Honda was born.

The 1980s, however, saw a different kind of movement take place. Companies like IBM and Macintosh were making computer technology available to the general public. As the demand for more efficient computers grew, technology began to advance exponentially. The auto industry had already been using computers and robots for some time, and was in a position to incorporate new technological breakthroughs to help design cars more quickly, and bring them to production in a more timely manner.

The motto of the 1990s could easily have been: "Better and Faster." Our lives consisted of cellular phones, FAX machines, Fed-Ex, e-mail, gigabytes, and nanoseconds. We put increasing emphasis on the value of our time and the efficiency of our machines. The result was an overall attitude of impatience. Some people even experienced anxiety waiting for the light to come on after they had thrown the switch.

This lack of tolerance for inefficiency, however, wasn't all bad. Japanese auto companies had long adopted a doctrine of open-minded productivity, and were in position to embrace this "better and faster" philosophy.

The first shot in the import performance movement was fired by Honda in 1984 when it introduced the CRX. The once "practical" Civic of the 1970s had evolved into a competent sports car. By the time the hopped-up CRX Si hit showrooms in 1985, people like Oscar Jackson (Jackson Racing) and Doug Peterson (Comptech) were already finding ways to make Hondas go faster and handle better.

Comptech and Honda's efforts in research and development benefit the average driver in ways that are often too subtle to detect. Engine design and testing, on the other hand, is usually more in the forefront. Their combined efforts have resulted in many world championship race cars. *Comptech*

Form versus Function

In the beginning, when it came to hopping up a Honda or Acura, traditionally the first thing the car owner needed to resolve was the dichotomy of form versus function. In the past, form was often diametrically opposed to function, and the car owner had to choose one over the other based on the intended use of the vehicle. Would the goal be good looks, or would it be performance? One of the first companies to resolve this dilemma was Mugen; however, the solution came at a price—a very high price that was out of reach for many Honda and Integra owners. But thankfully, the import movement of the 1990s grew so large and created so much competition among aftermarket parts manufacturers that car owners now have many choices when it comes to selecting affordable performance parts that possess both function as well as form.

But the "form versus function" conflict exists on yet another level, which can be exemplified when considering what kind of wheels and tires to buy for your car. 19-inch wheels are not meant for racing, but 13-inch rims are no longer cool. They don't fill up the fender wells, unless you lower the car to the point where you can't drive it anywhere without ripping the exhaust system off. But as you increase rim diameter and decrease tire section height, you reduce the size of the air chamber, which decreases load capacity often resulting in diminished handling (see chapter 4). So how do you choose?

First decide whether your goal is "form" or "function." If you can't make up your mind, buy two sets of rims, one for racing and one for show.

Unfortunately the form versus function debate will persist even after you resolve the wheel and tire dilemma. The sad fact is that race cars don't make good street cars. They are too stiff, don't always idle well, get poor gas mileage, and have few creature

Form or function? Street, race, or dual duty? The 1985 Honda CRX Si on the right is a full race machine, while the 1988 Honda C-Rex on the left is an excellent example of a street car that can perform dual duty as a weekend autocrosser/drag racer and a weekday driver.

comforts. On the other hand, great street cars don't usually make good race cars. They are too heavy, and they have softer suspensions and stereo systems. An exception to this rule is the new "street touring" classes adopted by the Sports Car Club of America (SCCA) in 1998. They allow many of today's popular hopped-up imports a chance to be competitive in Solo II autocross without sacrificing streetability.

Many years ago, my now ex-girlfriend laughed at me when I told her that, despite my mistakes of the past, this time I really would build a car that could be a competitive race car, yet remain fun and practical to drive on the street. "Sure," she said, "You're going to turn another perfectly nice car into an overpowered monster with the suspension characteristics of a lawn tractor." (So what's her point?) Shortly afterwards, she spent both road time and track time in the car, and emerged with the shocked declaration that, from her point of view, I had actually met my goal: a car that is a terror on the track, but not on the way to the grocery store. Having bonded with the car, she then proceeded to name the CRX "Fred," although I was leaning towards "The Mutilator."

I must confess that, even with the best intentions, many of us go too far and build cars that end up turning into race-only vehicles. It must be a male hormone thing. But by exercising some margin of restraint, a Honda or Acura can be built to serve both purposes very well. Learning from the mistakes and successes recounted in this book, you should be able to build an awesome street car capable of blowing the doors off of many other cars on the road.

But to return to the fundamental dilemma, before undertaking any type of performance improvement project, a car owner really needs to make a decision as to whether or not the priority will be based on form or function.

Once a decision is made, this book will provide some guidance to help you realize your goals. Most chapters cover form as well as function. Street racers will be able to take advantage of the latest good looking "go fast" and handling modifications, while pure

Examples of Acura form versus function: A third generation Acura Integra for the street, contrasted with Jerry Lustig's GT3 third generation Acura Integra for the track.

Form meets function in both the Honda S2000 and Acura NSX (no hop-up needed). The Honda S2000 couples a 245-horsepower engine with precise handling all wrapped up in this beautiful package. The Acura NSX is a factory race car that feels as comfortable on the track as it does driving to the track. This 1999 Alex Zanardi Edition is slightly lowered, has a stiffer suspension, and is capable of 290 horsepower. Although the Honda S2000 is 300 pounds lighter, it is still left in the dust by the NSX, due to the much higher torque of the Acura V-6 powerplant. *American Honda Motor Company, Inc.*

racers will be able to access practical information to help their cars become more competitive.

This book assumes that anyone planning performance improvements to their car already has a workshop manual. This book is in no way intended to replace or supersede any information in a Honda or Acura workshop or owners manual. For that reason, it is devoid of the boring charts and schematics that often fill the pages of typical aftermarket performance handbooks. Exploded views of your car's suspension or engine are already in a typical workshop manual.

Don't look for discussions about highly technical information,

or demonstrations of any internal engine modification procedures, such as cylinder honing or three-angle valve grinding. Attempting to machine a cylinder head by yourself is a waste of both time and money. You could easily end up ruining an expensive head. Engine rebuilding and head porting should be left to the experts, and there are many competent Honda and Acura specialists out there. In any event, 99.9 percent of the people who buy this book don't have the equipment to do this type of job properly, and if you are the 0.1 percent of the people who do, then you don't really need the book.

You will find this book concentrates more on what the average weekend mechanic can do to improve the performance of his or her car. Countless aftermarket parts are discussed, and many do-it-yourself projects are reviewed. The first step in any project, however, is setting priorities, such as "form" versus "function." Chapter 1 will help you make some preliminary decisions and get you started on your way to a great experience in the realm of Honda and Acura performance. The rest of the book won't help anyone with their journey to achieve meaning in the new millennium, but it could be a fun diversion along the way.

Chapter 1

So You Want to Hop Up Your Honda?

Welcome to the fun world of high-performance Hondas! By following the suggestions in the subsequent chapters, you should be able to transform your Honda or Acura into a vehicle that will give you so much pleasure and pride that you wouldn't want to trade it for anything except maybe a night out with a supermodel. Seriously, creating a hot Civic, CRX, Accord, Prelude, or Acura is a rather simple process. Often, the end result is so rewarding, that the bond you form with your car will rival that blind dedication you see in British car owners, with two big differences: Your hopped-up Honda will be able to blow the doors off of those British cars, and it will start when you turn the key.

Examples of two of the most popular Hondas typically chosen for hop-up projects: Woody Donnell's 1992 Honda Civic DX (foreground) and Rudy Zierden's 1988 Honda CRX (background). Both cars are lowered, fitted with custom wheels, and contain many of the modifications discussed in this book.

Even some of the "super cars" (as nice as they are to look at) can't make that same claim. It causes one to wonder why a person would want a car that seems to spend more time in the shop than it does on the road. Their parts cost a fortune, as does the auto insurance, not to mention the initial purchase price. But with a hopped-up Honda, an enthusiast gets remarkable reliability and great performance, all at an affordable price.

Lesson 1: Throw This Book Away and Buy a Honda Someone Else Has Built

Few things in life are as rewarding as turning the key and driving down the road in your newly completed Honda project car. After all, it was your sweat, blood, time, and money. The only thing more rewarding is to buy someone else's completed project!

You've seen the ads: *"1988 Honda CRX. Excellent condition. Lowered, headers, trick intake, Mon-*

Civics are not the only cars that are popular with the high performance Honda crowd. Pictured are fifth generation Accords: a two-door coupe (foreground) and a four-door sedan (background).

ster throttle body, limited-slip, ported and polished head, custom exhaust, Momo steering wheel, Recaro seats, 17-inch custom wheels with new low profile Yokohamas. Spare engine and tranny. Over $12,000 invested. Sacrifice for $4,700."

No, you didn't build it yourself. Yes, it's probably in less than perfect shape and may need some minor work, but *you* couldn't build one for less money. So what about that wonderful feeling of accomplishment you won't get to

Depending on your budget, a third generation Acura Integra may be the best choice for a project car because it already possesses a powerful 1.8-liter engine that will respond well to modification.

experience? I don't know about you, but I've been able to get over that. Add a few customizing touches, and you will soon forget that someone else did all of the work and spent all the money.

After you own the car for a few years, it will begin to feel like it's part of the family. And the best part is that if you get sick of it in the future, you can always sell it without taking a big loss.

This rust-free, lowered, supercharged 1988 CRX Si was purchased for under $5,000.

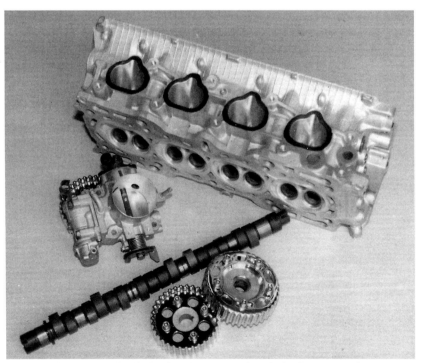

A polished and ported cylinder head, monster throttle body, cam and adjustable sprockets will eat up a significant portion of your budget, but they can add the power you need to be competitive. *J.G Engine Dynamics*

Lesson 2: Be Prepared to Spend Money on Your Car That You'll Never Get Back

If you insist on hopping up the car you already have, then you must be willing to accept this fact. Now don't take this wrong; the process may be worth the price you pay. Even with all of the free parts I have managed to scam as part of being an "author," I have over $10,000 of my own money into each of my two favorite Hondas. What could I get if I ever wanted to sell them? Probably less than $6,000 each. Of course that won't happen, since my buddy and I plan on being buried in the cars, although our wives may have something to say about that.

But most of you know what I am talking about. That's why we choose to take a financial loss and put money in the cars that we can never get back out. This process forms a bond between the car and owner that nonenthusiasts can't understand. It also forms a bond between you and your Master-Card! So if you choose to take this path, hold on to this book. It can help you get the most for the money you spend on performance improvements.

Lesson 3: Start with the Right Car

Before you begin a project, the first step is to decide what you want to do with the car. *Then* you can decide on the car you want. The biggest mistake most people make is to start with the wrong car. Whether intended for the street or the strip, the wrong car will add many unnecessary hours of labor and expenditures to your project. Know where the project is going, and buy the right car. If an engine swap is one of the goals, keep in mind that certain Honda or Integra models easily accept upgraded engine transplants, while others don't.

Whether you hope to transform your car into a weekend warrior or a serious racer, mistakes can be avoided at this early stage. Many entry-level racers tend to make modifications on their cars before they read the rules of the class in which they wish to compete. The most common error is the addition of a performance camshaft. This one change to original specs could cause your car to be placed in a class with fully-prepared race cars.

Another common mistake is to buy bigger and wider wheels. Most SCCA stock classes restrict wheel size to the factory diameter and width. Although somewhat easier to reverse than mistake No. 1 (upgrading your camshaft), wider wheels will often bump you out of a "stock" class, where most beginners will find the best chance of winning.

Lesson 4: Establish a Budget for Your Money and Time

When you start out to build the project car of your dreams, you should set a budget. Even if money is no object, a budget can be extremely helpful. A budget sets limits, and limits will help you to prioritize the way your money will be spent, based on the upgrades that are most important to you. Even large, multibillion dollar corporations have budgets to help keep the companies focused on their goals. Most of us are dealing with a limited amount of time and money, so building a project car often involves compromise.

Compromise No. 1: Money

Many auto enthusiasts make the mistake of buying their car, and immediately purchasing a cool set of rims, a slick-looking rear wing, and installing a killer stereo. A few months later, as their project car starts to come together, they decide to do some amateur racing. That cool wing may then become a wasted expense, and will likely result in exclusion from the stock or entry-level classes. How often do you see nearly brand new parts being sacrificed by people who did not take the time to plan out their project? If you plan your project well, their loss can be your gain. It's important to have the overall picture in place before you go out and buy film.

Compromise No. 2: Time

Besides finances, the other thing that needs to be budgeted is your time. In a perfect world, you could wake up in the morning, go out to the garage, and work on your car all day. But, unfortunately, most people have to go to work. Then there are friend and family responsibilities, and all of the other time constraints that come with life in the twenty-first century. Don't underestimate the importance of setting a time budget. Personal relationships are often put into some degree of jeopardy when people take on an automotive project. Fear not. There are ways to avoid these potential problems.

First, limit the time you work on your car when your spouse is home. If you have children, try to involve them in your project. Most important, though, empower your significant other. Give her or him the power to decide, for example, how long you will work on your car on a given day. Let the person know that she or he is more important to you than your car. Explain what aspect of the project you'll be working on today, with an estimate of the time it will take. Usually you will be able to find an appropriate stopping point and get cleaned up in about 30 minutes from the time you're asked to come back into the house.

From a completely different point of view, time management is important when it comes to deciding on the amount of time that you want to spend on specific phases of your project. Spending five hours wrestling with the installa-

As discussed in Lesson 2, many Honda/Acura owners will put money into a car that may never be recovered upon resale. All of the performance improvements and body modifications that have been done to this Del Sol have not added substantially to its resale value. *Mike Louie*

tion of an exhaust system, for example, may not be worth the $100 you could spend to have it installed at a muffler shop in 45 minutes.

Some people from the East Coast actually have towed their vehicles across the country to places like J. G. Engine Dynamics in California, just to get them tuned properly. It appears that this is time and money well spent. That's because hours and hours on a dyno will do no good unless you know what to do with the information you are receiving. That's the mistake I made with the EFI project car (see chapter 10), and if I could do it over again, that puppy would be on the doorstep of J. G. tomorrow. But isn't this sacrificing all of the valuable knowledge that could be gained by doing a project by yourself? Absolutely, and if this is one of your priorities, then go for it. If not, you need to decide which aspects of your project you want to do yourself, and which you should assign to an expert.

A Sample Budget

A budget can be a very personalized thing, but all budgets should take into consideration the basic components of your car. To get started, you should first take a look at all of the chapters in this book and decide what your car needs—based on exactly what you want to do with your Honda or Acura. Suspension, engine, intake, exhaust, ignition, and appearance should all be listed as categories in your budget. Even if you are not anal retentive, making a list can be very helpful, especially if you have a computer. Start by listing these categories, then add subcategories based on the sections in each chapter. For example, under "Suspension," you should have springs, shocks, sway bars, wheels, and tires. Even if you already have a nice set of wheels, enter a "$0" on the line next to "wheels." Under "shocks and struts," however, you may want to upgrade to an adjustable Tokico or Koni system, so about $500 should be budgeted.

This itemization will also serve another purpose. If you are using a computer program that can calculate your expenditures, you will have a running total of what you've spent on your car. This will help keep your head out of the clouds and your feet on the ground, protecting you from spending more money on the car than what it's worth. It will also help you to keep track of exactly what you have done, essentially giving you a readout of your car's modifications.

Finally, the budget could help with your insurance claim if your car were stolen. Receipts for both aftermarket parts and labor should be kept in a folder accompanying the hard copy of your budget. Put a "before" photo of your car in the folder. Those who take the time to compile this information will be glad they did when their project is completed, as it will serve as a tribute to the time, effort, and money that went into their Honda. And if the day ever comes that you decide to sell your baby, prospective buyers will recognize that you are a detail-oriented person who likely took good care of his car. It will prove, for example, that there actually is a limited-slip installed in the transaxle, or that the engine really was completely rebuilt a year ago, or that the timing belt was just replaced at 60,000 miles—all claims often made, but rarely substantiated.

Lesson 5: Read the Whole Book

Although the performance parts and modifications outlined in this book have been proven to work, your results may vary. Your particular car, depending on its age, engine size and efficiency, gearbox, and a variety of other variables, may respond differently to performance modifications described in this book. Bear in mind that the addition of a single performance component may not yield the targeted performance improvement. There can be many reasons for this, but often it's that all the components in a system (for example, the intake, exhaust, and

One solution for a budget-conscious racer is to buy a used Formula Ford Formula Vee, and *tow* it with your Honda. This beat-up 1984 Civic DX towed an 1,100 pound Formula Vee (pictured) across the country and back several times, even with a bad clutch.

combustion) need to be properly matched. For example, horsepower gains often only occur when the individual performance parts in a system complement each other.

Because Hondas and Acuras are such great cars to start with, sometimes you can do more harm than good. The Honda engineers have already designed the engine components to be both efficient and powerful. But you would think that by adding a hot camshaft, you could increase performance, and for the most part, you would be right. But this is more of an absolute for older models. A pair of Honda engineers recently decided to put together a racing effort, and started with the wonderful 1.6-liter VTEC (variable valve timing and lift electronic control) engine to power their late-model Civic hatchback. After trying two different aftermarket camshafts, they found that the best performance was achieved with the stock camshaft.

A final thought: If a particular type of performance part is not mentioned in this book, it's probably because it doesn't work. Don't listen to the claims made by some companies that boast of horsepower increases that seem too good to be true. They probably aren't. Even "dyno-tested" claims can't always be trusted. Under the right conditions, using an engine dyno, someone could probably show that adding dirt to your engine will increase power. The real test involves putting the engine in the car and driving it over a period of time. Only then will a chassis dyno plus some serious track time tell you if a product passes muster.

All of the parts discussed in this book have been dyno tested or road tested. Be skeptical of claims made by some manufacturers. There is no bolt-on $50 part that can increase horsepower by 5 to 10 percent, unless it's a used air velocity intake.

So the best advice is to read this entire book before you get on the phone to start ordering parts. You could save yourself a lot of time and money.

Lesson 6: Keep Up with Current Product Information

Unfortunately, this book can only provide information based on technology that was current as of 1999. While it is likely that what is contained within these chapters will remain valid for many years to come, there will be new developments in motorsport technology. An updated web page (www.hondabook.com) will provide news and advice for Honda/Acura tuners, with information on new performance products and ongoing tricks.

Additionally, two magazines are essential additions to any Honda nut's library. *Grassroots Motorsports Magazine* has been covering Hondas and Acuras since the mid-1980s. From the latest project cars to tech tips, *GRM* is one magazine that any Honda tuner will enjoy. If speed is your goal, *Turbo Magazine* will take your breath away with some of the coolest Japanese cars on the planet. Along with helpful how-to tips, *Turbo* gives no-nonsense advise on how to improve Honda and Acura performance.

If you enjoy this book, then these two magazines will blow you away. To get a free sample, or to subscribe to *Grassroots Motorsports Magazine*, go to www.grmotorsports.com, or call (904) 673-4148 and say, "Send me a free issue." For *Turbo* subscriptions, you can log on to www.turbomagazine.com, or call (800) 94-TURBO.

Chapter 2

Honda History:
From the 600 to the 2000

In the beginning, there were cars, and then there were Hondas. Motorcycles, that is. Honda was a relative latecomer to the automobile arena, but in the 1960s, plans were put into motion that would change the car industry forever. After years of success in motorcycle racing, Soichiro Honda and his engineers set out to design an engine for a Formula 1 car. Mounted in a Cooper-Climax chassis, that first Honda racing engine utilized 12 carburetors to feed 12 cylinders, each of which displaced 125 cc. Not your typical 1,500-cc design! Although this initial effort was not entirely successful, it was the spark that ignited plans for vehicles with four wheels instead of two.

Soichiro Honda assembled a team of engineers who had a profound impact on both Detroit and the American consumer. Nowadays, it's hard to imagine a world without Hondas and Acuras, but initially, nearly everyone believed that Honda's efforts would never amount to much more than building novelty vehicles. When the first Honda automobile hit the U.S. shores in 1970, the American manufacturers did not feel that the smaller Japanese cars would ever be a threat to their market. But in the meantime, Honda began to listen, learn, and quickly respond to what the American car buyer wanted in a vehicle. In fact, Honda seemed to know what Americans wanted before *we* knew. As the quality began to improve, auto magazines began to take notice. The U.S. auto consumer had never been exposed to the high quality, reliability, and economy that Honda was offering.

But those first Hondas were ugly (or cute, depending on your perspective) and far too small to gain the loyalty of the American buyer. Sure, they were extremely reliable and cost efficient, but there was one big problem that couldn't be overlooked. They were slow. And few really cared about economy back then, when the price of gasoline was as low as 30 cents per gallon. All that changed with the energy crisis of the 1970s.

When the U.S. manufacturers began to notice that people were starting to buy Hondas, their response was too little, too late. The Ford Pinto, Chevy Vega, and AMC Gremlin would go down in history as cheap and unreliable vehicles. Meanwhile, Honda had introduced the CVCC engine in a more esthetically pleasing design, and the Civic was born.

Still, the biggest difference between Hondas and the U.S. manufacturers was not in *what* they produced, but in *how* it was

The U.S. market's first glimpse of a Honda automobile came in the form of the Z600 coupe.

produced. From the U.S. point of view, it appeared that Honda was treating its workers better than its American counterparts were treating theirs, and this caused some dissension in the "Big Three's" rank and file. The United States began to hear strange stories about Japanese auto workers who loved their jobs, and how management loved them. Japanese workers and managers did morning exercises in a large group before starting their day's work. Management meetings included assembly plant workers. Managers encouraged their workers to make suggestions on how to improve operations and design. And management listened.

The Honda Motor Company, along with many other Japanese corporations, approached business in a way that was philosophically different than companies in the West. Long-standing Eastern cultural and religious traditions formed the basis for the Japanese business philosophy. This philosophy taught, among other things, that all people and creatures should be respected. Japanese companies, like Honda, treated their workers with respect, allowing them to feel more involved. The result was obvious: increased productivity.

The final component that allowed Honda to adapt so well to the U.S. market was that it listened to the American consumer. Often, Honda made changes to its automobiles in midyear, reflecting the opinions of both the U.S. buyer and Japanese assembly workers. Conversely, the American automotive bureaucracy was so big and unresponsive that it traditionally took years for a simple idea to filter up through the many levels of management. Of course, now the Chrysler Corporation has gained recognition for getting a car from the drawing board to the assembly line in record time, but

Nearly 30 years later, in the summer of 1999, Honda came full circle, bringing the S2000 to U.S. shores. *American Honda Motor Company, Inc.*

Although Honda was not successful in its initial F1 effort, that would all change in the 1980s. Comptech and Honda developed this rocket, which turned out to be a real winner. *Comptech*

with little change made to the initial fresh design.

In the past, a good-looking prototype (picture a Ferrari) would go through so many changes as it passed from one conservative committee to another, it would end up looking like a Corvair. Honda's management philosophy was quick to respond to change. This outlook both rewarded and encouraged new ideas.

Still, in the late 1970s, Honda was not yet a big threat to the industry, except when it came to the overseas market. Europe began to embrace the little Hondas, and U.S. exports began to slow. Then, Honda delivered the blow that would forever change the face of the auto industry. Honda unveiled the Accord in the United States in 1977. Immediately, demand far exceeded supply. Americans who wanted to buy an Accord were sometimes faced with a waiting list of up to a year. The Accords were good looking, economical, roomier, and for the first time, quicker than most of the compact U.S. cars. The press bestowed "best car" honors on the Accord and the tradition continues today.

Soon thereafter, the Japanese business philosophy swept across the Pacific and reached American shores. Cars that Ford, Chrysler, and GM produced began to reflect a high degree of quality, and today are designed to last. But the credit for these changes (which came to fruition in the late 1980s) rests squarely on the management model created by companies like Honda during the 1970s. Honda became the standard by which all other cars would be judged. "Made in Japan" no longer means "cheap imitation."

The First Honda Motorcars

The world had its first glimpse of Honda's intentions to seriously enter the automotive market at the 1962 Tokyo Motor Show. It would also be a hint that Honda was interested in performance, and these first cars were designed to compete with Datsun and British Leyland in the growing Japanese sports car market. Yes, the first Honda motorcar was a sports car. Fed by four carburetors, the S-500 cranked out 44 horsepower at 8,000 rpm.

Although never officially imported into the United States, the Honda "S" models (S-500, S-600, and S-800) were serious cars with potent, high-revving engines. Powered by a double overhead cam, four-stroke motorcycle engine, the chain-driven, rear-wheel-drive two-seater S cars quickly became favorites of Japanese sports car enthusiasts.

Over the next few years, the engines grew to 606 cc (producing 57 horsepower) in 1964, and then to 791 cc in 1966 (70 horsepower). Production continued through 1971, and by then the S car had undergone drastic and revolutionary changes. A live axle with coil-over shocks, trailing arms, and a Panhard rod replaced earlier model's independent rear suspension. Furthermore, the 70-horse-power engine was now able to propel the super-light 1,600-pound chassis to 60 miles per hour in just over 13 seconds.

Although nearly 27,000 S cars were produced from 1963 through 1971, they remained rare in the United States, occasionally brought home by soldiers who discovered these treasures while stationed overseas. The popularity

This modified S600 has had several owners over the years. At the time this photo was taken, the car was being raced by Pat and Ed Bochenek of Ohio, who had it in their family for many years. They sold it to Shigeri Honda in the late 1980s, but bought it back in 1990. It now has a new owner and resides in Texas.

This near-mint example of a Z-600 coupe belongs to David Scatena, who uses it as a daily driver.

of the S cars in Japan and Europe gave Honda high expectations as it set its sights on the United States.

The Honda 600 (1971–1972)

Not to be confused with the rare and beautiful S-600, the Z-600 Coupe and N-600 Sedan were the first Hondas officially imported into the United States. They were so small and slow, they should have come equipped with a big wind-up key on the rear hatch. At some point, every Honda nut should come face to face with a 600—and try to keep a straight face. That said, the 600 marked the first invasion of Hondas into the United States, and what Honda learned over the next decade would be used to grab a major portion of the U.S. automotive market.

Powered by a 598-cc, two-cylinder, four-stroke, air-cooled motorcycle engine, the 600 was able to squeak out a whopping 36 horsepower, with 0–60 times in minutes, not seconds. Interior space, however, gave the American buyer a glimpse of what was to come. Despite a tiny exterior, the interior was spacious! The back seats could even fit two adults without much cramping. Fuel economy was over 30 miles per gallon, but a tiny 6-gallon gas tank restricted cruising range. The engine compartment revealed a tiny, single carburetor (which was often mistaken for a fuel filter), headers, and a highly restrictive air cleaner system. With all of its faults, however, the 600 Sedan and Coupe remain special vehicles. There are many 600-based clubs on the internet. Parts are not as difficult to find as one may think. There are even hop-up kits and complete engines available, which can nearly double horsepower. In a 1,300-pound car, 65 horsepower transforms the "cute" little 600 into a pocket rocket.

Under the hood of David Scatena's Z-600 lies a 598-cc two-cylinder engine (note the carburetor). But don't let the silly looks fool you. This is one durable engine. I recently purchased a Honda Z-600 for restoration where the fuel tank had rusted internally, contaminating the entire fuel delivery system. Even though it had been sitting for years, after one spray of Gumout into the carb, that sucker fired right up.

The Honda Civic (1973–1979)

In 1973, the first *real* Honda hit the shores of the United States. Suggesting that the Japanese design engineers finally decided to finish the thought they started above, an actual rear end was added to the tiny Z-600, and it was given a real engine. Although the 600 and the new Civic hatchback clearly looked as if they came from the same family, they were actually extremely different automobiles. The primary difference between the Z-600 and the Civic was in the engineering. From top to bottom, the Civic was a small car, rather than a big motorcycle. With the introduction of the Civic, Honda made a firm statement that it was going into the business of building automobiles.

The first generation Civic had another impact on the automobile market, in that it was engineered differently from the automobiles Americans had come to expect. The Civic brought to America an overall difference in quality, originating in the inherent sense of cultural pride that the Japanese factory workers put into their product.

The first engine design was a 1,170-cc, four-cylinder, single overhead-cam (SOHC) design that was to serve as the prototype for many Honda engines. For the first time in a Honda, the camshaft was driven by a timing belt that was connected to the crankshaft. The timing belt, as it would in future Honda engines, performed additional duties. In the early Civics, it drove an oil pump, while the other end of the camshaft also turned the distributor.

Other innovations were used in later applications as they evolved. The 1973 Civic was first to utilize a transmission design that would constantly undergo improvements, and still remain virtually the same over the years. The outer aluminum housing contained

Adam Malley successfully races his first generation Civic in SCCA's H Production class. He routinely thrashes 1960s British roadsters.

both a transmission and a differential. Gears were lubricated with common engine oil, rather than heavier gear fluid. Both the engine and transmission were rotated at a 90-degree angle, perpendicular to a conventional rear-wheel design, and were placed transversely between the front wheels. The other unique feature of this powerplant was the universal joints that transferred rotational torque to the front wheels. This constant velocity (or "CV") joint allowed consistent operation despite the movement of the front suspension.

This first Civic underwent so many changes in so little time that parts from cars built within the same year often do not interchange. The biggest change during this early period occurred in 1975, when the CVCC engine was introduced. CVCC stands for "Compound Vortex Controlled Combustion." This engine utilized a small extra prechamber, where a richer air/fuel mixture was ignited. This flame then spread to a main chamber, where

the mixture was rather lean and could not easily be ignited by just a simple spark. By using such a lean mix in the main combustion chamber, emissions were greatly reduced, and gas mileage was improved. This design required a special three-barrel carburetor that proved to be a weak link in most of the non–fuel-injected Hondas through 1987. The 1975 CVCC engine was nearly 1.5 liters, but could only manage a little over 50 horsepower.

The other engine offered through 1979 was referred to as the 1200 (1,237 cc) and was fitted with a two-barrel carb feeding a non-CVCC head. By the end of its first generation, the 1979 Civic hardly resembled the original 1973 version (that is, underneath the body). For this reason, it is probably a good idea to stay away from this generation when selecting your project car.

Overall, this first Civic was generally very reliable and clearly built to last. But the United States was not yet ready for this type of

car, and little notice was taken by the American public. Only the minority counterculture (the same people as the VW Bug crowd) seemed to embrace it. But all this was about to change.

The Honda Accord (1977–1981)

In 1977, the world stopped making fun of the Honda Motorcars, and started lining up in the showrooms to purchase the new Accord. Most of the time, they had to go home empty-handed, with only a promise that when another shipment arrived, they would be called in the order in which their name appeared on the massive waiting list. Car lovers from around the world hailed the Accord, with its bigger engine and sporty exterior, as one of the best-built automobiles of 1977. It was introduced as a hatchback, with a four-door version following in 1979. From that point on, GM, Ford, and Chrysler knew that they had to do something to compete with this new threat. The Honda seemed to have snuck up on them. That's because they weren't paying attention in the first place, and although they began to take Honda, Toyota, and Mazda seriously in the late 1970s, it was "too little, too late." The cocky attitude of the Big Three would be their downfall in the 1980s. Chrysler barely survived. This arrogance allowed Honda to steal a huge piece of the U.S. market that it would never concede.

Looking back, the first generation Accord seemed more like a fancy Civic than what it would become: Honda's flagship automobile. Eventually fitted with a 1,751-cc version of the CVCC engine, the 1981 Accord didn't exactly tear up the street, managing only about 70 horsepower. But perhaps one of the most memorable impacts that the Accord made on the market was that it was offered fully loaded. In the past, auto manufacturers seemed to charge extra for everything from side mirrors to a gearshift knob. The Accord, on the other hand, was offered as one of the first affordable cars to come standard with all of the good stuff already included.

The Honda Prelude (1979–1982)

Although it is a rather rare vehicle today, the first generation Prelude did not stand out at the time of its introduction, since it was overshadowed by the Accord's popularity. But Honda didn't seem to care that the Prelude was not attracting attention in the showrooms. Despite sluggish sales through the end of the century, Honda still continues to use the Prelude to showcase their new technology.

Honda used the original Prelude to help launch the second generation Civic. The two cars shared much of the same mechanics. In Honda's first attempt at building a sports coupe, the Prelude was fitted with the Accord's 1,751-cc engine and a rear sway bar. Nevertheless, the Prelude did not impress the enthusiasts, since acceleration still did not crack the 11-second barrier!

The Second Generation Honda Civic (1980–1983)

The second generation Civic continued to improve on the reliable foundation that was started in 1973. From a distance, the eye could see few changes between 1979 and 1980, but the new Civic grew in length, width, and sophistication. Besides the hatchback, a nice-looking four-door sedan was offered, along with a station wagon! Honda was beginning to make an impact in the U.S. auto market, and this generation Civic (borrowing from the refinement of

After rust began to claim too much of the body, this first generation Accord lived out the remainder of its life as an autocross vehicle.

the Accord) was clearly targeted to steal customers from the Big Three.

Engines began to grow in both size and horsepower. Nevertheless, the newly redesigned 1.5-liter could still only manage 0–60 times of 12 seconds. A new, five-speed transmission available in the GL model helped overall performance.

Looking back, the Civic made remarkable progress during its first 11 model years. Now, however, performance parts are scarce, and technology has long since left this era in the dust. Modifying a 1973–1983 Civic can prove to be a frustrating endeavor indeed, but some have successfully done it. I suggest that if you have an undying love for these early Civics or S-series coupes, you would be better off buying one from someone who has already seen the project to its fruition. You will save a lot of money and time.

The Second Generation Accord (1982–1985)

The goal of this new generation of Accord was refinement. For the first time, Honda aimed to build an automobile that would appeal to the midsize car buyer.

The usually mild-mannered first/second generation Civics take on a whole new personality when modified for competition.

Looks alone will tell you that this model was the one that would set the standard for all future Accord generations. Although smaller than today's Civics, the four-door Accord seemed large to the typical Honda lover. Honda, continuing to generate money for the company with the award-winning Accord and universal appeal of the Civic, was able to fund research for new projects. Much of the money went into a continuing quality improvement program that always seemed to keep the Accord one step ahead of the competition. This second generation effort exemplified this commitment, as the car was given nearly a complete overhaul.

The Third Generation Accord (1986–1989)

Clearly, the third generation Accord was the most street-worthy car Honda had introduced to date. The 1986 Accord was an instant hit with the automotive public. This car was a little tighter, the ride was much smoother, and the interior looked more like a fine European luxury car. Using the same suspension as the 1984–1987 Prelude, handling was also improved despite a heavier body. To make up for the weight gain, Honda fitted the Accord with a slightly larger 2.0-liter engine that was rated at 110 horsepower. As usual, the press hailed this car as reliable, classy, and a "best buy." The third generation Accord, as well as the 2G Prelude, formed the foundation for the much-improved fourth generation Accord that would carry Honda into the last decade of the twentieth century.

The Third Generation Honda Civic Hatchback and First Generation Civic/CRX 1.5, and CRX HF (1984–1987)

When the Volkswagen introduced the GTI a year earlier, the public knew that Honda wouldn't be far behind. Although the first generation GTI is a good car, it does not compare to the engineering that went into these Hondas. The third generation Civic and first generation CRX came with a newly redesigned 1,500-cc engine coupled with an excellent suspension, clearly making the 1984–1987 Civic a better choice.

The interior of the new Civic was both comfortable and practical, as opposed to the GTI, which was cheap and somewhat tacky. The seats looked comfortable enough, but the GTI side support cushioning was hard as a rock and would dig into your side as you entered and exited the vehicle. Not

so with the third generation Civics. Another big difference was the handling. Many VW owners will rave about how well the GTI handles, but back before the GTI Golf was born, the GTI Rabbits could not compare to the precision and responsiveness offered by both versions of the Civic. With torsion bars up front and a coil-over shock design for the rear, the rack and pinion steering made the car feel as if you were driving a more expensive European car. The big problem with this generation Civic was that they were prone to rust. And when they rusted, unibody rigidity became compromised.

A fuel saver version of the CRX was also produced from 1985 to 1987. The CRX HF (high fuel) had the best gas mileage to date of all production vehicles, but was capable of only 58 horsepower. These bodies are still in demand for use in project cars, because they weighed in at just over 1,700 pounds. That was 80 pounds less than the 1984 Civic 1500, and 150 pounds less than the DX hatchback, which came with a five-speed.

Also offered in the 1984–1987 Civics was a 1,300-cc engine that produced 60 horsepower. The Civics came with four-speed trannies, and surprisingly, there is still some demand (primarily with Sports Car Club of America [SCCA] racers) for these smaller-engined Hondas. They are not popular choices for transplantation, however. Their slightly domed pistons have been put in the 1.5-liter block in an attempt to increase compression. But don't waste your time, as the 1.3-liter pistons have one less ring per piston, and oil seems to find a way to sneak by unless your cylinder honing is meticulous.

The weak link in the 1984–1987 non-Si Hondas were their carburetors, which were unreliable and often ran too lean. The

Mike Berrington's 1984 ITB CRX has been modified to SCCA IT specs (stiff suspension, roll cage, Weber carb, etc.). His rush hour takes place on weekends, and is usually spent by working his way through a pack of RX-7s.
Roz Rosintoski

Gary Graf's 1984 CRX has been modified to SCCA IT specs (stiff suspension, roll cage, Weber carb), but slap on some wide Revolutions and it easily makes the transition to Solo II.

The first generation CRX Si combined form and function into this neat little package. Light and quick, it ate Rabbits for lunch. The 1985 model came with 13-inch instead of 14-inch alloys, and was nearly 100 pounds lighter than the 1986–1987 CRX Si.

CVCC-type head (12 valves plus 4 auxiliary valves) further complicated this lean condition, which led to overheating. When the aluminum head was exposed to rapidly changing temperatures, it would warp. Often the head gasket failed. This is a fairly common condition with high-mileage carbureted Civics. In retrospect, the only thing that VW GTI had over these Hondas was fuel injection. If you have ever owned a mechanically fuel-injected vehicle, though, you know how crude this type of system is when it comes to precise fuel delivery. When running properly, however, the 1.6-liter VW engine did seem more competent than the Civic and CRX.

Despite their weaknesses, these new Civics were, and still are, bargains considering what you get for your money. Very popular with IT roadracers, the third generation non-injected Civics and first generation CRX 1.5 will remain in demand.

Although these cars were produced in massive numbers, one model from this generation, the 1984–1985 Civic S, remains somewhat rare and deserves mention. With a stiffer suspension and a five-speed transmission (also used in the Civic Si), the "S" option proved to be well worth the extra initial cost. Honda could do even better, however, and used this competent base to launch its first true high performance cars.

The Honda Hall of Fame

Although these early Hondas were somewhat popular with the hop-up crowd, they are not considered good project cars any longer, due to a diminished number of available aftermarket parts. If you want to start with the right car, you are better off sticking with the models that follow. Some are harder to find, but many are in excess, and prices are all over the map. So in this author's humble opinion, when it comes to easy hop-ups, the models to look for are listed in this "Honda/Acura Hall of Fame."

The Second Generation Prelude (1983–1987)

It took 12 years after the first Honda automobile was introduced in the United States before Honda gave us the gift of its first true sports car—a reliable, high-quality,

high-tech car that could break the 10-second barrier. Besides another suspension redesign, this Prelude also introduced a new 12-valve cylinder head (see 1984–1987 Civic). Both the head and the suspension carried over to the new-carbureted Civic and CRX. The power was generated by a new 1.8-liter engine fueled by dual carbs. But in 1985, the era of fuel injection finally came to Honda, as the Prelude Si, Accord SEi, and CRX Si were born. Fuel injection meant the elimination of the old faithful CVCC-type head in favor of a new 12-valve design. Gone was the tendency to run lean and blow head gaskets. Air/fuel mixture was run by a small computer, located under the passenger seat. This programmable PGM FI system worked flawlessly and delivered consistent power throughout the torque curve, *even at low rpm*. With the introduction of the Prelude Si in 1985, 0–60 times were cut by nearly a second.

The Honda CRX Si (1985–1987)

When the 1985 CRX Si was introduced, it seemed as if Honda was making a statement to VW GTI dealers around the planet. It quickly became popular with import enthusiasts and remains one of the most popular Hondas of all time. It's a cheap, competent little car, and is the model that really started the "Pocket Rocket" revolution. Enthusiasts do recognize that the CRX owes its existence to cars like the Austin Mini Cooper, but Honda took the concept much further.

In 1985, Honda took an already great car (the CRX 1.5) and gave it an injection of steroids. The 1985 Si was light (plastic front fenders and lower door panels) and had plenty of power to launch its anorexic 1,850-pound chassis. With 91 horsepower on tap, the 1985 CRX Si was much quicker than the non-Si version and edged out the 110-horsepower Prelude Si in a straight line.

As for hop-ups, the 1985 Si is easy and fun to modify. However, limitations include an outdated suspension design (front torsion bars, solid rear axle), as well as a limited number of performance modifications available for the 1.5-liter engine. The coolest headers, turbos and superchargers seem to be reserved for its 1.6-liter successors. From a performance standpoint, what really sets the 1985 CRX Si apart from the 1986–1987 is that the 1985 was much lighter and came standard with 13-inch alloys, instead of the 1986–1987's 14-inch wheels. The smaller-diameter wheel, coupled with the magnificent CRX Si gearbox, gave extraordinary torque and quicker 0–60 and quarter-mile times than the 1986–1987 models. However, if you are planning to do some major modifications, any CRX Si would be a good choice.

All CRXs owe their heritage to the Austin Mini. The late Bobby Eakin, a long-time autocrosser and vintage racer, is shown charging toward the finish line in his Mini Cooper at a Solo II Divisional Championship in 1990.

The Honda Civic Si (1986–1987)

Similar to the CRX Si, the Civic body style offered a slightly longer wheelbase, better balance, and more room. This car is a cheap and fun daily driver. An additional advantage that the Civic had over the CRX was its ability to haul stuff. The phrase "everything fits into a Honda" mutters forth from owners' mouths whenever they are astonished by the Christmas tree, couch, or lawn mower that actually did fit into the hatchback. When I was building a deck one summer, I found it easier to haul lumber in the Civic than in my Ford Windstar. The 16-foot

Derek Francis' Civic Si collected many SCCA ProSolo wins in the late 1980s. This Civic ran in the stock class, which allows minor modifications.

sections of decking wouldn't allow the Windstar's heavy hatch to close, and it was very difficult to tie down, but the lumber easily hung out of the back of the Honda.

A major drawback inherent in all 1984–1987 Hondas is rust, especially around the rear fender wells, sunroof, and floors. Carefully inspect the undercarriage of any 1984–1987 Honda before buying it as rust could compromise the integrity of the unibody and often cannot be repaired. It was also a shame that the Civic did not come with alloy wheels, although the CRX Si did, making them cheap and easy to find. Hondas are also the universal recipient for 4x100-millimeter wheels. For instance, VW wheels will bolt right on to a Honda (Scirocco alloys look particularly good), but a Honda rim will not clear the VW axle hub. Most Civic and CRX parts made during this period are interchangeable, except for some exceptions such as seats, torsion bars, body panels, and doors (obviously).

The Second Generation Honda CRX Si (1988–1991)

If you could only have one car to hop up (wouldn't that be a cruel world!), this final generation CRX Si would be near the top of the list of choices. Almost every Honda fan is still mad about the corporate decision to discontinue the CRX line. It was also a disappointment that the meanest CRX models were never imported into the United States.

Sure, with a lot of time, sweat, and money you could transform your CRX into a VTEC or a twin-cam model, but wouldn't it have been great to be able to buy a factory version of these cars? Imagine up to 180 horsepower in a stock CRX! There wouldn't be much reason to do anything else to it with that kind of power.

The 1988 CRX Si was one of the quickest pocket rockets ever built, due to the 108-horsepower, 1.6-liter, SOHC engine, coupled with lower weight (100 pounds less) than the 1989–1991 CRX. They also made great race cars. Terry Tzechman held several Solo I records in his second generation CRX, despite the fact that the car had only modest suspension and intake and exhaust modifications. *Roy Snyder*

Andy and Ann Hollis ruled SCCA's Solo II E Stock class in the late 1980s with their second generation CRX HF. The car was very light, nimble, and handled extremely well with just minor strut and shock performance upgrades.

Well, it's nice to dream. But 130-plus horsepower is easily within reach if you start with a second generation CRX Si. The 1.6-liter engine is calling out to be modified, and performance parts manufacturers have heard that call, answering with a ton of great bolt-on stuff that can put this CRX in the same quarter-mile second as the $100,000 super cars. And with available suspension mods, the car can be made to handle, as well as go fast in a straight line.

There are few suspension designs that are as efficient, neat, and easy to work on as the second generation CRXs. As for the engine, you can find turbochargers, superchargers, nitrous systems, cams, and the coolest headers on the face of the earth just waiting for your phone call (and credit card number).

It doesn't really matter what Honda does in the future, nothing will ever take the place of this great little car. It is destined to become a classic. Buy 'em up, but stay away from all non-Si models unless you plan to make radical changes. If so, look for the HF. It is much lighter (almost 180 pounds), but you will want to swap the 1.3-liter engine for a 1.6.

The Third Generation Prelude (1988–1991)

On the surface, the 1988 Prelude did not look much different than the previous generation. The lines were slightly refined, but no one had a hard time recognizing it as a Prelude. That didn't happen until the following generation.

The major technological advancement in the third generation (3G) 'Lude involved the introduction of a concept that sat on engineering drawing boards many years, but was never imple-

mented until 1988. Four-wheel steering was the "gimmick" that would always be identified with these third generation cars. Although never a factor in high performance driving (or in regular street driving, for that matter), four-wheel steering used the Prelude's rear double-wishbone suspension to turn the rear wheels in the same direction that the front wheels turned.

Actually, it had to do with how much you turned the steering wheel, because on a tight turn, the rear wheels would end up pointing in the opposite direction of the front. Sounds like it would work, but it didn't. Most drivers couldn't even tell the difference between the 4WS and the non-4WS Preludes. (Both were offered in this generation.) It's not often that Honda misses the mark, but this was one of those times.

The 1988 Prelude was a sharp car right out of the showroom. The new body design was a major styling change over the second generation car. This one-of-a-kind third generation Prelude is sporting a custom aero kit. *Diamond Star Creative Group*

But the third generation Preludes weren't a complete wash. A lame, carburetted, 12-valve engine was offered on the standard version, but the Si was a much more competent machine. A newly designed, 16-valve, twin-cam 2.0-liter (1,958-cc) produced 135 horsepower, and had excellent low-end torque (127 lb-ft at 4,500 rpm). In the final year of production, 100 cc was added to this Si powerplant, with an added bonus of 5 horsepower.

This was also Honda's first use of the dual-stage intake manifold, in which a second intake tract opens at high rpm. A vacuum-controlled valve allowed more air when the tach hit 5,000. This system re-emerged after further refinement on the 1994 Integra GS-R.

Sean Christie's street prepared 1990 Civic Si is shown attacking the pylons at the 1998 SCCA ProSolo II. The fifth generation Civic Si makes an excellent race car, due to its light body coupled with the easily modified 1.6-liter engine.

The Fourth Generation Accord (1990–1993)

Honda's attempt to merge luxury and performance reached a high point with the 1990 Accord. A 2.2-liter, SOHC engine capable of 125 horsepower was featured in the DX and LX models. Lucky EX, and later, SE buyers received a little more power. Honda gave the F22A engine (the same as offered in both the DX and LX) a trick exhaust manifold, boosting the horsepower to 140. Now that's more like it. Back in the Japanese market, four-wheel steering was offered on the 1990–1993 models, and it didn't catch on with the Accords either.

The Fourth Generation Honda Civic (1988–1991)

Historically, the fourth generation Civics are often viewed as stepping stones to the 1990s, when Honda and Acura turned up the heat and created some real factory hot rods. There were some positive changes made over the 1984–1987 Civics, the best of

which was the powerplant. The 1988 Civic Si came equipped with the wonderfully responsive 1.6-liter engine (identical to the second generation CRX Si) that reacted well to modification. This is the engine that set the pace for the Honda and Acura engines of the 1990s. Soon after the 1988 Civic Si was introduced, aftermarket parts manufacturers began to focus on the 1.6-liter, 16-valve engine, and stopped producing go-fast parts for the previous generations of Hondas. Honda parts manufacturer HKS recently delved into its dusty back rooms, looking for any turbo components that would fit a 1985–1987 1.5-liter Si engine. HKS once marketed a complete bolt-on turbo system for these cars, but not a single exhaust manifold could be found. It took weeks on the net before one could be located, and then the cost was high. And why not concentrate on this new generation powerplant? It produced 108 horsepower stock, but with all of the aftermarket parts that became available in the early 1990s, you

could easily end up with a supercharged 180-horsepower beast that was so well-mannered on the street you could loan it to your mom.

In fact, all of the new generation Civics were fuel-injected. However, the base Civic and DX were fed by a throttle body, dual-point injection system, while the Si, HF, and 4WD wagon had Honda's great multiport PGM-FI. Only these last three models contained the new 1.6-liter, 16-valve motor.

Another great change was replacing the front torsion bar suspension with a slick, double-wishbone system. Overall ride was improved, and more options were available when it came to the handling.

The major drawback over the previous generation Civic was the added weight (over 200 pounds!) and the bland, conservative styling. The 1984 CRX looked like nothing that had come before it, and Honda had a history of being slightly unconventional. It got back on the right track with the introduction of the radical (love it or hate it) 1992 body style, but this generation Civic seemed to just fade in to the background. One problem may have been that the 1988–1991 CRX got all of the attention (what a great body style). Still, the fourth generation Civic had such a competent engine, it is hard to understand why one doesn't see more of them on the race track.

While not as popular a choice for hot rodding, these fourth generation Civics do receive attention from the hybrid crowd. The main reason for this is that in Japan, the Civic and CRX Si models came fitted with the now-infamous 1.6-liter, twin-cam ZC engine. Some of these motors, referred to as the Honda Civic Si16-1.6i and CRX Si16-1.6i, have made their way to the United States, thanks to engine importers like HASport. The ZC is a relatively uncomplicated bolt-in swap for the 1988–1991 Civic and CRX that will net nearly 140 horsepower. That ought to more than make up for the increase in weight over the previous generation.

Woody Donnell's 1992 Honda Civic DX effectively incorporates many of the performance improvements outlined in this book.

Ralph Weaver's 1995 Del Sol Si is only lightly modified. High performance wheels and tires have been stored for the winter, and only an air velocity intake, strut tower stress bar, and performance exhaust have been added.

The Fifth Generation Honda Civic (1992–1995)

Proof that Honda continues to get better with time is the fifth generation Civic. By far the most popular chassis for the engine transplant crowd, the "jellybean" hatchback has already become a classic. With a body that, for most people, becomes more appealing the more you look at it (in other words, it looked kind of silly the first time I saw it), the 1992–1995 Civics have been more highly modified than any other Honda in history. Hop-up parts are everywhere, and when it comes to engine swapping, it almost seems as if these Civics were built with transplantation in mind. This is probably because this chassis, which is very strong and rigid, can support a number of different powerplants.

Besides the gas-saving, SOHC, 8-valve, 1.5-liter, 70-horsepower Civic CX, there is a 16-valve, VTEC-E (economy) Civic VX rated at 92 horsepower; an LX/DX package (102 horsepower); and finally an energetic SOHC, VTEC Civic Si and EX (125 horsepower). If that's not enough, Honda offered a Japan-only engine. Never officially imported into the United States, this same body supported a 1,595-cc, DOHC, VTEC engine with a 10.4:1 compression ratio capable of producing 160 horsepower.

At some point, possibly because the U.S. buyer felt cheated, someone attempted to put a 1994 Integra GS-R into this generation Civic and discovered that the motor mounts for the 1992–1995 Civics and second generation Integras were nearly the same. Hence, this extremely popular hybrid project was born.

These Civics also have had much success at the race track, especially the ones with no turns. This car was largely responsible for the increased popularity of drag racing in the late 1990s. At many of the drag strips in California, import drivers now outnumber the traditional American musclecars. Not only are they popular, but more and more Civic hybrids are breaking into the 10-second barrier (remember, the car is front-wheel drive). If anything will let enthusiasts forgive Honda for the death of the CRX, it is the introduction of the fifth generation Civics.

The Del Sol (1992–1996)

When Honda introduced the first Del Sol in the United States as a replacement for the much-loved CRX, reaction was mixed. At first, the word of a two-seater, mid-engine sports car excited many Honda lovers, but when they rushed into the showroom to test drive the new baby Honda, many walked away disappointed. That's because the U.S. market only received the low-power version of what Japanese enthusiasts got to play with.

Using the same engine as in the 1992–1995 Civic DX (1.6-liter, SOHC, PGM-FI), the "sports" car only was capable of 108 horsepower. That would have been enough for a 1985 CRX Si, but this new Del Sol weighed nearly 400 pounds more! VW Golfs were pulling away from them at red lights. Meanwhile, the Japanese kept the big motor for themselves.

Reaya Reuss' 1995 Del Sol VTEC. She is the president of Capitol Sol, which is open to residents of the greater Washington, D.C., area. *Reaya Reuss*

Honda owners weren't the only ones to be disappointed by underpowered Japanese sports cars. The introduction of the Mazda Miata in 1989 started the current modern roadster movement, but had enthusiasts wishing for just one more thing: power. One would think that the motoring public would be grateful that roadsters were again being mass produced, but the Miata, as well as the Del Sol, were described with an adjective that sends shivers up the spine of most sports car owners: *cute*. You don't usually hear people describe the NSX, Twin turbo Supra, or Porsche 911 as "cute." Most of us don't want to be driving a "cute" car. We want to be driving a *mean* car. A car isn't cute if it can beat a Mustang Cobra in the quarter-mile. Without the new roadsters, the car world would be boring, but without horsepower, they seem nothing more than show. Throughout the 1990s, Mazda continually updated the Miata to the point where it became less cute in both looks and power, but the Del Sol did not keep pace.

The United States received an Si version of the Del Sol with slightly more horsepower (125), but it still wasn't enough. It wasn't until Honda added a VTEC motor, that the Del Sol evolved into a competent sports car. Equipped with one of the best motors to come out of Japan, the B16A3, the Del Sol VTEC cranked out 160 horses, more than enough to leave those Golf owners scratching their heads at red lights. But just when Honda started to get it right, the Del Sol VTEC was no more. Whether due to its funky styling or lack of interest by serious auto enthusiasts, sales were poor, and Honda chose to end production in 1996.

The Fifth Generation Accord (1994–1997)

After much anticipation, Honda finally put the second generation Legend 2.7-liter V-6, tweaked slightly to 170 horsepower, into an Accord, but it didn't happen until 1995. This was a nice increase in power over the 145 horsepower, SOHC VTEC that was standard on the base DX. As if the V-6 option wasn't enough, the Accord was redesigned for the better in order to keep pace with the Camry and Maxima, both of which also received nice makeovers during this period. The Accord V-6 continued to use this Legend-based engine

Del Sol owners seem particularly loyal. Club Sol has helped over 10,000 Del Sol owners since its conception, and is the largest Honda club in the country. Visit the Del Sol web site at www.clubsol.com.

throughout this generation. For the home market, Honda offered a Japanese-only version, called the Accord Si-R, which was equipped with a 190-plus horsepower, 2.2-liter, twin-cam powerplant.

The Fourth Generation Prelude (1992–1996)

When the new body style Prelude was introduced in 1992, not everyone was impressed. The rear end was somewhat controversial, and then there was the engine. Many were hoping that the Prelude would get a new V-6 powerplant, but Honda surprised everyone by using a four-cylinder VTEC engine. This engine design had been around in Japan for a couple of years (1990 Civic and CRX Si-R), but in the form of a much smaller, 1.6-liter block. Honda applied this revolutionary engine design to a larger 2.2-liter powerplant, and to everyone's de-

light, it produced 180 horsepower out of a lousy four-cylinder engine. From 1994 to 1996, the engine was slightly tweaked each year to produce even more horsepower, eventually delivering 190 in the 1996 Prelude VTEC. This kind of normally aspirated power had previously been achieved in four-cylinder race cars, but only after considerable modifications. But the Prelude VTEC was being offered to the general public as an exciting, high-revving, factory hot rod.

The other Preludes were not so lucky. The Prelude S used a SOHC 2.2-liter, and the Si was powered by a twin-cam, 2.3-liter engine. Horsepower ranged from 135 to 150, depending on the model. Honda didn't sell many fourth generation Preludes, proving they weren't very popular with the general public. A Honda vice president confided that the

One of the only Hondas participating in SCCA Pro Rally is the 1993 Prelude VTEC owned and piloted by Jim Anderson. Usually, all-wheel-drive cars make the best rally cars and are the top choice for professional drivers. But don't tell that to Jim Anderson, who raced his Prelude to a National Championship in 1996. *John Wynn*

car was designed originally to target women, who actually did buy more than 60 percent of these automobiles. The new 'Lude, however, is targeted at men over the age of 40.

The Fifth Generation Prelude (1997+)

Many people already miss the half-moon rear end of the 1992–1996 Prelude. It was dropped in 1997 when Honda made a scheduled design change for the fifth generation Prelude. The new exterior is somewhat reminiscent of a third generation Prelude, but that's where the similarity ends. Under the hood is a slightly tweaked 2.2L VTEC engine that could produce 195 horsepower. Also new was a smooth 4-speed, automatic sequential sportshift, one of the first times this type of option was offered on an affordable sports car.

Long before the 1997 Honda Prelude was introduced, some automotive journalists, including myself, were given the opportunity to put it to the test at a Detroit race track (we beat the living hell out of the car!). Honda also let us compare this 'Lude to the fourth generation car. It was no contest. Although both cars easily tamed the race track, the 1997 Prelude was faster simply because it was able to get more power down to the pavement. The reason for this lies in a new piece of technology designed by Honda engineers specifically for the Type SH (a very desirable option for the fifth generation Prelude).

Honda always seems to be on the cutting edge of automotive science, and they traditionally use the Prelude to showcase new technology much as GM uses the Corvette. Anti-lock brakes, 4-wheel steering, and the VTEC engine are some good examples of Honda setting

Two fifth generation Accords: a 1997 model (top) and a 1996 (bottom). Both cars were modified by a company founded by Neil and Gene Tjin, called Star Performance Accessories. For more information, send e-mail to veilsidetl@aol.com. *Neil Tjin*

the standard that other companies must try to follow. The gimmick for the 1997 Prelude type SH was ATTS (Active Torque Transfer System). Working much like a limited slip differential, the 5 extra horsepower offered on the 1997 seemed more like a 10 horsepower improvement over the 1996 (see chapter 13 for a more detailed description of ATTS).

Even the non-type SH models are an improved machine. You may or may not like the redesigned rear end, but 4G lovers can take heart that thanks to the

1997 body style change, the 1992–1996 Preludes are starting to become more affordable.

The Sixth Generation Honda Civics (1996+)

With the death of the Civic Si at the end of the 1995 model year, the Honda EX took over bragging rights as top dog in the Civic lineup. The Civic DX and LX retained a slightly tweaked version of the D15 powerplant, but the CX was upgraded to the same 1.5-liter, SOHC engine, which was rated at 106 horsepower. The new HX

It didn't take long before the new fifth generation Preludes became victims of "hop-up fever." With an extra five horsepower on tap, optional sport shifter, and ATTS, the 1997 Prelude raised the technology bar another notch. . . and just when the U.S. automakers were beginning to clear the mark set by the 4G Preludes! *Diamond Star Creative Group*

model received a VTEC-E engine (economy version), and the EX was fitted with a redesigned version of the SOHC, 1.6-liter VTEC motor (D16Z) called the VTEC-II. Very similar to the powerplant in the 1992–1995 Civic Si, this new VTEC added 5 more cubic centimeters and gained 2 more horsepower. Other than a small change in styling, along with some added weight, there is no big difference between the fifth generation and sixth generation Civics. The Civic Si, powered by a 170-horsepower, twin-cam VTEC engine (nearly identical to the B16A3 motor that drove the Del Sol VTEC), continued to be offered in Japan and was powered by a 170-horsepower, twin-cam VTEC engine (nearly identical to the B16A3 motor that

drove the Del Sol VTEC). Although promised to the U.S. market since 1996, we finally received our own version of this car (officially named the Civic Si-RII in Japan) in February 1999. The 160-horsepower U.S. model retained the name "Civic Si," carrying on the tradition that began in 1985, when the CRX Si launched Honda's pocket rocket movement.

The 1998 model year also introduced (to Japan) the Civic Type-R, promised to the United States for mid-1999. Further advancement of the B16 powerplant has resulted in a 1.6-liter, normally aspirated, twin-cam VTEC engine that can produce 185 horsepower in stock trim, and has a redline of over 8,000 rpm. These performance models (Civic Type-R and

Civic Si) should help the sixth generation cars stand out when twenty-first century historians look back at Honda development. Prior to this, this sixth generation Civic had not made the same impressive technological leap that traditionally occurred between generations. As 1998 drew to a close, the U.S. market's top-of-the-line Civic EX didn't get to the finish line much faster than the now–technologically challenged 92-horsepower 1986 Civic Si, mainly because it weighs nearly 400 pounds more. However, one thing has remained constant—the Civic line remains affordable to first-time car buyers.

Of course, the hybrid crowd embraced this generation just as it did the 1992–1995 Civics. Even before the warranties expire, you see 170-horsepower versions of the 1994 1.8-liter GS-R (B18C1), 1995 1.6-liter Del Sol VTEC (B16A3), or imported Civic Si RII engines fitted into these sixth generation Civics. Actually, if you think about it, these enthusiasts aren't necessarily crazy for voiding the warranties. What good, really, is a Honda warranty since you never have to use it anyway?

The Sixth Generation Accord (1998+)

The 1998 Accord was a much-anticipated vehicle and quickly became a top seller. As in the past, Honda offered it in four models (DX, LX, EX, and SE) with a choice of powerplants. The DX retained the four-cylinder, 2.2-liter, SOHC, 135-horsepower VTEC motor, but the LX and EX came with a hopped-up four-cylinder, 2.3-liter VTEC that was capable of 150 horsepower. But once again, the star of the line-up was the Accord V-6, which abandoned the 2.7-liter Legend-based powerplant in favor of the 3.0-liter engine used to propel the Acura CL. This fine specimen pumps out a healthy 200 horsepower, making the Accord more competitive with the Camry and Maxima.

Honda changed the exterior as well. The sixth generation Accord now resembles many of the other sedans on the market. The 2-door EX Coupe, however, is an exception as it has bold, exciting lines. It seems Chrysler is the only major manufacturer venturing to design cars that look a little different than the mainstream. Even Saab conformed in 1998! Nevertheless, the Accord's body hides a redesigned, slightly stiffer suspension. The major drawback was that the 1998 V-6 was only available with an automatic transmission, a weakness that was corrected when a five-speed became available the following year.

On the Japanese home front, the Si-R was upgraded with a 200-horsepower engine for 1998. Rumors continue that an Accord Type-R will be introduced to the United States in the year 2000.

The Acura Hall of Fame:
The Acura Legend (1986–1990)

Honda may have been afraid that its loyal Accord and Prelude owners would feel devalued if a line of upscale Hondas were introduced. In reality, however, the company knew that if it failed to introduce a Honda luxury car to compete head-to-head with the fine European sedans, the "Honda" marque would not be taken very seriously. Hence, it launched the Acura division. Toyota (Lexus) and Nissan (Infinity) soon followed suit, with all three finding success in the market traditionally dominated by Saabs, Volvos, and BMWs. The first of these new

Acuras to come off of the assembly line was called the Legend. Although a competent car, it was not exactly designed to be a sports coupe. Instead, it emerged as one of the better luxury sedans ever made. The 10-year history of the Legend reflects typical Honda development. The Legend may be remembered for one other feature: the first Honda V-6 engine.

Drawing on lessons learned in Formula 1 racing, Honda designed a completely new powerplant. The 2.5-liter, 151-horsepower V-6 was used to launch the new luxury Honda. Somehow, driving around in a luxury car with an engine inspired by a Formula 1 race car made drivers feel slightly wild.

In spite of Acura's engineering focus on styling and luxury, the Legend's powerplant also managed to gain significant technological advances over its 10-year history. In 1988, the 2.5 gave

The Japanese FWD 10-second drag club is usually dominated by lighter late-model Civics, but there is one competitor who gives Acura fans something to cheer about. Tony Fuchs manages to drag his substantially heavier, first-generation Integra body across the finish line as quickly as those hybrid Civics. His 10.67-second time at 133 miles per hour is accomplished thanks to a turbo-charged, J. G. Engine Dynamics–built powerplant capable of over 400 horsepower. *Tony Fuchs*

A sixth generation Civic. See what fun you can have with some Stillen body modifications? *Stillen*

way to a 2.7-liter V-6 capable of 161 horsepower, and an attractive two-door coupe was introduced. This engine went on to find happiness in the 1995 Accord V-6, where it remained until 1998, when the Accord switched to the 1996 Acura CL, 3.0-liter VTEC engine.

The Acura Integra (1987–1989)

Considered to be an entry-level Acura, the Integra more closely resembled the 1986–1987 Civic Si than it did its big brother, the Legend. Using the same suspension and fuel injection system as the Civic Si, the Integra packaged these components into a redesigned, sportier body. More importantly, the Integra gave the United States its first look at the 1.6-liter, twin-cam engine that was available only in Japan for the

The Civic Si returned for 1999 sporting a twin-cam, 1.6-liter VTEC engine (similar to the Del Sol VTEC), which produces 160 horsepower. We are still waiting for the Si in hatchback trim. *American Honda Motor Company, Inc.*

1986–1987 CRX 1.6i-16. At 113 horsepower, this upscale pocket rocket could reach 60 miles per hour in well under nine seconds. Of course, this engine does fit into a U.S. CRX or Civic with just a little effort. The same computer also powers both engines, so it too could be swapped into a Civic/CRX Si to help raise the rev limit and offer better high-end torque (see chapter 5). As for modifications, the Integra responded similarly to the Honda Si, and remains a very popular project car. Many still prefer the first generation's styling to the more popular 1990 model.

Second Generation
Acura Integra (1990–1993)

The Integra LS and RS were slightly redesigned for 1990, containing a reworked version of the 1.6-liter engine that came in the previous generation Integras. This motor, which became known as the ZC, is still one of the most popular engines Honda ever made. The hybrid crowd, known for fitting Integra powerplants into Civic and CRX bodies, found that the ZC could be transplanted easily into a 1988–1991 Si. That's because this engine was shared by the second generation, Japanese-only Civic and CRX 1.6i-16.

The Integra GS also made hybrid history because it was equipped with a 1.8-liter, DOHC engine. Although it had less overall horsepower then the LS and RS, the GS carried more torque and was reworked in 1992 to deliver 140 horsepower. These B18B engines also find comfortable homes in Civics, because they respond somewhat more enthusiastically to performance modifications than do the ZC powerplants, mainly a result of their great low-end torque. No wonder it's one of the most desired transplant donor engines around.

The 1998 two-door Accord EX is one great four-cylinder coupe. It hides a 2.3-liter VTEC engine that cranks out 150 horsepower. Even in stock trim, this is such a capable car that the Mid-Ohio Drivers School uses them exclusively to teach prospective SCCA racers high speed driving techniques. Of course the car is also available with a V-6. Both engine options are also offered on the 1996+ Acura CL, which is built off of the same platform as the Accord.

As if this wasn't enough to make the second generation Integra a hit, the one thing that will make them stand out in automotive history was revealed when the first Integra GS-R was introduced in 1992. In place of the B18-type engine, the GS-R came equipped with a smaller, but much more powerful 1.7-liter, DOHC VTEC powerplant that cranked out a whopping 160 horsepower! This was Integra's version of the Honda Si, and gave us a sign that the Acura division was also committed to producing hot rod versions of its cars. Indeed, 1992 was a good year for engines, as Honda went on to produce several versions of the VTEC and fit them into everything from the Del Sol (VTEC and Si), Civic Si and EX, Prelude VTEC, and even an economy edition of the VTEC in the Civic VX. As usual, Japan played with this revolutionary new engine design a couple of years before the United States, as

the B17A first appeared under the hood of the now-infamous 1990 Civic and CRX Si-R (never imported to the United States).

The Acura Vigor (1991–1994)

Appearing briefly in U.S. showrooms, the Acura Vigor was not enough of a financial success to live past one generation. Part of the reason may have been that it had a weird five-cylinder, 176-horsepower engine. Built off the Legend platform, the Vigor was a heavy car that was not as reliable as the mid-1990 Hondas and Acuras. Due to its unusual design, it has developed somewhat of a cult following and used Vigors remain in demand.

The Second Generation
Legend (1991–1995) and
First Generation RL (1996+)

In typical Honda style, improvements continued for this new generation Legend. A beautiful exterior makeover of both the Sedan and Coupe helped the Legend gain significant ground in the European luxury car market. Things were changing under the hood as well. The 2.7-liter V-6 was replaced with a much more competent 24-valve, DOHC 3.2-liter that cranked out 200 horses. In 1993 it was tweaked to deliver 230 horsepower, and was capable of going 0–60 in 8 seconds.

With a top speed of 150 miles per hour, this 2G Legend could cover the quarter-mile in 16 seconds. This nifty 3.2-liter engine eventually gained new life under the hood of the Acura TL sport coupe.

Although the Legend was officially retired in the United States and Canada, the model marque continues throughout the rest of the world. For the U.S. market, however, the "Legend" was renamed the RL (road luxury), and was refitted with a 3.5-liter, 24-valve V-6 that had more torque, but less horsepower than the Legend configuration.

Third Generation
Acura Integra (1994+)

Sporting a dramatic change in body style that did not gain immediate acceptance by Integra fans, the 1994 Integra made a clear statement that this was going to be a completely different car. Underneath the exterior, there was a more rigid suspension and stiffer unibody, enabling this new Integra to out-corner the first two generations. Based on the Civic, the 1986–1993 Integras improved on basic Honda structure, but in 1994, ground was broken for a completely different foundation. The Integra established itself as a unique entity.

Development continued on the B18 powerplant, which was now offered for all third generation Integras. Gone was the popular ZC-type, D16A 1.6-liter, replaced by the 142-horsepower engine first offered in the 1992 Integra GS (B18B1) (dropped for 1999). The exception to this rule was the second generation GS-R, which added more than 100 cc to the B17 engine for the 1994 version. Although both third generation Integra engines have B18 classifications, the GS-R more resembles the B17 platform. It revs much higher than the GS, LS, and RS B18B1 (8,200 rpm), and has the same compression ratio as the B17 (10.0:1). Horsepower is similar, but those extra 100 cc are responsible for 10 more ponies (170 horsepower) plus an added bonus of better low-end torque. Honda reintroduced a much-refined dual stage intake manifold system, borrowed from the third generation Prelude Si, in

The first generation Integra was an upscale third generation Civic, with the suspension of a fourth generation Civic, and the motor that was used in the Japanese version of the first generation CRX Si.

The second generation Integra was a beautiful car, and many still prefer the 1990–1993 front clip to the round dual headlight design that replaced it in 1994. This beautifully maintained example of a 1993 Integra belongs to Angel Rojas, Jr. *Angel Rojas, Jr.*

which a second intake tract opens to allow the engine to breathe better at high rpm. Thanks to this high-revving VTEC engine, this beast can get to 60 miles per hour in under eight seconds. All in all, the 1994 GS-R B18C1 powerplant is a work of art and has become, by far, the most popular engine for transplantation.

Honda wasn't through with these third generation Integras when it came to hot rod development! In 1997, the entire automotive community took notice when the Integra Type-R was offered to the hungry motorsports community. With 195 horsepower on tap, this reworked version of the GS-R's B18C1, twin-cam VTEC easily burned up the quarter-mile in under 15 seconds. It set the standard by which all future four-cylinder engines would be judged. The Japanese version of the Type-R is equally potent, but 200 pounds lighter, since the United States requires more emission and safety equipment. The Asian version also shows off a newly designed front clip. Gone are the dual round headlamps. The Japanese version looks slightly more distinguished. A new version Type-R will squeeze 210 horsepower out of a 1,797-cc motor! For those who didn't believe that Honda's commitment to racing would directly benefit the average car buyer, this certainly is indisputable proof.

But the best thing about the Integra Type-R is that it was not intended to be a race car. It's street legal and is available (with some luck and a good credit rating) at your local Acura dealer. Already a hit with the autocross community, the Type-R scored a big win in the Sports Car Club of America's (SCCA) G Stock class, previously dominated by V-6 Camaros. In 1998, Neal Sapp, in one of his first times piloting an

One of the biggest facelifts in Japanese automotive history came in the form of the third generation Integra. This beautiful example belongs to Mark Mawhinney, who has it detailed several times a week and parks it in front of the audio shop he owns to help attract customers. (We stopped!)

Darren Mass waits at the starting line of the 1998 SCCA ProSolo II, behind the wheel of his 1995 GSR. (Pay no attention to the "Type R" badge on the rear of the car.) Second generation Integra owners report that the third generation cars seems to have more inherent body roll than the previous generation.

Acura, just missed the National Solo II title by less than 0.4 second driving a bone-stock 1998 Integra Type-R. This car will no doubt go on to experience much more success both on the road and on the track.

The Acura 2.7 TL and CL (1996+)

Equipped with the same engine as the 1993–1995 Legend, the TL cranks out 225 horsepower in stock trim. The body is sleeker and more sporty than the Legend

Coupe, but underneath, it is built on the same platform as the Legend. With double-wishbone suspension, traction control, and a sequential sportshifter (used on the Prelude Type SH), this isn't "your father's Legend." This is probably the classiest pocket rocket ever built. Who would have thought that the lowly Civic and CRX Si would give birth to this technological marvel? The TL was instantly popular with the hop-up crowd. G-Force makes a chip that can further boost power, and most of the other engine goodies (not to mention body kits) are widely available.

The 1996 Acura CL and the 1998 Honda Accord shared the same 3.0-liter, single-cam VTEC V-6 that produces 200 horsepower.

Although it carried the Acura name, it is more closely related to the Accord because they share the same platform. The CL is also available with a 2.3-liter, 16-valve VTEC, similar to the Accord LX and EX.

The Acura NSX (1991+)

Out of reach for most automotive enthusiasts both for initial investment and yearly insurance, the NSX is the culmination of all Honda development since the 1950s. Who would have thought that its initial failures in racing would lead to domination of the sport in the mid-1980s, and to the closest thing to a street legal Formula 1 car, the NSX? Soichiro Honda would be proud. Led by one of Honda's most creative engineers, Shigeru Uehara, the NSX project came to fruition in 1990, becoming the first Acura to carry the trademark "A" symbol. It remains the benchmark by which other super cars are judged.

During the developmental stages of the NSX, Honda engineers came up with an engine design that would change the face of Honda and Acura powerplants for years to come. The VTEC engine was first designed as a 24-valve, DOHC V-6, but soon emerged as a twin-cam, 16-valve, four-cylinder engine that reached production before the NSX. Labeled the "ZCG" engine, it was used to power the Civic and the Japanese-only-release CRX SiR.

Although the NSX is worth every penny, the problem is that it takes too many pennies (over 8 million of them, or $80,000) before an Acura dealer will let you take one home. That's why there are not even 10,000 lucky drivers in the world who have an NSX in their garage. Extremely light and nimble, the first NSX was powered by a 3.0-liter Acura V-6 engine that

The Integra Type R came only dressed in white, disproving the belief that nice guys finish last. It takes the solid foundation of the GSR, and adds 25 horsepower boosting power to 195. Right out of the showroom, it can do the quarter mile in 14 seconds and some change. That sounds like a muscle car to me. *Reaya Reuss*

Star Performance Accessories also can help you modify your Acura TL. This 1996 3.2-liter V-6 model sports a custom-made ground control kit, 18-inch wheels, cross-drilled rotors, Tanabe exhaust, and it receives a power boost from a G-Force chip. *Neil Tjin photos*

The NSX is the pinnacle of Honda power and technology, other than Honda's F-1 racing development. Acura only released 50 of these 1999 Zanardi Editions to the public. *American Honda Motor Company, Inc*

Honda and Comptech have gone hand in hand since the mid-1980s. When the two worked together to develop Honda's F1 program, everyone knew that all that technology would eventually trickle down to the general public. *Comptech*

Comptech technology is not just for the major players with big bucks. Weekend racers, as well as nonracers, can benefit from its engineering developments. Soon, most Acura and V-6 Honda owners will be able to buy a Comptech supercharger for their cars.

was capable of producing 270 horsepower. The same V-6 continues in today's NSX, but it has been slightly tweaked from year to year, making it capable of nearly 300 horsepower! Imagine going 0–60 in less than five seconds driving a stock Honda!

What could it do with a little tweaking? Why anyone would want to hop up this rocket ship is beyond belief, except for those owners who want to achieve even further exclusivity. Now, thanks to Comptech, you can do just that. For years, Comptech has been helping Acura owners reach for that extra bit of performance.

Behind most performance companies there lies a former race car driver, and Comptech is no exception. After a successful racing season behind the wheel of a Honda CRX, Doug Peterson and Comptech went on to help define Acura Integra performance in the mid-1980s. Clearly, the most knowledgeable and successful Acura tuner in the industry, Comptech continues to work hand-in-hand with Acura to ensure that all of their hop-up parts maintain the high standards to which Acura owners are accustomed.

The same is true for the way Comptech has developed performance products for the NSX. Comptech offers everything from billet brake calipers to rear bushing kits that correct the radical factory toe-in—serious parts for serious drivers, and at serious prices. The brake package, which includes cross-drilled rotors, retails for over $12,000. Comptech also offers a supercharger for those who feel that their NSX is a little sluggish in stock trim. With 0–60 times in under 5 seconds, and quarter-mile ETs of 12, you can own one of the most powerful "Hondas" in the world. This epitomizes the racer's credo: "How fast do you want to spend?"

This just goes to show that even if you have the top-of-the-line Honda sports car, you still can have the urge to hop it up. Even though most of us will never own an NSX, or even drive one, it is an important car for us regular Honda and Acura owners. The car stands for what Honda has achieved in its first 50 years as a company. That level of quality is reflected even in the more Civic and Integra models. Most Honda owners like to think that there is a little bit of NSX in their own car.

The Future of Honda: The Honda S2000

In October 1998, Honda made up for the untimely and unpopular termination of the CRX Si in

What can we say? Honda came full circle in 1999 when it released the S2000 as the first Y2K Honda model. Power, performance, and looks—a far cry from the Z and N600 (the first Hondas exported to the United States) but true to the origins of the first Honda motorcar, the S series. Is this the shape of things to come for Honda? Will the S2000 set the standard for Hondas still on the drawing board? The author's guess is: Absolutely!

1991. Introduced in the United States in mid-1999, the S2000 two-seat roadster was worth the wait. Throughout the late 1990s, Honda lovers had to bite their tongues as their BMW and Porsche friends bragged about the Z3 and Boxter. Finally, Honda enthusiasts have a car that will blow the doors off both these European marques in both performance and value.

Yes, Honda has come full circle. Those early S600 twin-cam, four-cylinder motorcycle engines have evolved into four-cylinder, SOHC, 2.0-liter VTEC automobile engines. On paper, the S2000 doesn't seem like the culmination of 30 years of Honda technology. But cars aren't driven on paper.

Actually, about the only thing that the S2000 has in common with its early "S" car ancestors is the name. The 2000 turned out to be everything that Honda and Acura lovers had hoped for, and more.

Leading Honda into the next millennium, this new sports car was aptly named. The new 2,000-cc powerplant will define the future of Honda for the year 2000 and beyond.

The technology found under the lightweight shell is also worthy of the twenty-first century. In a world where we want to go faster but need to preserve our environment, Honda designed an engine capable of 1.5 horsepower per cc that is also kind to the planet. The S2000 is a low-emission vehicle, meeting standards that haven't yet been EPA-set. With a nearly perfect weight distribution front to rear, the 2000's powerplant was designed to balance the car for precise handling. Most of us would have tried to shoehorn an NSX V-6 into this beautiful convertible, but then the carefully designed weight parameters would have been compromised. The 2.0-liter, SOHC inline-four sits a bit

Just in case you weren't on the list to receive the NSX Zanardi Edition, Comptech can fix you up. Perhaps we should say Comptech can fix up your present NSX. If the 300-plus-horsepower DOHC V-6 seems a little sluggish, then call Comptech and get yourself a supercharger. How does 425 horsepower sound? That ought to leave that new little pesky S2000 in the dust. The one modification all NSX owners should consider is the rear bushing kit, which helps correct the factory toe-in problem. *Comptech*

further back than in most Hondas or Acuras, making two extra cylinders seem unnecessary to achieve remarkable performance.

The big weakness of previous VTEC powerplants was that big torque was only available at high rpm. But this 2.0-liter VTEC has been joined to a new six-speed transmission, so that torque can be found at all speeds. And speaking of rpm, the redline of this combination is set at 9,000, epitomizing the automotive definition of "screamer."

Incorporating a very rigid body supported by the NSX-type double-wishbone suspension, the 2000 is the best handling Honda to date. The high-revving engine

feels like you are driving an early Lotus Elan as opposed to a new Mazda Miata, except with more power (and considerably greater reliability). Whereas other manufacturers (except maybe for Chrysler) often lose some heart when taking a car from the drawing board to the assembly line, the Honda S2000 retains the spirit of a true race car. Honda lovers should be grateful to Mazda for resurrecting the roadster, but the Honda S2000 is the car that the Miata should have been.

One of its best features may be that the S2000 is rear-wheel drive. Much of this book is designed to help Honda and Acura owners correct the factory understeer that

seems to come as standard equipment on most FWD vehicles. The S2000, on the other hand, can be put into a power drift around the first turn you encounter while leaving the showroom, pink slip in hand. (I advise waiting a few days before you find an autocross course.)

So what will the future hold for Honda and Acura? Count on more efficient powerplants, smoother designs, and consistent quality. In other words, depend on all that we have come to expect from Japan's premier auto manufacturer. Perhaps this book will need to be revised at some point in the near future to include subjective test data on a new CRX Si. We can only hope!

Chapter 3

Handling

In building a performance race car, the first item on the agenda should be handling. Obviously, if drag racing is your thing, you may want to skip this chapter and come back to it later. For all other applications, since most fuel-injected Hondas are already fast, light, competent little beasts right off of the showroom floor, some minor suspension tweaks can help you make better use of that power.

If Hondas and Acuras have any weakness at all, it is in the way the suspension is set up by the factory. There are several reasons why such a conservative approach is taken, the least of which is to maintain a smoother ride. Hondas, like most front-wheel-drive cars, are *designed* to push, or plow. Engineers must feel that, for the average driver, this condition is easier to control than having the tail hang out around every turn, so they purposely induce understeer.

This is accomplished by fitting the front end with stiffer springs than the rear. The best handling setup for a racing Honda or Acura is actually opposite of this philosophy. The springs in the rear should be stiffer than in the front. Since this is contrary to what the manufacturers recommend, you may find that many aftermarket parts distributors will try to talk you out of making the rear stiffer. This may be because they are fol-

One of the best handling Hondas in the nation lifts its rear wheel in a 1992 SCCA ProSolo event, with Jim Leithauser (now an SCCA board member) at the wheel. Since the mid-1990s, this car has been codriven by Steve Mieritz and Stacey Despelder. It consistently brings a podium finish to its drivers.

lowing your car's original suspension design. The springs they may send you will probably make your car lower, but not completely correct the understeering condition. They may be okay for the street since you don't want to feel every bump in your daily driver, but for racing, you will need a heavy rear sway bar to provide additional stiffness. A good parts distributor should be able to quote you the spring rates of the suspension package you want to order. If they don't know the spring rates, than they are probably poorer quality

springs and will not give you the handling you desire.

A second word of caution: A competition spring setup is not for everyone. It takes a good driver to properly take advantage of a properly balanced suspension. The best way to sort out which suspension setup may be right for you is to take your car out to a local autocross. If the understeer you experience causes you to yearn for a more balanced car in the turns, then you may be ready to change your stock spring setup.

The best handling Hondas and Acuras have less understeer

Lightspeed makes competition springs for 1988+ Civics, 1990+ Accords, and 1994+ Integras for less than $200. *Lightspeed*

An adjustable spring perch system allows easy height adjustment, which can turn corner weighting into a simple task.

(push) and will actually oversteer (rear end rotation) when driven with some degree of skill. This chapter can help you transform your daily driver to a weekend racer, as well as give you better control on the street. Of course, I do not endorse fast street driving. Racing should be reserved for the track, and not done on the road. But a better balanced vehicle will offer better control, and could help you avoid obstacles in the road, getting you out of dangerous situations.

Rear Suspension

The biggest problem with understeer is that, when entering a

A typical stock spring (right) compared to a cheap variable rate "performance" spring (left).

turn carrying too much speed, there is little chance of being able to negotiate the turn. The reason for this is that the front tires will screech, lose traction, and tend to want to go straight. This could put you into the weeds (or worse), because when you lock up the front tires, you won't be able to steer the car.

If, on the other hand, traction is lost with the rear tires, steering is still possible. That's why a little oversteer (in the right hands) will enable you to go around turns carrying more speed, with more g-force, and under better control. And the best way to reduce understeer is to start with the rear suspension. In fact, if you are on a budget, money could be saved by leaving the front suspension alone and just making the rear a little stiffer.

All Hondas utilize a rear suspension design in which the shock/strut sits inside the spring. The 1984–1987 Hondas and 1G Integras, however, have a one-piece tubular rear axle as opposed to the more competent independent rear suspension that came on later models. Thankfully, there are still affordable rear suspension upgrades available for the earlier cars. Aftermarket competition springs can be found for as little as $100/set, but most only lower the

car about an inch, and do not correct the inherent understeering problem. Owners of 1988+ Hondas and 1990+ Integras have more choices when it comes to purchasing aftermarket springs. The double wishbone rear end is much more responsive than the earlier design, but most aftermarket suspension manufacturers still don't make springs that are stiff enough to decrease understeer.

If you cut the springs to lower the car (not recommended, but widely practiced), the shock itself may compress too far, resulting in restricted piston travel. This can essentially render the shock useless. Another big problem with the cheaper aftermarket springs is that they are not much stiffer than the stock units. (They won't even tell you the spring rate.) For racing, Honda experts recommend a spring rate of at least 300 pounds, and you can't find springs anywhere with that rate that will still fit the Honda perch.

You could have them custom made (big bucks), but still not escape the "compressed shock" problem. Even with an adjustable perch setup, when weight is taken off the rear wheels, the spring will fall down to the bottom of the perch. This phenomenon is further exaggerated when using a stiff rear sway bar. Autocrossing a FWD car will demonstrate the problem of having a spring that is too short. It is common for one of the rear wheels to lift off the ground during hard cornering. When that happens, the spring may fall onto the bottom of the perch (referred to as "spring slop"). Then when the rear wheel returns to earth, the spring has to find its way back into position at the top of the shock tower. Sometimes it doesn't seat properly for a few seconds, causing the back end to become unsettled for an instant.

This may be acceptable for Solo II, but with the higher speeds encountered in Solo I and roadracing, that instant of instability can be even more unsettling for the driver. Tom Fowler along with OPM Motorsports was one of the first to give us a solution to these problems. Systems like the OPM model don't compress the shock to the point where it becomes useless, nor do they create spring slop when the car is lowered, since the springs don't have to be cut. The OPM system utilizes a smaller-diameter spring than the stock setup, and aluminum adapters are used to help the system mount in the stock perch. Some second generation CRX racers use 500-pound springs in the rear, removing the front sway bar completely to reduce understeer.

Koni also recently introduced a fully adjustable spring perch system for 1992+ Civics and all Del Sol models. Each corner comes with an externally adjustable Koni strut, a performance spring that will lower your car between 1 and 2 inches, plus a fully adjustable threaded lower spring perch that can change height by plus or minus 5 inches. Progress Technology offers a similar set-up for Integras and Accords, as well as late-model Civics—expect to pay more than $1000.

For street applications, an adjustable spring perch system may be overkill. Any of the aftermarket springs available through reputable Honda/Acura performance shops will likely serve your street project well. Even though the rear springs will not be stiff enough to effectively deal with the factory understeering problem, there are other ways to address this issue while retaining streetability.

Adjustable shocks and struts, for instance, can help fine tune your vehicle's handling. In the end, however, you will likely end up with a stiffer ride, but steering feedback will improve as will your car's stability. Tokico Illumina shocks and struts have long been favorites for Honda and Acura drivers. We have used nothing else but Tokicos on our project cars due to the simple fact that they are externally adjustable.

Now, Koni also offers externally adjustable units for 2G+ Integras and 5G+ Civics, all Del Sol, as well as for 1990–1997 Accords, but unfortunately not for Acura TL/CL/RLs. Konis are "infinitely" adjustable by turning a knob at the top of the strut. They also offer the option of lowering your car an additional 20 mm by removing an insert prior to installation. It is not as easy to keep track of your settings with Konis, but most Honda racers feel that Koni shocks are the top of the line. The best price for Konis can usually be found at Overseas Auto (800-665-5031), a Koni dealer for 40 years. For street or dual driver 3G and 4G Civics, all CRX, and 1G Integras, Tokico still seems to be the best choice. Either way, expect to spend around $500 for a set.

Koni offers a fully adjustable threaded spring perch system, incorporating a high quality, externally adjustable shock/strut, performance spring, and a threaded height adjuster. *Overseas Auto*

Ingalls' "FastCam" replaces the stock strut or shock bolt and can also be used to adjust camber. *Ingalls*

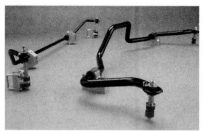

Lightspeed makes sway bars that help keep your car connected to the ground. They fit most late-model Civic, Del Sol, and Integra models, and cost from $365 (Integra) to $440 (Civic). They are excellent for drag racing, autocross, or roadracing. *Lightspeed*

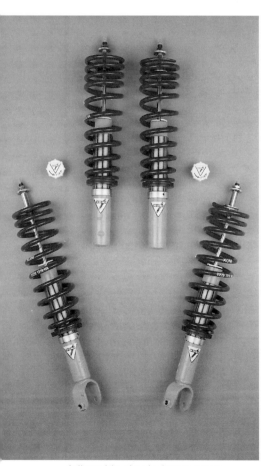

Adjustable shocks/struts are a must for any suspension project. Costing $500 per set, they're well worth the money if you are serious about handling. These Konis can be easily adjusted externally with a simple twist of a knob. *Overseas Auto*

One bit of caution when replacing shocks. Many CRX and Civic owners may run into a hard time when removing the bottom rear shock/strut bolt. The head either snaps off leaving the remainder of the bolt still in place, or the bolt turns as if it were stripped but won't come out. This is because rust has welded it to the inside of the shock bushing. At this point, the only option is to cut it out, which can take hours. Sometimes this problem can be avoided if you soak the entire assembly in Liquid Wrench every day for a week before you attempt removal. If you have an older model Honda or Integra, however, the best strategy is to take your new struts to a muffler shop and have them do the installation That way they can get out the plasma cutter if they run into a problem.

The final component to a trick rear suspension is also the simplest to install. A sway bar is one of the best ways to keep the rear of your car under control while reducing its tendency to plow. Some models, such as the 1984–1987 Hondas, did not come equipped with a factory rear bar. But, since they share the same chassis, a sway bar from the rear of a 1G Integra will bolt right onto a 3G Civic. Call your local junkyard before spending big bucks on an aftermarket bar. Addco bars are another inexpensive alternative, and in the past they have been distributed by the J. C. Whitney Co. for under $70.

For 1988+ Hondas and all Acuras, rear stiffness can be increased by replacing the rubber sway bar bushings with polyurethane. There are also many aftermarket rear sway bars from which to choose. Most import performance shops have them in stock. Another inexpensive and effective way to address rear stiffness is with the addition of rear upper or lower stress bars. The upper bars can also be homemade rather easily.

Whether your goal is to drive an excellent-handling street machine, or a full-blown race car, the quest for neutral steering is often realized only with the installation of a fully adjustable rear sway bar. Besides the higher price ($200+), welding and/or hole drilling may be required before the new bar is in place. But then the fun begins. If the rear bar completes your suspension package, then a trip to the a local autocross should be next on the priority list. Start with the bar in a loose setting, then tighten it up until you begin to feel the rear end bite. If the car becomes too unstable or spins, simple loosen the bar a notch until there is a compromise between understeer and oversteer. In the event that you are someday faced with having to perform a high speed emergency maneuver on the street, you'll be glad you first sorted the car out at the local autocross.

For pure race vehicles, many drivers prefer having predictable oversteer as opposed to neutral handling. With some left-foot-braking practice, you can learn to make the rear of the car slide out

If you want to learn how to properly handle a Honda at speed, then the Mid-Ohio Drivers School is for you. You don't even need a helmet or driver's suit to join in on the fun.

upon command while simultaneously keeping the throttle pegged. Done properly, there are few thrills in life that compare to this experience.

Front Suspension

When it comes to the front suspension, major changes took place in both Honda and Acura models in the 1980s. All of the 1984–1987 Civics (including CRXs) and 1986–1989 Integras were fitted with struts connected to torsion bars via a lateral link control arm. This was a departure from previous generations, and set these models apart from every other Honda product.

All other Hondas and Acuras use a strut/shock and coil spring design in the front. Because of the major differences between the torsion bar set-up and the coil/strut design, two distinct approaches are required when discussing handling improvements.

1984 Civics/CRXs and 1986–1989 Integras

No matter how you feel about torsion bars, they are good for one thing—they can raise or lower a car in an instant by the simple turn of a nut. For dual-duty cars, you can lower the car at the track while you are changing tires, then raise the height back up before you go home. The main question you face when considering suspension modifications is what size torsion bars to use. The 20-mm stock bars

are great for the street and OK for the track, but allow too much body roll. After experiencing both the 23-mm and 24-mm bars, the 23-mm bar appears to be the best choice for a 1G CRX, and the 24-mm bar is preferable for the 3G Civic and 1G Integra. Many performance shops stock these aftermarket torsion bars, manufactured by Sway-A-Way bars, which sell for around $250 a pair.

One problem with the torsion bars on 1984–1987 Hondas and 1987–1989 Integras is that they are often difficult to remove. Our advice: refer to your workshop manual, buy a pair of snap ring pliers, and keep a sledge hammer handy. Here are a few additional tips: Once your car is up on jack stands, it may

Just in case you get a little nervous when spinning a car out of control, the Mid-Ohio Drivers School offers a Civic equipped with training wheels. Actually, this vehicle is used in their teen training program.

be helpful to position another jack under the control arm so that you can raise it slightly. This will cause the torsion bar to rotate slightly in the tube until you can find a position where there is no longer any pressure applied to the splines of the torsion bar. Sometimes that doesn't even help because they may be rusted in place (hence the need for the sledge hammer).

Once the bars are out, remove the tubes that hold the torsion bars in place. Put these tubes in a vise with the rear of the tube facing

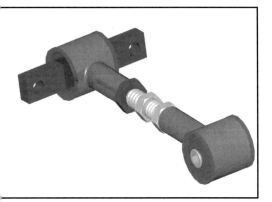

A rear camber adjustment "SmartArm" for 1988+ Hondas and 1986+ Acuras. *Ingalls*

you, and file off the keyway on the inside. By doing this the torsion bar can be installed into any number of positions.

Clean out the tubes and apply some anti-seize before installation to make it easier to get the torsion bars out again. It may be necessary to remove them and reinstall them several times until your car is lowered to the desired height. Mark the position of the former keyway with white paint before putting the tubes back on the car. That way you can easily spot the stock position of the torsion bar in relation to the tube.

Gradually jack up the control arm, and partially install the correct bar for that side (they are marked L and R), lining up the keyways at the front of the car. Then, look at where the keyway on the rear of the bar lines-up with the paint mark on the tube. We found that jacking up the control arm until the bar is one spline away from this white paint mark results in the car being lowered satisfactorily. Two splines can make the car too low for the street, and three . . . (well, never mind). Once lined up

in the new position, you can tap the bar back into place and replace the snap rings. The front of the bar is secured with a different type of snap ring that can be removed and refitted with your fingers alone. Remember to turn the adjustment nut on the end of the tube all the way up before taking the car off the jack stands. If you don't, you may not be able to get the jack out from under the car if you decided to lower the front suspension by two or three splines.

When it comes to sway bars, the ideal set-up for autocross is to throw away, or loosen, the front sway bar to improve turn in, and put a thick, adjustable sway bar on the rear. Roadracers often choose to retain their front sway bars, and some 1984–1987 IT racers even use a thicker 19-mm front sway bar from a Honda Civic Wagon. This can serve to keep the front tires more firmly planted, allowing better traction when exiting the turns.

Moving on to the front struts: Another trick (which we learned the hard way), is to grind 1/2 inch off the locator tab at the bottom of the front strut. This will allow the strut to drop further into the receiving sleeve. Any guesses as to why? When the front of the car is lowered with the torsion bar adjustment, the shock (in its standard location) may compress too much, resulting in restricted shock travel. The strut will essentially "bottom out" and not be able to rebound correctly. On bumpy pavement, the tires may not be able to extend quickly enough to meet the ground, resulting in lost traction. Dropping the strut further into the sleeve will help correct this problem, but be aware that the front end will be lowered even further. That's why you should stick to the "one spline" rule regarding the torsion bars.

The final step before installing the strut is to grind a small concave groove (similar to the one already at the bottom of the strut, but 1/2-inch higher up) to allow clearance for the securing bolt to be easily refitted. Be aware that strut manufacturers do not typically endorse any of these modifications, so you should weigh the risks and benefits before getting out your grinder.

Once the old front struts have been removed, camber plates can be homemade by enlarging the inside part of the stock plate and elongating the two bolt holes on the strut tower to allow for inward movement. This way the front alignment can be adjusted so that your Honda won't eat tires on the street. On race day, however, the plates can be loosened and the strut position changed to obtain up to 1.5 degrees of negative camber in the front. Real camber plates will allow for more negative camber adjustment, but cost around $150.

1988+ Civics/CRXs, 1993–1997 Del Sols, 1983+ Preludes, 1986+ Accords, 1990+ Integras, and all Acura TLs, CLs, RLs, Vigors, and Legends

The double-wishbone-suspension design that is popular today originally debuted on the 1983 Prelude. That's no surprise, as the Prelude is often the first Honda model to showcase new technology. Unlike the torsion bar set-up above, the suspension geometry of a double-wishbone design requires a completely different approach when addressing alignment changes. Newer Honda and Acura models have a strut that sits inside a spring assembly and is sandwiched between an upper and lower A-arm. Camber adjustments cannot be made at the top of the strut, and therefore must be performed from under the car. In order to make precise changes,

you will need to spend between $150 to $250 on aftermarket adjustable A-arms, control arms, or camber adjusters (depending on your make and model).

For example, 1983–1991 Preludes have nuts on the upper control arm that can be loosened and allow the suspension to slide in or out. An aftermarket adjustable control arm mount is available for 1986–1989 Accords. However, if you own a 1996+ Civic, you need to purchase a replacement upper A-arm that has been modified to allow for adjustability. Although costing $250 for both sides, it does make camber changes rather simple. Most other models use an adjustable control arm anchor bolt, which is a simple installation and makes for a somewhat cheaper conversion ($150).

Of course, all of these newer Honda and Acura models can be lowered by installing aftermarket performance springs (just as in the rear suspension). For that reason, it is usually not necessary to induce negative camber since it naturally occurs as a result of the

lowering process. For example, Ingalls Engineering points out that if you lower your car by 1 inch, you can expect a camber change of between -3/4 to -1 degree. Lower the car 2 inches, and you are looking at -2 degrees of camber. A full 3 inches of height change can result in nearly 4 degrees of negative camber that will wear out the inside of your new gumballs before you get home from the tire store. Race cars don't even use that much negative camber. Therefore, if you are planning to use your car on the street, you will want to reduce the negative camber that has occurred as a result of lowering your car by using the products outlined above.

Final Suspension Tweaking (All Models)

If externally adjustable struts are installed, such as Tokico Illuminas, start with a setting of #1 (full soft) in front, and #3 in the rear when you are driving on the street. If you decide to try your hand at autocross, front and rear stiffness can be changed in as little

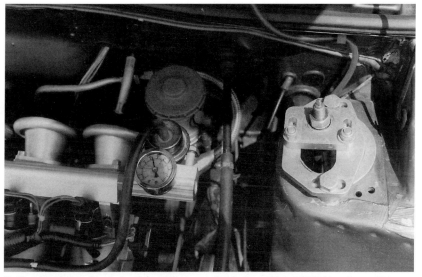

Fully adjustable front camber plates, available for 1984–1987 Hondas, allow up to a three degree adjustment. Castor can also be changed by moving the plate forward or backward.

as 60 seconds. A good baseline is #3 in the front and #5 (full hard) in the rear. It may take some trial and error before you find which settings are best for your driving style. Koni also makes externally adjustable shocks for most of the later-model Hondas and Acuras, but it is harder to keep track of your settings.

There is an excellent assortment of adjustable strut tower bars on the market for around $200. These not only look sharp, but they add structural rigidity to the front end.

For earlier Hondas and Integras, strut bars can also help make camber adjustment very simple. With the camber plates in the stock setting, have your local alignment shop add 1/16-inch toe-out on the front to help the car turn in quicker. *Sit in the car* during this process to ensure true settings.

With the alignment apparatus still attached to the wheels, slide the camber plates inward as far as they will go, and see how much negative camber you can get while insuring equal readings on both sides. Marking the "street" and "race" location of the camber plates is helpful if you plan on changing back and forth between races.

Changes in the front suspension are relatively simple to make, but that's not the case for the rear. If you own a Honda/Integra with a one-piece, solid rear axle, you will need a sledge hammer to make any adjustments. Still, some drivers choose to induce negative camber and toe-in by use of the sledge-o-matic, but this should be reserved for race-only vehicles. We don't recommend it.

Late-model cars may not be able to benefit from the adjustability of a front strut bar; however, aftermarket camber kits are available for the rear of most 1988+ Hondas and 1990+ Acuras. These kits will allow the camber to return to the stock setting to compensate for any change in height that resulted from lowering the rear. Race cars may want to retain some negative camber depending on the front settings, but daily drivers will find that the car will turn in better if the rear is returned to zero.

A final touch that I enjoy doing (partly because it looks so cool) is to relocate the battery for better weight distribution. Drag racers may want to keep the weight up front to improve traction, but roadracers and autocrossers often put the battery on the deck behind the passenger seat, or directly over the rear axle between the wheels (hatchback models). For CRX and pre-1992 Civic owners, this will also make additional room for access to the

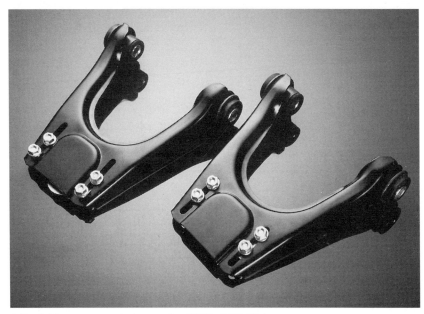

Adjustable upper control arms for 1996–1999 Civics

For 1988+ Hondas and 1986+ Acuras, camber cannot be adjusted from the top of the strut. Ingalls makes a control arm and adjusting bolts to allow for increased negative camber, or more commonly to correct for excessive negative camber that results from lowering the car. This kit is designed for 1988–1995 Hondas. *Ingalls*

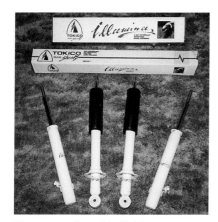

Five way adjustable Tokico Illuminas can help you fine tune your car's handling with just the turn of a screwdriver, without even getting dirty.

A strut tower bar such as this one from GAB for a 1984-87 Honda can significantly minimize your car's front body twist.

distributor and/or the addition of an air velocity intake. Since the battery for most late-model cars is positioned up against the fire wall, it usually need not be moved.

Balancing Act

In racing, a poorly balanced car could shave some time off your life, especially in Solo I or roadracing. Downshifting and hard braking at 100-plus miles per hour will exaggerate any weight imbalance your car may have, even though you may not have noticed it at slower speeds. Trail braking and heel/toe downshifting can help, but a properly balanced car will react in a much more predictable fashion, allowing the driver to push the limits of tire adhesion without excessive twitch and roll.

So, what does it take to engineer a well-balanced machine? For many vehicles, all it takes is access to accurate scales, help from a friend, and about an hour of your time. Assisting me on the job was suspension expert, Mark Hopkins from Carrera. The other item that made things easy for me was that my test vehicle was a

The popular Neuspeed strut tower bar fitted to a 1993 Del Sol.

1985 CRX, which has a fully adjustable suspension.

One of the few good things about torsion bars is that you can raise or lower the front of the car in seconds by turning an adjustment nut under the chassis. Match this with a Carrera/OPM rear suspension kit, and you too can have a fully adjustable 1984–1987 Honda. Acuras and 1988+ Hondas will need to get the kit for all four corners to achieve total adjustability.

With pen and paper in hand, to record changes from inside the

cockpit while Mark read the weights, we pushed the car onto the scales. Figure 1 of table on the following page indicates the dry weight of the CRX (without driver). These numbers aren't of much use unless you're planning to pilot your car by remote control. The heaviest weight you will ever add to your car is *you*, so *you* should be in the driver's seat when the car is on the scales. Figure 2 shows the difference in weight distribution by adding a driver. But look carefully. Where

Figure 1

Weight Distribution—dry weight

LF: 602 lbs	RF 519 lbs
LR 318 lbs	RR 415 lbs

Figure 2

Weight Distribution—with driver

LF: 669 lbs	RF 544 lbs
LR 393 lbs	RR 462 lbs

Figure 3

Weight Distribution—change rear

LF: 665 lbs	RF 564 lbs
LR 414 lbs	RR 437 lbs

Figure 4

Weight Distribution—lower front 1/4"

LF: 639 lbs	RF 568 lbs
LR 420 lbs	RR 424 lbs

Figure 5

Weight Distribution—lower front 1"

LF: 613 lbs	RF 602 lbs
LR 440 lbs	RR 409 lbs

Figure 6

Weight Distribution—lighter driver

LF: 577 lbs	RF 588 lbs
LR 418 lbs	RR 380 lbs

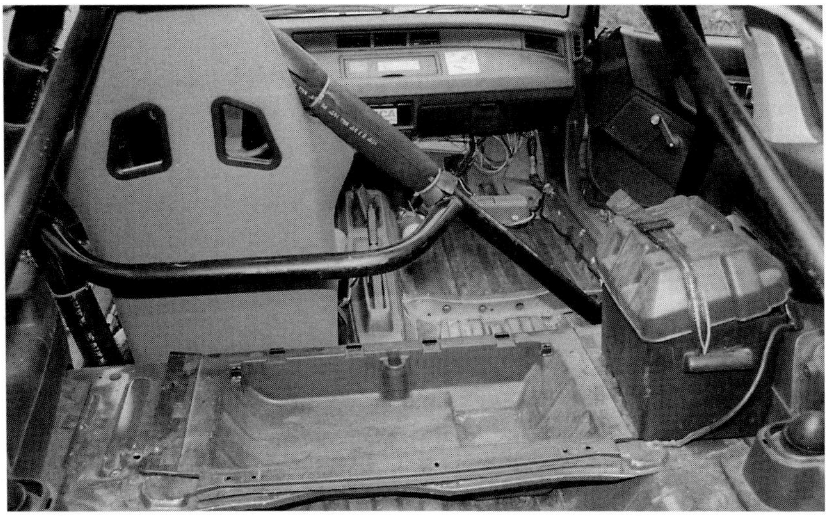

Only recommended for racing (nondrag) applications, battery relocation can help with corner weighting by distributing some weight to the especially anorexic rear of the first generation and second generation CRX. Civics also will benefit.

did the majority of the weight go when the driver sat down in the car? Surprise, nearly 60 percent of the weight went to the rear! Mark Hopkins immediately put me to work lowering the RR (right rear) and raising the LR (left rear). Two principles are at work here. The first is that vehicle weight is not balanced from one side to another, but on a diagonal. For instance, if your car is relatively well-balanced, except for the LR which is too light, you can't just add some weight to that corner and expect to solve your problem. If you do, prepare for a shock. Sure, some of the weight will go to the LR, but the RF (right front) will also increase substantially (more on this later). The second principle is that raising a corner will make it heavier. Does that make sense? It does if you think about it in terms of what is happening to the wheel. You're not raising the car as much as you are pushing the wheel down towards the ground. Mark at Carrera gave me a very easy way to remember this principle: Lower is lighter.

So, back to the CRX. After the initial adjustment in the rear, the weights changed as indicated in figure 3. Note that the front changed only slightly, but the rear differential (left to right) decreased from 69 to 23 pounds.

I recommend that you don't drive yourself crazy trying to reach a "zero" differential, since changes planned for the front will significantly effect the rear numbers. I was happy with this improvement, and therefore moved on to the front corners.

The torsion bars were then cranked down on the RF and up on the LF, changing the ride height by about 1/4 inch on each side (see figure 4). No big deal here, as the differential went from 101 to 71 pounds. Mark urged me to go further, and away I cranked until the RF was lowered and the LF raised by over 1 inch each. But look at the results (figure 5).

With the differential reduced from 101 to 11 pounds, Mark happily informed me: "now you have a race car." And although the rear numbers were negatively effected, they remained in an acceptable range, showing an overall change from 69 to 31 pounds.

Next, just for fun, I took my heavy body out of the driver's seat and replaced it with the much lighter frame of Solo II multi-National Champ Jean Kinser. This was to demonstrate what happens to the weights based on the first principle of diagonal transfer. With a 100-pound difference, check out figure 6 to see how the weight was distributed.

The most weight came from the LF and RR (36 percent + 29 percent, respectively, = 65 percent), while the least was relocated along the opposite diagonal (14 percent (RF) + 21 percent (LR) = 35 percent). As you can see, weight can be added (or removed) to make subtle changes in your car's balance, but never add any weight beyond the axles.

Relocating or changing the size of the battery is a common trick that will shift weight from one corner to another. Experiment by placing the battery in different locations before bolting it down. Hint: the best place isn't always behind the passenger seat.

Corner-weighting can be a relatively simple procedure if you have an easily adjustable suspension. But if you can't take advantage of the aftermarket suspension systems and/or are not permitted to alter ride height, don't be too discouraged. There are still some options available.

For example, experimenting with different spring rates can also change the balance of a vehicle. This would involve much more time, since the springs would have to be removed and replaced, then the car reweighed with each combination you attempt. In principle, the stiffer the spring, the less the spring will be able to compress, resulting in more weight transferred to that corner. But is it a good idea to have different spring rates on each corner of the car? Wouldn't that *create* instability? As Johnny Carson would say: "wrong, shock absorber breath."

Circle track drivers have been doing this for years, as have road-racers. Even in stock classes, some car builders shop for natural variations that can occur in stock spring rates, and bias the car based on these variations. Another trick is to use older, worn "stock" springs in some corners, and fresh new

springs in others to create the desired effect. There are also variations in the thickness of "stock" strut tower bushings, which can alter ride height.

So will all this actually make your car handle better? If the car is poorly balanced (like my CRX was), the answer is yes. But if the weight is already within 2 percent from the left side to the right side (that's about 60 pounds in a 3,000-pound car), then be prepared to accept a trade-off if changes are made.

Remember the cardinal rule of fine tuning: changing one thing usually effects something else. So if you car understeers when turning right (a common FWD problem), you can improve this situation if you are willing to sacrifice some the good handling you are experiencing when turning left. Here are a few lessons to keep in mind when approaching this project: 1) have a definite plan in mind before you begin, and 2) don't make too many changes at one time. Remember, there's more to corner-weighting than meets the eye.

For drivers who do not intend to race their vehicles, one of the current trends involves being able to change the height of your car so that you can clear speed bumps during routine driving. However, upon arrival at a car show or club meeting, your car can be lowered several inches. Firestone makes these Airride rubber air shocks, and ChassisTech has adapted them to fit your Honda/Acura.

This 3G Prelude begs the question: "How low can you go?" Usually, a car that has been lowered to this extreme has form as a priority over function.

Chapter 4

Wheels and Tires

Nowhere does the difference between form and function become clearer than when selecting wheels and tires. For the cool street look, there are many options from which to choose. Making a selection is similar to deciding which speakers you want to buy for your stereo. A look that will complement your car's personality is usually the driving force behind which manufacturer you choose.

On the other hand, if function is your priority, the selections are more limited. Wheels for racing have an emphasis on function, and are generally not as attractive as those for the street. In this case, the type of racing in which you choose to participate will likely drive what type of wheel/tire combination you need.

Wheels for the Street

Never in automotive history has there been a larger selection of aftermarket wheels from which to choose. Prices can range from $50 each to upward of $2,000 per set. But how do you decide what wheel and tire combination is best for your car? There are several scenarios that can help make this often difficult, but mostly fun, decision.

If you have not set a budget for your project, then looks should be the priority. The particular design of the wheel selected should be one that enhances the overall look that you have planned for your vehicle. Then shop around, as prices can

Racing setup (13x9 Taylor Duralights with 225/45/13 Hoosier Autocrossers) versus street setup (15x7 TSW Blades with 195/50/15 Falken ZIEX tires).

vary as much as $100 per set for the more expensive brands.

But if you have taken the advice in chapter 1 and have created a budget, then this budget will help dictate what wheels will best meet your needs. After buying the stereo, spoiler kit, Akimoto intake, GReddy exhaust, and DC header, you may find that you won't have enough money left over to get the real expensive wheels if you want to buy some Nitto tires and a new driver's seat. Then again, wheels may be more important than the stereo. A budget is all about compromise, but it will help you to make sound decisions about your car guided by your head, and not so much by your heart (or the limit on your credit card). Remember, you need to have enough money (or credit) to go have fun with your car after the project is finished.

One of the big decisions that will come into play when planning a wheel purchase is the diameter of the rim. Keep in mind that the larger-diameter the wheel, the lower the final drive ratio. In other words, the larger the wheel, the less revolutions it will make compared to a smaller-diameter rim. The effects of this phenomenon are far reaching, impacting many of your vehicle's operating systems.

If you choose a larger-diameter wheel, your tires will last longer (unless you're doing burnouts). Caution, since tires come in different compounds, this point is only valid when comparing tires of similar composition. The car's speedometer will also be affected by using a wheel/tire combination that is larger than the stock diameter. The common result of this phenomenon is a speeding ticket. The reason for this is that the speedometer is tricked into thinking that your car is going slower than it actually is (since there are fewer tire revolutions per

17x7 Enkei-RS Evolution with Nitto Exit-GT 501 205/40/17.

mile). A positive effect of changing to a larger-diameter setup is that your wheel bearings may last longer, although you will be putting more stress on your transmission. It's much easier to turn a small wheel than it is to turn a larger wheel. That also explains why there will be a reduction in torque when you use a larger wheel/tire combination. The good news is that you may not be quicker off the line, but you will be able to hold first and second gear longer before having to shift.

This effect, however, is undesirable if you have a hi-reving VTEC engine under the hood. A smaller wheel will help keep those Integras up in the power band (between 5,000 and 7,000 rpm) under more circumstances than if a larger rim was being turned by the axle. So at any given point, acceleration will likely be more lively than with the bigger wheel.

Then there is the cost of the tires. Given the same brand and type of tire, the 13-inch size will be cheaper than the 17-inch version every time. Of course, some high

performance street tires do not come in 13-inch or 14-inch sizes, but even though the brand you want doesn't make a tire to fit your 14-inch rim, there are always alternatives. Just because a specific tire brand is "cool," doesn't mean that you won't be able to find a smaller size in a different brand that will match or outperform your friend's "cool" tire.

The main advantage of larger rims over smaller ones is that you can fill up your fender wells without having to lower your car to the point where you won't be able to straddle road kill. Your car will look lower than it actually is. Dropping a car too far has other disadvantages, as outlined earlier in this chapter, so to achieve that "racing" look, a larger wheel will help maintain the streetability of your car.

Tires for the Street
There is less of a selection in street tires than in cool wheels. The most often asked question is: What tires are best? In reality, the tire you select should be based on

Chris Simpson's 1992 Honda Civic is fitted with 16x7 TSW VX1 and Toyo Proxes 205/45/16.

what type of driving you want to do. Usually, you get what you pay for. But if you buy expensive tires expecting that they will be good for both the street and occasional track use, you will be disappointed. Tires come in different compounds. Simply stated, a softer compound will offer better handling, but will wear out sooner than a harder tire. And a racing tire may handle well on dry pavement, but not in the wet, and vice versa.

So how do you decide? Forget the hype that you hear claiming that one tire is so much better than another. When comparing tires with similar design and compound, there is usually no significant difference in the major brands. That is not to say that purpose-built tires are all the same. For instance, snow tires will provide better traction in the snow than will regular tires. So comparing a Bridgestone Blizzak with a Pirelli P6 is not a fair comparison. The P6 will outperform the Blizzak every time on dry pavement, but

won't get you stopped as quickly on an icy road. Off-brand tires, however, usually do not perform as well as the major brands.

But there is even a big difference within a major company's products. Take a BFG ZR and a BFG Touring TA, for example. Tire manufacturers offer many different designs and compounds, just as GM builds Corvettes and Cavaliers. So the top-of-the-line BFG ZR tire is a much better performer than the bottom-of-the-line "touring" design. However, the top of the line performance tire offered by BFG, Goodyear, Yokohama, Michelin, and Nitto all compare favorably. Once you narrow down all the brands that make a tire for the particular use you have in mind, then go pick the tire that is on sale, or that has a "cool" name. It's very similar to choosing which sneaker you want. Forget that crap about Japanese tires performing better on Japanese cars, because it is just not true. Some of the best handling Hondas in the country run on Hoosier racing tires.

So the first thing that you need to do before you choose a street tire is to decide what type of driving you want to do. If you don't plan on doing any racing, a harder compound will do nicely. Traction in the rain and snow will not be compromised as long as you stick with good name brands. If you care more about handling than tire wear, select a softer compound performance tire. Be careful, however, when using these softer compound tires on your daily driver. Performance in the dry will be superior (if not exhilarating), but under any other conditions, you could be putting yourself at risk. In other words, if you live in California or Arizona, go for it. But for Seattle and Pittsburgh residents, a more conservative compound would be a better choice. Ask your tire dealer about available compounds before buying.

The only problem is that it is not always easy to compare compounds from one brand to another. Each manufacturer has its own system of grading "wear," which is an indication of how hard or soft a tire may be. There is no standard. A "250" wear rating on a Goodyear tire may not compare to a "250" on a BFG. But within the same brands, the rating is more of a constant. For example, a BFG tire rated at 250 is softer than a BFG rated at 300.

Tire sizes can also be very confusing. For example, both a 225/50/15 and a 205/55/15 will fit on your 15x7-inch wheel. But you want the 50 series tire because it has a smaller overall diameter. That, however, would be an incorrect assumption In reality, they have the *same* overall diameter. Take another example: the wider 225/50/15 compared to a 205/50/15. The second number in this tire formula ("50") is a percentage of the width versus the height of the tire's sidewall (distance the tire extends above the rim). In other words, the tire "series" indicator (which is a percentage) is not constant. In this case, the height of our 225/50/15 is the first number (225 millimeters, the width) multiplied by the series number (50 percent), which equals 112.5 millimeters in height. For our narrower tire, the 205/50/15, the height is 205 millimeters x 50 percent, or 102.5 millimeters tall. So the 225/50/15 has a sidewall that is 10 millimeters taller than the 205/50/15.

That's why the only way to get a wide tire to fit on 19-inch rims so that the entire package will fit under your fender well without rubbing, is to go to a series 40 or even series 35 tire. The Michelin Pilot SX MXX3 or BFG Comp T/A ZR (excellent tires) both come in the popular size 255/40/19, which is only 102 millimeters tall. The sidewall is therefore a full 10 millimeters shorter than the above 225/50/15. As a comparison, if you did not want to go as radical as a 19-inch wheel, the Nitto Extreme Performance ZR and the Goodyear F1 GS (again, excellent products) make a 255/45/17, which has a sidewall that is approximately 115 millimeters tall. Michelin, BFG, Pirelli, Dunlop, and Yokohama also stock similar sizes.

Finally, in order to calculate the overall diameter of your wheel and tire combination, you need to convert inches (wheel size) to millimeters. One inch equals 25.4 millimeters, but don't get out the calculator yet. Let's say you and your friend have identical Integras. He has 17-inch wheels mounted with a set of 255/45/17 tires, and they look great. There doesn't seem to be any way to fit a larger wheel under the car without running into problems. But you want to go one step more radical than

T.J. Baker uses Avanti 17x7 wheels fitted with Nitto Exit-GT 501 205/40/17 on his 1996 Civic EX.

This standard three piece BBS racing wheel is held together by 16 bolts. Wheel manufacturers build wheels in this manner so that racers can custom order the exact width, offset and bolt circle of the wheels they need, saving the manufacturer from keeping hundreds of one-size only, one piece cast wheels in stock.

Brand new 225/45/13 Hoosier Autocrossers are one of the best choices for Solo I and II Hondas due to their extremely sticky compound. Although not intended for street use, they are Department of Transportation (DOT) approved. Hoosier has purpose-built this tire to be used in SCCA classes where non-DOT tires (racing slicks) are prohibited.

setup will be best for how you want to use your car. Then measure the opening you have to work with, do some of the math above, and call a reputable dealer and ask questions. Feel free to then shop around, but don't always go with the best price. Good customer service is also important. If the company with the cheapest prices can't answer your detailed questions, but a place like the Tire Rack takes the time to work with you, don't turn around and buy the stuff from the other guy just to save a few bucks. Chances are, the other guy won't be able to help if you run into problems.

Wheels and Tires for the Track—Autocrossing

Generally, if you want to compete in a stock class, you will be restricted to retaining your stock rim size. The Street Touring class, if offered by your local club, allows wider wheels. Check with the SCCA first before spending any money. This is one of the newest classes, and there were several changes made over the first two years of its existence.

Since alloy wheels are lighter than steel wheels, they are recommended. The factory Honda and Acura alloys are excellent choices for autocrossing in stock classes. You would think that some of the more expensive aftermarket wheels would be lighter, but you would be wrong. Stick with the stock wheels. Mount up a low profile tire, and you are ready. Some clubs offer "street tire" classes, so you can use the same rubber on the track that you use on the road, saving you from changing wheels when you get to the track.

But, if you want to be more competitive, then here is the short list of tires with the highest percentage of stock class wins for the late 1990s: BF Goodrich R1,

your friend, and wonder if somehow there's a way a 19-inch rim could fit. So, let's do the math. The wheels you want to buy are 2 inches larger than his, but in reality, only 1 inch will stick up into your fender well. The other inch will lift your car off the ground by an extra inch. That's because the distance from the center of a 17-inch wheel to the outer edge of the rim is only 8.5 inches. On the other hand, the radius of a 19-inch rim is 9.5 inches. So, overall, your 19-inch wheels will only reach up an extra inch toward the top and sides of your wheelwell.

Now for the hard part. In order to retain the same overall look, what tire size must you use? Let's try out the sizes discussed earlier. We know that the 255/45/17 has a 115-millimeter sidewall. Add 216 millimeters to this (8.5 inches x the conversion factor of 25.4 millimeters) and you get a 331-millimeter radius. With the 255/40/19, you add the height of the sidewall (102 millimeters) to the radius of the 19-inch wheel (9.5 inches x 25.4 millimeters) and you get a radius of 343 millimeters. That's an extra 12 millimeters, or a little less than 1/2 inch. If you don't think that will fit, you could raise your suspension an extra 1/2 inch (if you have an adjustable suspension), get different springs, or consider an 18-inch wheel with a 255/40/18 that will be essentially the same size. But here's the kicker. Some tires seat lower in wheels than other tires (like the Michelin Pilot). Also, if you buy a wider wheel, the tire will usually seat lower than with a narrower rim.

Since there are several factors that come into play, the first decision to make is what suspension

Hoosier Autocrosser, Hoosier Radial, Kumho Victor, and Toyo Proxes. The Nitto R-type drag radial also shows some promise, but Nitto is still behind BFG and Hoosier in soft compound race tire development. During the late 1990s, Goodyear stopped making a competitive, soft compound autocross DOT radial, and Yokohama made little changes in its first generation A008R, choosing not to keep pace with the top dogs. Since the race tire market changes from year to year, you may want to check with your local autocross club to see what the current hot tires are, or you can go online with one of the autocross discussion forums like www.team.net.

There are several differences between the top three brands, BFG, Hoosier, and Kumho. Kumhos wear better, and will last much longer. For that reason, they are an excellent choice if you decide to add some track events to your autocross schedule. Hoosiers and BFGs tend to be too sticky for drivers schools and track time events.

BFG lays claim to the most stock class wins since the mid-1980s, but unless they are properly heat cycled (it's complicated—ask BFG), your tires could develop the dreaded "groove of doom." A brand new tire could begin to separate near the center treadline, exposing the steel cord below. Once your tires show cord (anywhere), you will not be allowed to compete until the tire is replaced. Hoosier radials made an impact on autocrossing in the late 1990s, but will sometimes wear inconsistently, or wear out too quickly. The most consistent performer of the group, and in my opinion the stickiest gumball you can buy, is the Hoosier Autocrosser.

I have long been a believer in the bias ply Hoosier Autocrosser, especially if you race a Honda,

Taylor Duralight wheels are the best three-piece racing wheels the author tested. Pictured are 13x9 rims, one of the most popular sizes used on street prepared autocrossing Hondas.

Acura, or other light, front-wheel-drive car. The Hoosier's nonradial, bias ply construction has clear advantages over a radial, the best of which may be its weight. In the very popular 225/45/13 size, Autocrossers weigh nearly five pounds less *per tire* than the BFG R-1, Kumho, or Hoosier radial. All of these tires are excellent examples of racing rubber, but they are heavy and add rotating weight to your car. (For a racer, this is the worst kind of weight.)

Hondas and Hoosiers have long been a good match, since Hoosiers stick nicely even while cold. Many FWD vehicles have very little weight bearing down on the rear tires, which often don't reach proper operating temperatures on an autocross course.

If you choose to leave the stock class and move up to street prepared, then there are no restrictions on wheel size. SCCA street prepared history has proven that, for Hondas and Acuras, the best choice in wheel size is 13 inches.

This is because the smaller-diameter wheel will provide better low-end torque, a very valuable commodity in autocrossing.

Specifically, 13x9 or 13x8 for the front, and 13x8 for the rear is a great combination. One of the best wheel distributors in my opinion is the Taylor Corporation. Bryan Taylor distributes Duralight and Lite Speed modular racing wheels, which in the size above weigh only 12 pounds each.

These wheel sizes were carefully chosen, based on extensive testing with FWD vehicles. And although Revolution Wheels are the most popular choice among autocrossers, the Taylor rims are the best-constructed wheels I have ever seen. The problem is that they can be pricey (nearly $200 each). On the other hand, a used set of 13x8 Revolutions can often be found for around $400, and this would be a great choice to get started. But don't go smaller than 8 inches, unless there is a wheel restriction in your class (as in

These are 13x8 Revolutions with 225/45/13 Hoosier Autocrossers. This complete set of four Revolutions mounted with brand new Hoosiers were found on sale at a race for only $500, the cost of the tires alone.

Sticky racing tires, like these Kumho Victors, significantly increase the g-force exerted on your suspension. Sometimes, weak points in the system can give way to this increased stress.

SCCA's Solo II Prepared class, and the Roadracing IT and GT classes, which typically allow no more than a 7-inch-wide rim).

So why a 13x8 wheel? I actually tested 7-inch, 8-inch, and 9-inch wide wheels mounted with the same size and brand tire. The test car was a 1988 Honda CRX, weighing in at 1,200 pounds front, and only 850 pounds in the rear. On a 60-second autocross course, I found that there can be as much as a 2-second difference in times between the wheel sizes, depending on driving style. This was true for both radials and bias ply tires.

And forget about the FWD myth that the rear wheels don't do as much work as the front, therefore the front tire patch is more important. Not true—in fact, one of the largest gains was in the rear, when I replaced the 13x7s with a wider 13x8-inch wheel. The 13x9 seems to be overkill, and can cost a lot more than the smaller sizes (but they look really cool, especially before they have tires mounted on them).

Why not 14-inch or 15-inch wheels? Simple. For most autocross applications, the smaller-diameter wheel will change your final drive ratio. This will give you more torque coming out of a turn, and in accelerating. If you don't believe this, go to a drag strip (as I did) with both 14-inch and 13-inch wheels on hand. The 13-inch wheels will usually give you faster quarter-mile times.

But, there are applications where a larger-diameter wheel would be preferable. Some high speed courses may require an extra shift before a particular turn, often requiring an immediate downshift before exiting the turn. That can waste precious time. Sometimes, however, there isn't much choice. You can't afford to ride along on the rev limiter for more than a second, or you will waste *more* time. In this case, a larger-diameter wheel could be used to change your final drive in the other direction, helping you to avoid that extra shift. The only problem with putting this sound theory into practice is that you have to bring along an extra set of wheel and tires to events.

Racing Slicks

At events or in classes where the use of DOT (Department of Transportation)-approved tires is not required, racing slicks are an even better choice. They can also be much cheaper, especially if you buy used. It is not often that one service stands out above all others, but when it comes to used slicks, you should contact John Berget Tire (414) 740-0180, out of Wisconsin. The price of new slicks is usually more than $130 each, but you can get two for that price through Berget. John also has access to new slicks at discount prices. They are sent COD to your door in only a few days, and for good customers, he will often throw in a free tire from time to time.

But are slicks that much better than the DOT-approved autocross tires mentioned above? Yes, and for one good reason. They have no tread. The tread on a tire will bend slightly when you throw your car into a hard turn, causing some slippage and loss of friction. Since slicks have no tread, they avoid this problem.

So if you are new to the sport, I recommend that you don't go out and buy a new set of street tires to use for autocrossing. A full-treaded tire will slip and screech all over the track, and although this can be entertaining for the spectators, it does not translate into fast times. If you are on a very tight budget, use the baldest used street tires you can find, as long as

RWS 13x7 Alleycats with 20x8.0x13 Goodyear racing slicks. Since slicks have no tread that can bend under hard cornering, these tires maintain a better contact patch than DOT tires. Some SCCA classes restrict wheel size to 7 inches. Tire companies have designed tires to make up for this restriction. Cantilever tires, like these slicks, will fit on 7-inch, or even 6-inch rims, despite the fact that they have an 8-inch wide contact patch. Slicks, however, are not legal for all classes.

they don't show cord (this can be dangerous, as exposed cord can cause a blow out). You won't be competitive, but you will sure have fun.

There are several good slicks on the market, and despite the esteem in which Hoosier Autocrossers are held, the nod goes to Goodyear when it comes to pure race tires. Over the years, the Goodyear slicks have demonstrated two big advantages over their competitors. First, they resist heat cycling. This is also a problem for the BFG DOT R1 tires, but unlike Hoosier Autocrossers, Hoosier slicks seem prone to harden once they have been heated and cooled several times over several races. The other problem with Hoosier slicks is that the sidewalls are so thin, they tend to leak air directly through the sidewalls, often as much as five pounds per hour. As

far as rubber compounds go, both Hoosier and Goodyear offer some excellent choices. From super sticky (used for qualifying or autocrossing) to endurance tires (harder, tend to last longer), there are several compounds from which to choose. Typically, the lower the compound number, the stickier the tire. Of course, the stickier the tire, the quicker it wears out.

Roadracing

You shouldn't run the same tire for autocrossing as you would when roadracing. After several hot laps, a sticky tire will often overheat and become "greasy," thus losing traction. Nor will the softer compound tires last the entire race. Autocross compound tires, however, are often used for qualifying. When you can start in front of the pack, there is less chance of getting taken out by one of the many passing mishaps common in roadracing. Most of the race tire manufacturers already mentioned make tires for roadracing. The only difference is usually compound. Roadracers using slicks have additional choices in how soft they want their tires to be. Besides that super sticky autocross compound, there are usually intermediate soft and full hard tires.

Sometimes, Mother Nature will challenge a roadracer's driving abilities. For this purpose, there are rain tires. Made out of a super sticky compound, rain tires have grooves (you could call them tread) that are designed to channel rain and optimize contact with the pavement. Despite these "grooves," the rain tires are not DOT approved. Class permitting, autocrossers also use these rain tires when the going gets wet.

Drag Racing

When it comes to tires, drag racers have choices similar to what the autocrossers face. Do you go with a street/drag tire, or with a pure race tire? Or, do you just use what you have, and head out to the strip. Entry-level drag racers can have tons of fun with little or no money in their wheel/tire budget. But in order to bring down those quarter-mile times, a good FWD drag tire is needed.

The most popular drag tire with the Japanese import crowd is the Nitto Drag Radial. This tire is constructed with "R" compound rubber, and is the stickiest DOT-approved tire that Nitto makes. The only problem is that there are only a few sizes available. In my tire testing, it was no faster than the BFG R1 or the Hoosier Autocrosser, which come in a larger variety of sizes. And if your goal is to reduce your quarter-mile times, and you want to use an "R" rated tire (which will wear out quickly on the street), then you should have an extra set of wheels so you can more easily change over from your street tires to the racing rubber.

If this is the case, you should try to fight the urge to look cool with a 17-inch wheel, and drop down to a 13-inch wheel, which will increase your low-end torque and give you faster quarter-mile times. The only problem with this setup is that it may require you to make an extra shift before the finish, which will cost some time. If you have not yet started seriously drag racing, just bring your car to the track in street trim, and observe the cars that are similar to yours. What size wheels and tires are they using? Are they crossing the line under high or low rpm?

If they made their final shift just before the finish line and end up crossing at lower rpm, then a smaller-diameter wheel may provide them with enough time to get the car's power band after that final shift before crossing the line. It will also provide more torque at the starting line. On the other hand, if the car you are observing is crossing the finish under high rpm (without bouncing off the rev limiter), they probably have just the right wheel/tire combination for their car.

For the most part, unless your quarter-mile times are under 13 seconds, stock wheels and tires for the rear of the car will do fine. But once you are breaking the 100 miles per hour mark, stick in the rear is also important. Since most serious drivers set up their cars so that the front end is heavy (especially if there has been a more powerful and heavier engine transplanted), that leaves the rear end light. There may come a point at which the rear becomes too

J. G. Engine Dynamics builds many of the engines you will find in West Coast–based drag cars. Many are 1.6-liter and 1.8-liter blocks that can put out well over 500 horsepower. For that reason, the list of FWD Civics/Integras that can do the quarter mile in less than 11 seconds is growing monthly. *Turbo Magazine*

light, which could be dangerous without sufficient rear end stick.

When it comes to pure drag tires, there are only a few choices. Mickey Thompson has long been one of the most popular tires among drag racers. And even though there are sizes available for the formula cars that compete in autocross, you rarely see them amongst the pylons.

These slicks require much less air pressure than the tires discussed above, so review this with your tire dealer before starting out. The heavier your car, the more air pressure you will need to run.

Tire Pressures

The previous chapter covers many ways to improve your car's handling, all of which involve spending money. In this section, we'll discuss one of the most effective and cheapest ways to fine tune your car's handling.

Many people both overlook and underestimate the effect that tire pressure can have on handling. But when it comes to changing handling characteristics, adjusting pressures is one of the best tools you can have at your disposal.

For racing suspensions, a good starting point for most 2000 lb. and under Hondas using bias ply tires is 27 psi in front and 25 psi at the rear. Radials require slightly higher pressures (2 to 3 pounds). If you find your car pushing itself around the track, then you should change your settings to 29 front and 24 rear. With heavier cars, such as Accords, you may want to start with 40 front and 30 rear.

If the car is "loose as a goose" (oversteer—rare with stock Hondas and Acuras), then lower the front pressures and add air to the rear. The theory to keep in mind

for most motorsports is that increased pressures result in increased traction. (However, for some reason, dirt-trackers find that the reverse is true.) Adding air to the front tires will cause them to stick better, and your car will pivot around that point and cause the tail to swing out (oversteer). Increasing pressure to the rear will cause the back end to stick better, and will induce some plowing (understeer).

Drag racers tend to run very little air in the front tires. This is contrary to the theory above, but drag tires need to flex, so that initial grip can be maximized.

For the most part, Hondas come standard with understeer at no extra cost. But by following the guidelines outlined in this chapter, your Honda can be transformed into a well-balanced and more predictable creature.

In this case, a racing wheel was not able to tolerate this extreme g-force. It snapped off, sending the outer portion of the wheel hurtling toward a course worker, who tackled it before it could smash into a competition vehicle waiting at the starting line.

Andy Hollis checks tire pressures for his wife, Ann, between runs at an Akron Sports Car Club autocross. This is done to ensure that the correct pressure is maintained from one run to the next, allowing the car to exhibit predictable handling throughout the day. The reason pressures can change throughout the race day is that as the tires heat up, pressure increases. A codriver will often adjust the pressures for their fellow driver just before a competition run begins. Following the initial runs of the day, as the driver(s) receives feedback on how their car is handling, pressures are changed in order to fine tune handling characteristics (induce or eliminate under or oversteer).

Chapter 5

How to Get More Out of Your Stock Fuel Injection System

This chapter was developed as a result of frustrations faced when trying to hop up a stock fuel-injected engine. A hot ignition and header were added and the intake system modified to make it more efficient. The result was increased air flow, which changed the fuel mixture so that it became slightly leaner. Although still within specs that could be managed by the Honda's computer, the addition of that hot ignition resulted in a much more efficient combustion of the fuel mixture. So efficient, in fact, that not enough gasses were left over to help cool the cylinders between firing. And although the car wasn't overheating, the spark plugs *were*, to the point that they literally began to melt.

Being one of the weaker links in the combustion loop, the spark plugs are likely to manifest the first signs that an engine is running too lean. A colder spark plug helped to slow the meltdown process, but obviously did not address the lean problem. A big part of the problem was probably a bad head—one with stripped spark plug holes that had been replaced with a Heli-Coil insert, or similar product. In any event, there were many questions that arose regarding this situation, which led us to an investigation of ways to gain some better control over stock fuel injection systems. Better to cover this information early in the book before you make modifications

An early version of a K&N air/fuel meter. Newer versions now available through companies like Racer Wholesale can also measure fuel injector efficiency.

that create a "too lean" condition, resulting in piston meltdown.

Some aftermarket computer chips available for the newest model Acuras and Hondas will increase performance, although most readers probably own a 1985+ fuel-injected car that will not accept a chip. Does this mean that you are stuck with the limitations that have been built into this sealed system? Not necessarily.

There are ways to alter the computer management system to improve performance. But how can you be sure that changes made to the system are actually effective? Experts in the field, including Tim Marren (Marren Motorsports), Joe Pondo (MSD), and Russ Collins (RC Engineering), advise you cannot trust your "gut" when it comes to analyzing your car's performance when making changes to an EFI system. And don't think you can simply pull the spark plugs to check for leanness—variations in brands of unleaded gasoline will provide inconsistent readings. So what can you do?

To minimize "subjective" ratings, the first thing to do is install an air/fuel ratio monitor. Inexpensive monitors are available through companies like Racer Wholesale (800-886-RACE) for between $100 and $150. These units easily tap into your existing oxygen sensor, and are highly recommended for determining whether the desired effect has been achieved when a change is made to the injection process. But don't think that what works for one car will work for another. All fuel management systems are slightly different (since individual engines operate in various stages of efficiency), so the results may vary even between vehicles of the same make, model, and year.

Trial and error can be a long and costly process. Here are five

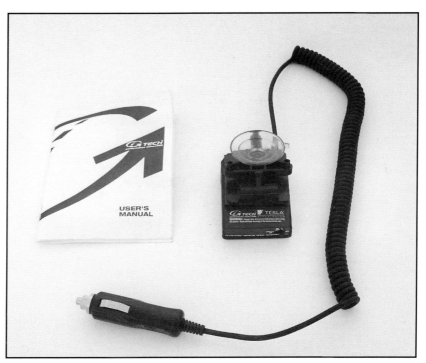

Tesla's G-TECH onboard dyno helped determine what changes were effective in getting the most out of a stock fuel injection system.

popular theories on ways to squeeze additional performance out of a stock fuel injection system.

Legend

The EFI systems of the early Hondas and Integras were examined to demonstrate these theories. Each theory will first be followed by a "wallet indicator," ranging from "inexpensive" (one dollar sign) to "open your wallet wide" (four of them). Then, there will be an indication as to whether or not the particular theory "holds water." Just for fun, instead of water, let's use mugs of beer. Four mugs of beer denotes that the theory is great; one mug means it isn't worth your time.

Theory No. 1:
Modify or Substitute the
On-Board Computer

If your car had carburetors, the solution would be simple: just install larger jets and watch the

air/fuel meter. With any EFI system that has increased air flow (header, Iceman intake, bigger throttle body), you have to find a way to tell the computer to "loosen up" and provide more fuel for the cylinders to burn. These compact computers (found under the passenger seats of most Hondas and Acuras) are programmed by the factory to provide an adequate amount of performance without compromising fuel economy.

In the 1980s, most auto manufacturers decided that a car (especially the econobox models) delivering 40 miles per gallon with 95 horsepower would sell more units than a car that produced 130 horsepower but only got 20 miles per gallon. Thankfully, things have changed, but if you have a mid-to-late 1980s EFI Honda or Acura, what can you do?

Since often there are no "performance chips" available for these vehicles, there are some

This computer from a 1987 Integra five-speed is a direct plug-in substitution for the computer that controls the injection system of a 1985–1987 CRX Si and 1986–1987 Civic Si.

companies that are working to alter the stock computer so that the car's full potential can be realized. Research in this area is resulting in some strange bedfellows: computer hacks working closely with gear heads. This will hopefully result in a trick computer that increases horsepower, or it will further burden the justice system with lawsuits filed against frustrated mechanics by computer programmers for reimbursement of proctology fees for the removal of said computers.

In the meantime, the brain used in a 1.6-liter 1986–1987 Acura Integra five-speed can be interchanged with a 1985–1987 CRX and Civic Si. A source at Honda stated that these cars were designed first for economy and second for performance. But that is not true for the Integra, whose brain unit will keep the CRX injectors open for a fraction of a second longer. Reportedly, timing will be changed, and the rev limiter will increase by a few hundred rpm.

Computer modules from later Honda/Acura models (1988–on) will not work without modification,

since they monitor a crank sensor, which the earlier Hondas (1985–1987) don't have. This tends to make the computer nervous—since there will be no crank sensor input, it believes the engine is malfunctioning.

For all VTEC owners, there are extremely advanced fuel controller systems available from companies like Field, which can be programmed to modify your fuel delivery system throughout the rpm band. And for non-VTEC engines, there are also controllers available for late-model Hondas and Acuras. So, does altering or swapping the electronic control unit (ECU) work?

Wallet Indicator: $ $ ($100–150)
Holds Water:

You bet it holds water! The beauty of this trick is that it will take most people longer to brush their teeth than it takes to change the computer on a 1985–1987 Civic or CRX Si. The Honda connectors

plug right into the Integra unit, and there is no sign that the CRX is rejecting its new organ. The EFI indicator on the dash doesn't even light up. Just plug it in and drive away. Used computers can often be found in the boneyard, costing approximately $100. Make sure that the ECU you are purchasing is from a 1986–1989 Integra five-speed.

For late model Hondas and Acuras, the expense of gaining better control of the EFI system is greater.

Another option is to rewire, or essentially reprogram, your stock ECU. Many unsuccessful attempts were made to do this during the first two generations of Honda fuel-injected engines. Now, however, there has been some success as a result of the popular hybrid movement. Check out the Hybrid web page (www.hybrid.honda-perf.org) for more information. You really need to be a computer engineer to understand the theory, but engine specific questions can usually be answered by these transplant experts.

Theory No. 2:
Install Bigger Injectors

When you add a heater, monster throttle body, or an air velocity intake, your car's EFI computer will try to compensate for the increased air flow into the engine by asking the stock injectors for more fuel, but that they just are not up to the task. Some racers believe that replacing the stock injectors with injectors that have a higher flow rate will increase performance. When it comes to injectors, there are only a few experts out there who really know what they are talking about. Two in particular seem to offer low-budget racers great bang for the buck. If you are looking to keep your car stock, have your old, worn fuel injectors balanced and blueprinted by Marren Motorsports. Tim Marren explained that after a few years, Honda injectors can lose their ability to flow properly. And even if they are flowing at 99–100 percent, the spray pattern may be less than 360 degrees, which will severely rob low-end torque. Expect to pay $150-$250 for this service, depending on the condition of your injectors. The result can be well worth the cost.

For more radical applications, Russ Collins of RC Engineering in Torrance, California, is an experienced engineer who has been tweaking fuel injection systems professionally since 1969. (He must have started at age 15, right Russ?) Russ can compute what injectors you need, based on a variety of factors, including estimated horsepower, how well your intake system flows, or how efficient your exhaust system is.

Most early Honda injectors flow at 175 cc per minute, so Russ sent out Nippondenzo injectors that were rated at 200 cc per minute. Lucas injectors are also available, and are the latest trick in competition injectors. They have rotating discs in the injector tip, which keeps them from clogging, but be careful, as they do not work with all systems.

By the way, why do the British drink beer at room temperature? Because Lucas builds all the refrigerators.

Actually, these new injectors are extremely reliable (didn't a Japanese company buy out Lucas?). Of course, you can always try to find used injectors at a junkyard (no easy task), but be aware that this option may not be as cost effective as you think. In addition to the purchase price, the used injectors should be flow balanced and blueprinted, since the car's computer will choke down the flow of all four injectors to match the least efficient injector in the set. One bad

Gude Performance offers this ECU upgrade for most 1990–1995 fourth generation and fifth generation Civics, and second generation CRX. It changes rev limit, fuel curve, and timing in a manner similar to the way the 1986–1987 Integra does it for the 1985–1987 CRX Si and 1986–1987 Civic Si. *Gude Performance*

apple can spoil the bunch. It will likely be cheaper in the long run to simply go with new injectors.

Wallet Indicator: $ $ $ ($150–300) Holds Water:

What a treat. The higher flow injectors that RC Engineering provided did the trick. The air/fuel meter finally lit up some LEDs that had not been seen before, and now there is a near perfect mixture being burned. As far as performance, there is improved low-end and midrange power, and in general the car is much quicker.

Theory No. 3:
Improve the Flow Through the Intake System

It is assumed that by improving the flow in the intake manifold and throttle body, performance

will increase. Various methods can be utilized to achieve this goal, with the newest trick being Extrude hone. To make sure this theory could be given a fair chance, I again turned to a tried-and-true formula developed by Russ Collins of RC Engineering. He believes that by helping the intake manifold flow better, and by increasing the volume and flow of the throttle body, significant performance improvements will follow. Russ did his magic on these components from the project carand mailed back the improved components (including a Monster throttle body).

Wallet Indicator: $ $ $ ($150–300) Holds Water:

Even if the RC throttle body didn't work, it would get points for

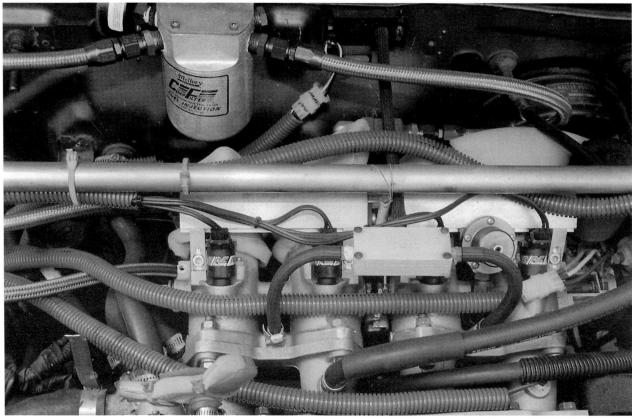

If the air/fuel meter determines that your car is running too rich or too lean, companies like RC Engineering can supply a variety of injectors to meet your car's fuel needs. There are injectors that are designed to flow at higher or lower rates to match modifications to your car's intake system.

looking "tough." One look into the engine compartment, and your competitors will start whining. The beauty of this all is that the throttle body does work, and work well. Performance improved, and in combination with trick injectors, our cute little CRX turned into a monster. The only negative point is that some low end was lost, since when you stomp on the accelerator, a rush of air enters the system, which results in a lean condition. This problem situation quickly turns into a bonus at higher rpm, and overall the CRX was much faster on both the autocross course and in 30–50 miles per hour trials.

One note of caution: If all you do is change the throttle body, you will likely not be pleased with this theory. Dyno testing on a twin-

cam Integra engine, with just the stock throttle body replaced with its Monster cousin, did not give significant results.

But if your car is running richer than stock, and if you have updated your air intake system and added a header, this step should be well worth the money. Remember, you may need to increase the size of your injectors to get the full effect.

Results are often not seen until you complete the final step of your project. Components need to be matched so that you can take advantage of all the modifications you have made.

Our favorite claim from fellow racers (and some manufacturers) is that they got a *15 percent* (add your own number) increase in horsepower when they added a

header (fill in the component). What they don't tell you is that the *header* or other component completed the system that included many other modifications. The benefit of all the other modifications they made was only manifested by the addition of that final component.

Theory No. 4:
Trick the Computer Sensors

This is a theory that many drivers endorse. The trick is to fool the computer into thinking that the engine is cold, so that it will respond with a slightly richer mixture, similar to when the car is warming up. In carburetor language, it is like pulling out the manual choke slightly. The car still runs fine, but the fuel mix is richer.

RC Engineering's Monster throttle body will allow a greater volume of air to enter the intake system. Often this will improve horsepower, but depending on other modifications (header, air velocity intake system), the RC throttle body may cause your engine to run lean, and horsepower will decrease. If this is the case, higher flow Injectors or a fuel pressure riser recapture the lost horsepower, and in most instances, add to your car's punch.

This is done by switching around the wires to the coolant sensor. The only real compromise is that the car will probably not get as good gas mileage.

A switch could be installed in the coolant sensor circuit so the circuit can receive correct readings when the car is started or driven on the street. Then when it was time to race, this switch could be flicked to reverse the readings, trick the coolant sensor, and get better performance.

Wallet Indicator: 0
Holds Water:

This sounds good in theory, but for most cars the increased performance you "feel" is all in your head. I hooked up a switch to test performance with the system getting both correct and incorrect information from the coolant sensor (at our discretion). But the air/fuel monitor and VC-200 don't lie. Hey, since it doesn't cost anything, what the heck. Throw that switch before your last run, if you think it will get you that extra 1/100 of a second. Who knows—it may help. Don't underestimate the power of positive thinking and self-confidence.

Theory No. 5:
Regulate the Fuel Pressure

Most onboard computers control how long the injectors

stay open (longer duration means more fuel into the cylinder), but don't monitor fuel pressure. Another way to fool the computer would be to install an inline fuel pressure regulator, and boost the pressure a few psi. You will have to disable, bypass, or remove the stock regulator, but after the adjustable regulator is installed you can increase the fuel pressure at the end of the injectors by simply turning a knob or screw. This could theoretically make your injectors behave as if they were bigger.

Several companies, such as Stillen, sell fuel pressure risers that will work on any injected Honda or Acura. Usually, the stock pressure regulator will not let the fuel pressure get above 45 psi.

Wallet Indicator: $ $ ($100–$150)
Holds Water:

Increasing fuel pressure will not necessarily result in a richer mixture, but it will cause the injectors to flow at a higher rate. The Stillen unit consistently added one-half of one horsepower throughout the torque band. The unit is easy to install, and does not require the removal of the stock regulator. The question is how far to go before you hit diminishing returns.

MSD offers computer software that can tell you what results to expect when changing various components in a fuel injection system, such as inlet temperature, size of the injector, fuel pressure, etc. This software could be helpful in determining how to proceed in testing the various theories listed above. As for the fuel pressure theory, the gain is enough to justify the expense, although the best way to provide more fuel to your engine is to install bigger injectors.

Conclusions

The Honda fuel injection system is hard to beat. It is both efficient and practical. But is it a match for some of the aftermarket EFI systems that are being offered? If you are willing to make some changes and use proven, matched components, the answer is yes.

For autocrossing, the best performance was achieved with retaining the stock Honda computer, matched with the RC Engineering high-flow injectors and Monster throttle body. For roadracers who need less low end and more throttle response above 4,000 rpm, the Integra computer is best. For serious horsepower gains, there is no substitute for the control offered by the aftermarket fuel and EFI controllers. Most Honda/Acura performance shops can install and tune them.

If you can't afford this setup, then using the Integra computer alone will likely result in both quicker autocross and lap times. Adding bigger injectors is the next step up, both in performance and money, but if you want to play with the "big boys," you will need the bigger throttle body as well. Good luck. I hope you also can "strike it rich."

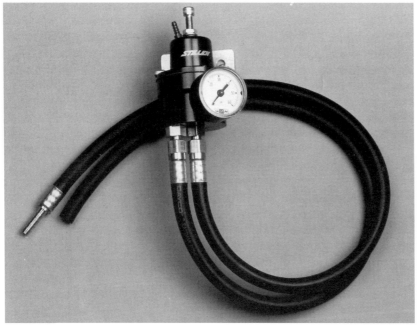

Stillen's fuel pressure riser system can cause your present injectors to flow at a higher rate (as if you have replaced them with bigger injectors). This will provide more fuel and help correct a lean running engine, which will add horsepower.

Chapter 6

Intake Systems

The Scoop on Air Velocity Intake Systems

When it comes to fuel-injected engines, of all the products tested over the past two decades, few have yielded more bang for the buck than the new air velocity intake systems. Usually when a company claims "instant bolt-on performance for very little money," the actual horsepower gain is negligible or nonexistent. "But on the engine dyno, we have proven a significant increase in power by using our product." I don't know about you, but I find that my engine is more useful in my car than it is sitting on a dyno stand. With some clever tweaking behind the doors of a sterile dyno lab, you could probably prove that adding dirt to your oil will result in a power increase. And sometimes when a company claims there is a significant gain in power by using its product, the small print may reveal that it is only under certain conditions, for instance at very high rpm using 100 octane gas.

But in the real world, with the engine actually in your car and hooked up to the alternator, cooling fan, power steering, etc., a better test would be how much of this "increased horsepower" makes its way to the drive wheels. Frankly, when it comes to product claims of "more power," I have been disappointed more than I've

Air Velocity Intake Systems come in all shapes and sizes, and prices. This LightSpeed intake was tested on several Honda and Integra motors, and it is a consistent performer.

been pleasantly surprised. But not in this case. I had to check the dyno several times to make sure that the numbers were correct. I double checked our baselines, installed and tested the intake systems, then removed them, restored the cars to stock, then retested the baselines. The result: a 7- to 8-percent increase in real horsepower was achieved by using a product that costs less than $200 and takes only minutes to install. And this increase was consistent all along the torque curve, not just above 7,000 rpm.

Why do these intake systems work so well? The main reason is not that they are highly advanced technological marvels. It's mostly that the stock intake systems they replace are restrictive and inefficient. So why do the automobile manufacturers make their stock intake systems so restrictive? The answer could be longer life for the engines, lower insurance rates for consumers, more business for the factory replacement air filter market, but these are not the reasons. The main reason is noise. The average car buyer wants a quiet car.

One of the most popular systems around is this Akimoto unit. The reason for this may only be brand name recognition, as most units we tested performed about the same.

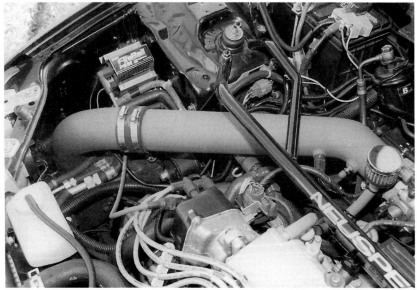

Also extremely popular is the Iceman system, which draws cold outside air instead of warmer engine compartment air. Both systems were tested on a chassis dyno, and there is no difference. This is because, in theory, the Iceman's advantage comes when the vehicle is moving. So it was tested with the trusty Tesla G-tech onboard dyno. The results—inconclusive. If there was a difference, it fell within the margin of error expected when using a device like the G-tech. One thing you can't take away from the Iceman: It looks meaner and, in theory, should add one or two extra horsepower, especially at higher speeds. Note the Crane Fireball coil.

A stock intake manifold is designed with resonating chambers, much like a muffler, so that noise can be kept to a minimum. If you don't believe that air intake can be noisy, you don't already have one of these performance air velocity intake systems. The first time you start your car after installing one, it will sound like a vacuum cleaner.

Another reason stock air intake systems are so restrictive is that they are designed to cut down on emissions. And finally, auto manufacturers often use the same intake manifold on all of their cars, including the "sport" versions, simply because it is cheaper to make just one for all applications.

After all, an engine is just a fancy air pump. Since these stock systems are so restrictive, simply increasing the air flow into the engine will help it breathe better and will usually give you better performance. Sometimes however, the vehicle's computer doesn't know how to manage this increased surge of air and will unsuccessfully try to compensate, resulting in a loss of power. This instance, thankfully, is not the common experience. So why should you spend money on one of these systems when you could just rip out the existing air filter and box, and put a sock over the remaining plastic intake tube. Wouldn't that serve the same purpose?

Yes and no. Usually, anything you do to help the stock system flow better will help. Simply replacing the stock air filter with a freer flowing K&N filter (or removing the filter altogether) will often net a couple of horsepower. But you have to understand the theories of velocity, turbulence, and air flow to see why the old "sock over the tube" deal won't give you what these tuned systems offer. Ed Chang at Twin Cam Motorsports (manufacturer of the

This is probably the meanest-looking intake system you'll see. It belongs to Jerry Lustig's GT3 Acura Integra. Why would someone replace the exceptionally efficient Acura fuel injection system with dual carbs? The answer is one that you will only find in the world of racing. The rules prohibit running fuel injection in GT3, so the car was converted over to Webers.

"Air Accelerator") explains that these units work much like a velocity stack on a racing carburetor.

When air entering the engine is flowing smoothly and consistently, it can be mixed more uniformly with fuel, allowing for better performance across all cylinders.

These aftermarket intake systems also decrease turbulence while increasing the velocity of the air (sometimes as much a two-fold) on its way to the injection system.

The old "sock" can't do either of these things. There are some slightly different systems on the market that draw cold air directly from outside of the engine compartment.

The systems described above draw both warm and cold air. The popular (and probably accurate) theory is that cold air is better for performance. And with the cold air induction systems, cold air flow obviously increases as the vehicle accelerates.

So which one of these systems should you buy? Depending on your car, you may have several choices. It could boil down to a matter of individual preference, price, looks, color, whatever. I routinely use a number of these systems on both our daily driver and racing vehicles. The bottom line is that you really can't go wrong with any of these products.

Chapter 7

Exhaust Systems

One of the most common modifications for the street and the track is the addition of a performance exhaust system. But with the huge selection available, how do you choose? Easy. Pretend you are shopping for a pair of speakers for your stereo. Seriously, there is a direct analogy.

If you have a cheap stereo, buying an expensive pair of speakers will not give you the perfect sound, and will underutilize the potential of the speakers. The reverse is also true. If you have an expensive stereo and you buy a cheap pair of speakers, you will not realize the potential of your stereo. But sometimes, you buy speakers just for looks.

The same goes for your car. Any good aftermarket exhaust system will likely help your car's performance. But, as with stereo components, they must be matched.

Putting a wide open exhaust on your stock Honda may help high-end torque, but your low end (our favorite kind) will suffer! And don't assume that the louder the system, the more wide open performance you will receive.

I did some dyno testing on one of the favorite exhausts around, the stainless steel Supertrapp. You've heard the claims: It is "the tunable exhaust." A lot of performance products were tested that day (only one exhaust system, however), but the only product that lived up to its claim was the Supertrapp. After starting with a 1995 Neon that had no exhaust except for a straight through pipe, I put the Supertrapp on the end.

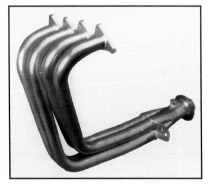

A header is the heart of a good performance exhaust system. An engine can't perform efficiently unless it can effectively and quickly remove exhaust gasses. A header, especially one that is coated on the inside like this one, offers much less resistance to escaping exhaust gasses than a standard exhaust manifold, and it's at least 50 percent lighter. *Stillen*

This Tenzo muffler is an excellent choice for adding some horsepower to the higher RPM range.

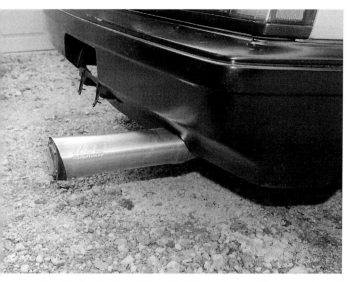

The lightweight and "tunable" Supertrapp. Discs can be added or removed at the tip of this glass-packed muffler. Removing discs provides less space for exhaust gasses to escape, restricting flow and slightly increasing low-end torque. Adding discs will do just the opposite.

There was no decrease in horsepower. At 7,000 rpm, 2 to 3 lb-ft of torque was lost, but the reward was a slight gain at 3,500 rpm. How can that be?

There's no big secret to what happened. The phenomenon is referred to as back pressure. All cars need back pressure to function, or the exhaust gasses that have just been burned in the cylinders will not be efficiently sucked out of the engine. Less back pressure equals more torque in the high rpm range. More back pressure equals better low-end torque.

Most good performance exhaust systems have been tailored to get the most out of your car. However, a Supertrapp is an excellent example of how to explain the above phenomenon, because Supertrapps can be tuned to adjust back pressure. At the end of a Supertrapp, you attach a stack of between 1 and 15 baffle disks. When many discs are used, there are more spaces *between* the discs, making it easier for exhaust gasses to escape and decreasing back pressure. Remove discs, and there is less space for the gasses to escape, which creates back pressure, helping low-end torque.

Once a standard performance exhaust system is on your car, you have no real options to adjust torque. But here's a reality check before the folks at Kirker performance (who make Supertrapps) get swamped with phone orders. The tunability of a Supertrapp covers a very small range of torque (plus or minus 1 to 3 lb-ft of torque). On the other hand, they are relatively cheap (under $150) and work with your stock pipes (replacing the much heavier OEM muffler).

The tail end of a Lightspeed exhaust system attached to the 1.6-liter motor of a second generation CRX.

But don't overlook some of the other systems on the market. NOLOGY, the "HotWires" company, has a self-tuning exhaust tip for street applications called the Shotgun. This tailpipe restricts exhaust flow at low rpm (decreasing decibels), but when you need more power, it swings wide open (loud). HKS is another quality tuner that has been making complete cat-back systems for Hondas and Acuras for a dozen years. GReddy/Trust also has several very cool-looking applications for Hondas, however, both the HKS and GReddy units are rather expensive, costing well over $400. Any of the Honda performance guys can sell you a great system matched for your model car. Choose your system based on what you want to do with your car.

Often, a performance exhaust will bring out the best in some of the intake, injection, carb, or engine mods you have made. Once your car is breathing better, you will begin to reap the benefit from all of your other hard work.

Headers

Most good headers will improve your car's performance, in both low-end and high-end torque, as well as overall horsepower. Due to increasing concerns regarding the environment, removing your catalytic converter is illegal in nearly all states, but a header unit will still help your car to breathe by allowing the exhaust gasses to escape more efficiently.

Most pure race cars that are only used on the track remove the cat and put on a total system from the header back. Which header would we choose if money were no object? Simple. The one

The complete, 100-percent stainless steel Lightspeed Megaflo Pro exhaust system. Dyno tests show a boost of between four and seven horsepower. Cost is under $600 for four-cylinder cars, and around $800 for 1998+ V-6 Accords. *Lightspeed*

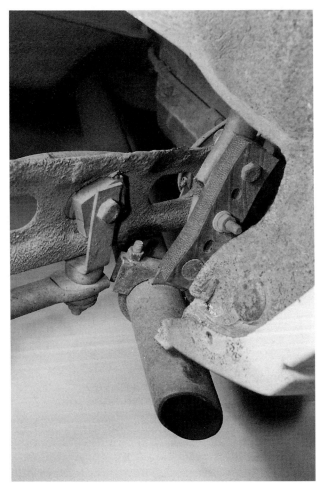

Above
For an inexpensive exhaust on a full-blown race car, simply connect a pipe to the end of the cat or header (with or without a cheap "cherry bomb-type" muffler, depending on your class rules) and make one bend so that it exits on the passenger side of the car in front of the rear wheel.

Right
A close-up of of the bracket that holds the tail pipe in place. Use stiff rubber brackets when possible, to avoid rattles. Note how close the muffler clamp comes to the sway bar end link. The muffler clamp should have been rotated to provide more clearance.

from DC Motorsports. Too bad they don't make them for the 1.5-liter engines, but they have to be one of the coolest engine modifications you can get for the 1.6-liter and 1.8-liter powerplants.

For all of you 1,500-cc guys, the best option is to call a company like Jackson Racing, King Motorsports, etc., and get one of their headers. They offer either a basic 4 into 2 into 1 system, or a more tricky 4 into 1. If the header you purchase doesn't come coated, ship it off to HPC or Jet Hot to have it coated inside and out, costing about $200. A low-budget alternative is to go with a Pace Setter system, $90–120, and have it Armor coated (ceramic coating, around $100).

Our HPC-coated header was done eight years ago, and even though the car sat outside in the Northeast winters, there is only a touch of rust starting to show. Without it, a header will rust in no time. The coatings come in colors, but they are not cheap. Expect to pay around $200 for the job, but you will find that it is worth the investment.

So what have we learned? First, that headers are a great modification that will increase the overall efficiency of your exhaust system. Check to see if local emission laws permit their use on the street. Second, performance exhaust systems are one of the coolest bolt-on hop-up presents you can give to your car. Don't just go to the local muffler shop, however, unless it is to have them put on your new Jackson Racing, HKS, or GReddy system. Call one of your favorite Honda performance shops and order an exhaust that will match the capabilities of your car. For highly modified engines, you can

A custom racing header fitted to a DOHC Integra VTEC motor. Racing headers typically use larger-diameter pipe, and are much noisier than conventional headers.

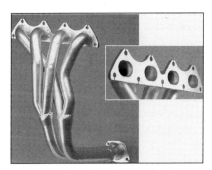

Lightspeed headers fit nearly all 1988+ Honda and 1992+ Integra models, and cost around $375, except for the 1996–1998 Civic, which includes a free-flow converter (not CARB legal) for around $450. *Lightspeed*

get away with a wide-open exhaust system, but without additional modifications to your fuel injection system, a wide-open system can hurt your performance, especially at low rpm. If you can afford stainless steel systems, and you plan on keeping your car for a while, the extra expense is worth it, even though it's often double what a conventional exhaust will cost. Third, it's hard to go wrong with a Supertrapp. They're light, cheap, look radical, and can help finely tune your torque curve.

The best way to find out about an exhaust part before you buy it is to look at data regarding how efficiently air will flow through it. At J.G Engine Dynamics, exhaust components are tested and flow rated. There is a direct correlation between positive results on this "Flow Com" and horsepower gains on the chassis dyno. *Javier Gutierrez*

Chapter 8

Ignition and Timing

An aftermarket ignition system is not a necessity in order to have a fun, competitive vehicle. The stock Honda ignition is an excellent system. Upgrading should only be a priority if you plan on powering a carburetted engine or building a race vehicle. Your decision should also be based on the intended use of the car. For example, if you intend to hop-up an "Si" model for the street, you don't need to spend money on an aftermarket ignition, as it could be spent in better ways. For the track, however, it can be well worth the investment.

There are basically two types of aftermarket ignition systems to consider, and they can be distinguished by their method of timing and distributing the spark. The most popular add-on ignition utilizes a Capacitive Discharge (CD) mechanism. Most Hondas come stock with inductive systems, which are designed to more efficiently burn fuel by supplying a long spark duration. A CD system, however, builds up energy in its capacitors, then the spark is discharged in one short, powerful burst of energy. A CD system will tolerate a larger spark plug gap and tend to be more accurate at higher rpm.

Let's get right to the point. I have tested a variety of the systems over the years, and for the most part, they are all the same.

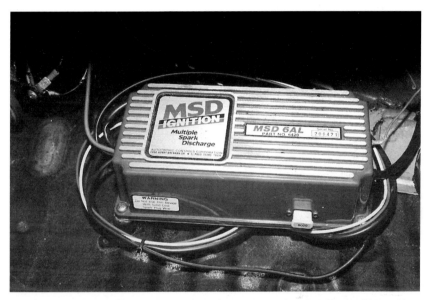

The ever-popular MSD 6AL has built-in rev limiter technology that utilizes chips (bottom right) to control the rpm limit. This unit also has an output lead that can be easily connected to a shift light.

There are many different systems on the market, but the ones to be discussed in this chapter have been proven to be an asset for most applications. The first system recommended is the ever popular MSD 6AL, which remains the preferred ignition for carburetted engines. This is the original multiple spark ignition. And, yes, it does spark several times per stroke and will burn rich mixtures more efficiently than a stock system.

Favorite aftermarket ignitions for fuel-injected cars include the Crane HI-6, which has a built-in rev limiter, and the Jacobs Energy Pack, which has a theft control feature, but no rev limiter.

The HKS Twinpower unit is slightly more unusual, in that it is made to work with your stock coil. Its multiple coil system keeps your stock coil charged in a way that the other systems cannot. All of the above ignitions come with easy-to-follow installation instructions written specifically for your model Honda.

The reason why the HKS unit addresses the weakness inherent in your ignition coil is because

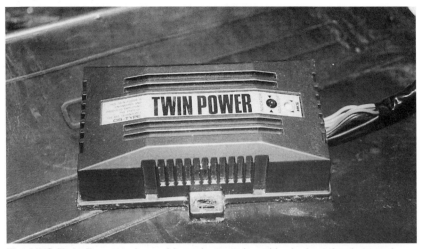

The HKS Twin Power unit provides a hot spark and is designed to be used with your stock ignition coil. The electronics inside the HKS ignition allow for quicker recharging of the coil, providing stronger and more consistent spark, especially at high rpm.

Possibly the ultimate ignition system is this Electromotive unit. There are two coils per cylinder to optimize coil recharge, as well as a direct crank-fire design that makes your distributor obsolete. It can actually be removed (and used as a distinctive paperweight), since the Electromotive receives feedback regarding when to fire the plugs directly from the movement of the crankshaft. This is much more efficient than a standard OHC distributor, because the crank must first turn the timing belt, which in turn rotates the timing gear, which turns the camshaft, only then providing input to the distributor as to the position of the crankshaft and pistons.

most coils cannot return to a full charge at high rpm. Both torque and horsepower curves can become erratic unless you have some help above 6,000 rpm. All of these systems will help flatten out that curve, and can increase horsepower 2 to 5 percent, as well as improve gas mileage by one to two miles per gallon. The best part is that they cost between $200 and $300, and install in less than an hour. Trust me, if I can do it, you can do it.

Last but not least, the other type of system to consider is the same one that revolutionized amateur racing in the 1990s. It is difficult to install and can cost between $300 and $500, but if you have the time and patience, there are rewards. Of course, this is the Electromotive HPV1.

This ignition distinguishes itself from the others in two ways: First, you won't need your distributor. (This is great, save some weight.) Second, it uses a multicoil setup. This allows one coil time to recharge while the others are working. When the installation is complete, your engine compartment will look cool, especially if you have relocated the battery to the rear. And the Electromotive system looks "bad." It's ugly, black, and begs the question from your friends: "Hey, what is that thing?"

The pain of installation involves converting your engine to a crank-fire system. This way of distributing the spark is much more accurate than a standard distributor. Hey, with the money you save on buying caps and rotors, this system could pay for itself in 50 years! Briefly, a standard Honda distributor is driven by the camshaft, which is turned by a timing belt that is connected to the crankshaft.

As you know, the crankshaft is driven by the pistons, which are pushed up and down by explosions in the cylinders. So timing

Under the right set of circumstances, a set of high-quality 8-mm wires can help boost spark better than conventional wires. Many theorize this is because they offer less resistance to electrical flow, therefore transferring more energy to the spark plugs. That sounds like a great theory, but in reality it's the quality of a wire's construction that will set it apart from the rest of the pack. For more information on this subject, check out Magnecor's web site at www.magnecor.com.

information is mechanically relayed from the crankshaft to the timing belt, then to the camshaft, and then to the distributor. With a crank-fire system, you eliminate this entire loop, because the Electromotive ignition receives its information *directly* from the crankshaft pulley.

The problems begin when you have to remove the pulley and fit it with a magnet, or use a special aftermarket pulley. Then you will most likely have to fabricate an aluminum mounting bracket for the engine block to support the sending unit.

As the magnet on the crankshaft pulley turns past the magnet mounted onto the engine block sending unit, timing information can be passed directly to the Electromotive system to pre-

cisely tell it when to send spark to the plugs. Some sending units are designed to read the teeth on degree wheel pulleys.

Getting the mounting bracket and magnets aligned can be tedious, but once your system is set, look out. Talk about a flat torque curve, even at 8,000 rpm! Only the Electromotive system can offer that. Of course once you have installed the HPV1, you will want to convert to Electromotive fuel injection. Pros and cons of this will be examined later in the book.

In conclusion, all of the systems outlined here should give you more horsepower, better gas mileage, and move you up a few notches on the "cool" list. But which should you choose? If you are looking at doing some serious

racing, then the Electromotive should be your choice, as it is probably the best. For performance street or autocross applications, choose one of the others. Yes, many Street Prepared and Prepared Solo II National Champions have the Electromotive system on board, so if you plan on becoming a national champ, then by all means, indulge yourself. If not, get real and go with one of the other CD systems. The free time you save on installation can be spent with your family.

Wires and Plugs

As you surely know, there are many simple little tricks that will get you more power, from adjusting timing to indexing spark plugs. Timing is discussed later in

NOLOGY wires have built-in capacitors that, in this case, are grounded to the valve cover. NOLOGY has its share of critics, but in a stock 1.5-liter test vehicle they were effective, especially at high rpm.

this chapter. Spark plug indexing is a trick that many drivers employ to get a little—*very little*—extra bit of power. Done mostly in stock vehicles (since rules are so restrictive in these classes), it is a waste of time because in modified vehicles, you can use an alternate ignition which will fire a plug even if it has been sitting in the bottom of your tool box for the past 10 years.

Briefly, the goal is to have the open end of the spark plug facing the intake valves. To do this (before installation), mark the position of the open end of the electrode on the white insulator covering of the plug so you will be able to see it when the plug is installed in the cylinder head. Make sure you have at least two sets of plugs handy. The rea-

son for this, as you will see, is that each plug has a slightly different orientation. You will have to try one plug after another until the line you drew on the cover of the plug lines up with the intake manifold. This usually requires installing and removing several plugs per cylinder before you find one that lines up properly.

Why don't I bother? Honda heads are made of aluminum, and repeated screwing and unscrewing will increase the chances that you will strip a plug hole (as I did once). And if I can do it, you can do it.

Probably the most common modification done to a car is the installation of a set of aftermarket ignition wires and plugs. But can these products really improve a car's performance?

Many race car drivers who compete in stock classes feel that they do. Stock classes don't allow many of the changes outlined in this book, but they do permit replacement of the stock ignition coil, wires, and plugs. There is much debate as to whether or not it is worth buying Splitfire plugs, high-performance wires, or super coils. Stock powerplants typically do not respond to these ignition upgrades as well as the more modified engines. The most one can usually hope for is a smoother torque curve at very high rpms.

On the other hand, carbureted cars will usually benefit more from ignition modifications than their computer-controlled, fuel-injected counterparts. The reason should be obvious. Fuel-injected cars have an oxygen sensor that provides feedback to the computer that controls the injectors, and therefore can provide a more accurate and consistent mixture of air and fuel into the cylinders. A carburetion system is much more crude, and in the event that the mixture becomes too rich, a stronger and more consistent spark can result in a more efficient burning of the mixture.

Fuel-injection systems that have been modified can also benefit from these products. Depending on what modifications have been performed, as much as 5 horsepower can be captured by utilizing a high power ignition module, wires, plugs, and a coil. The reason for this is because your stock ignition may not be able to keep up with the needs of the richer fuel mixture you are introducing into the cylinders. In fact, you may experience a decrease in performance if you install bigger injectors without making any other changes to balance out the system.

High power coils and special spark plugs are often overkill on standard EFI systems. Most ignition coils can easily supply the energy needed to fire a spark plug. Providing more juice to the plug will not necessarily create a hotter or bigger spark. This would be similar to putting 94 octane gas into an engine that only requires 89. Your car just won't be able to use that extra octane, just as your spark plug won't be able to effectively use the extra energy.

When it comes to aftermarket wires, however, there is considerable controversy. One of the more interesting products on the market today is from NOLOGY. They believe that instead of trying to burn fuel in the cylinder over a period of time, a more intense spark delivered at a shorter interval will produce a more powerful blast.

NOLOGY has built a capacitor into each wire, and an individual grounding strap that connects the negative end of each capacitor to the engine. Energy is accumulated in the capacitors (housed in the wires themselves) until the voltage reaches the ionization point. Then, all of the energy is discharged at once. Some Honda owners swear by the NOLOGY products. The drawback is that the system is expensive, costing nearly $300 for the coil, wires, and the special spark plugs that are required.

Another leader in ignition-wire technology is Magnecor. They concentrate on manufacturing high quality wires that are designed *not* to interfere with a vehicle's fuel management system. One of the side effects of using some of the "low resistance" wires on the market today is that many will emit electromagnetic interference. This can cause your EFI computer to misinterpret some of the signals it receives, resulting in anything from an occasional misfire to a rough running engine. Magnecor wires are designed to eliminate electromagnetic interference altogether, and are constructed better then most of the other products on the market. They also make no claims that their wires will increase horsepower. For this, they should be applauded. Most other companies state that their products have been proven to increase horsepower. That may be true under certain circumstances, but they have yet to

MSD has a alternative for those 1988–1991 Si owners who do not like the stock Honda ignition setup. On all 1988–1991 fuel-injected models, the ignition coil is located inside the distributor cap. MSD has an alternate distributor cap that, when used with their Blaster coil, replaces the Honda system with one that can produce a higher-energy spark.

pass our chassis dyno test. Over the years, we have tried many brands of wires on Hondas that have both stock and modified fuel-injected engines, and found little evidence to support these claims.

So where does that leave you? Probably confused, and that's because most ignition products can add, at best, only a couple of horsepower under certain circumstances. OEM Honda/Acura wires are excellent products, and usually never need to be replaced unless they wear out. If you install a high power ignition system, however, there is some evidence to support upgrading to a higher performance wire. Some stock wires have been known to fail under the more extreme conditions imposed by a hotter ignition. Then again, so have some high performance wires.

If you choose to invest in any of these ignition products, the "bang for the buck" quotient is not as favorable as other modifications found in this book. One additional bit of advice: Don't use solid core wires on fuel-injected cars. They are meant for carburetted race cars, and can play havoc with an EFI system.

Finally, to satisfy any curiosity readers may have, our highly modified 1985 CRX Si uses an MSD ignition, NGK wires, and an MSD Blaster coil. The Supercharged 1988 CRX Si project car uses wires from a company that is no longer in business. It has also been fitted with an aftermarket MSD distributor cap and Blaster Coil set-up, replacing the stock Honda coil that was incorporated in the distributor. The twin carb project car utilizes the stock Honda coil with an HKS Twinpower ignition and MSD wires. For all of the above vehicles, spark is provided by either standard NGK or Nippondenzo plugs. The SDS EFI project Civic uses the stock ignition to distribute spark, but incorporates a crank trigger. Magnecor wires and Split-fire plugs round out the system.

It's Just a Matter of Time

Racers and mechanics with all levels of expertise recognize that distributor (ignition) timing is one of the many components that can be adjusted to change the characteristics of your engine performance. The degree of adjustability, however, is often limited to: 1) this makes my car run good, or 2) whoops, now my car runs crappy. But in the battle for a "tenth of a second," distributor timing can make a difference.

Your car's engine produces a fixed amount of horsepower, and changing the timing will usually not affect this (unless you had crazy Darryl at the local muffler shop set your timing).

In that case, returning the timing back to the factory setting should recapture your lost performance. What changing the distributor timing will do is tell the engine *when* you want that horsepower to work for you. But first, put down that wrench. There is no escaping the basic law of timing:

When setting your distributor timing, especially when fine tuning an adjustable cam timing gear (as in the next chapter), Honda and Acura owners should always use a timing light (like this one from Sears) that has a degree advance dial. Hondas traditionally run well between -10 to -25 degrees BTDC. Trying to guess at the adjustment you want could cause you to miss out on some of the engine's potential. With this timing light, simply aim the light at the mark on the crank pulley that corresponds to TDC, then turn the degree advance dial until the mark lines up with the mark on the timing belt cover. Now just look at the degree dial setting and *voila*, it will tell you exactly where your timing is set. To make an adjustment, simply turn the distributor, then repeat the steps above to see how the degree dial reading has changed.

Robbing Peter to pay Paul could get Peter really pissed off.

Or put in other terms: If you want more power at low rpm, you will likely have to sacrifice some power and torque in the higher rpm band. It's simply a matter of being advanced or retarded, and in this case, being retarded is not a bad thing. The distributor decides when to send spark to the spark plugs. Although it seems instantaneous, from the time the spark plug fires, to the time when the air/fuel mixture is ignited, it does take time. Granted, this interval is measured in milliseconds, but it does take time, and that period of time remains constant (unless you use a better burning, higher octane gasoline, or are supercompressing the mixture). By moving the distributor in order to retard ignition timing, in essence you are allowing the piston to get closer to the top of its stroke (top dead center) before the spark plug fires and ignites the air/fuel mixture. As rpm increase, the piston is traveling up toward top dead center (TDC) at a higher rate of speed. Since the time it takes to ignite the air/fuel mixture remains constant, you need to advance the timing so that the mixture is ignited earlier, or before the piston reaches the top of its stroke. At very high rpm, as the piston speeds up toward the point where the distributor tells the plug to fire, by the time the air/fuel mix starts to burn, the piston will be long gone past TDC and on its way back down.

To retard the timing, you are adjusting the distributor so that the spark begins to ignite the fuel when the piston is much closer to top dead center, or in some cases, after

Often, small horsepower gains can be realized with simple and inexpensive modifications. Replacing your crankshaft or alternator pulley with a lighter (less rotating weight) or larger-diameter pulley (improved mechanical advantage, making it easier to turn) will usually net a couple of horsepower in most cars. Pictured are AEM Power pulleys. *Diamond Star Creative Group*

the piston moves past the top of its stroke. But why put a spark to the fuel before it is fully compressed?

Remember that even if you have your distributor timing set at -10 degrees BTDC (before top dead center), that doesn't mean that all the fuel will burn before the piston reaches the top of the stroke. The spark plug may fire at -10 degrees, but initially only part of the fuel ignites, which in turn causes the main mixture to explode. During that time, the piston has advanced much closer to (or just beyond) TDC. The point in time (relative to TDC) at which you choose to push the piston along its way will define certain torque characteristics along the crankshaft.

Autocrossers tend to be slightly retarded (sorry, couldn't resist) because retarding the timing will often increase low-end torque, enabling them to get more power coming out of a low-speed turn. Depending on the track and gear selection, roadracers spend much more time in the higher rpm band, and are willing to sacrifice power at 3,000 rpm to gain power at 6,000. For this reason, they advance the ignition timing. Drag racers follow the same philosophy as do the roadracers. As with any adjustment you make to your car, you should initially experiment with small changes and measure what effect they have on horsepower and torque throughout the rpm range. The only reliable way to do this is on a chassis dyno. You should only need about an hour to accomplish the fine tuning necessary to obtain your desired torque curve.

Chapter 9

Putting in a Hot Cam

In most cases, adding a high performance cam will increase horsepower. To what extent is often determined by what other modifications have been made to the engine. The best thing to do before you open your wallet is to check with the experts, or just ask the guys who are driving the same model car as you, but going faster.

Installing a new cam is a relatively simple operation, and should only take a couple of hours. Performance cams range in price from $150 to $600 (with exchange), and very often you get what you pay for. You can also select various levels of performance from mild to radical, depending on the specific operating range you want to improve. Be warned that a radical grind will cause a four-cylinder car to idle like a chain saw. Your favorite performance shop can help you select a cam to meet your needs. But for the most part, you will usually have at least three choices, based on the rpm range you wish to improve.

A wide range conservative grind will usually give you improved low-end torque, a nice boost in the middle range, as well as significant improvement in the high end. The more radical the cam, usually the less gain down low, and the more up high. I chose a mild grind from our friends at J. G. Engine Dynamics for the Honda project car. The cam was also very reasonably priced at about $200 (with exchange), as opposed to the high quality Mugen cams costing triple the price.

Cam choices are even more numerous for newer Hondas and Integras, including the twin-cam and VTEC engines. Prices, however, are slightly higher for these models. The twin-cam Integras seem to especially like to undergo a hot cam conversion, and horsepower can jump up 10 percent or more depending on what else has been done to the engine. Often, the addition of a hot cam will hurt performance if you are installing it before any other fuel delivery modifications are made. This is a common problem with stock VTEC engines.

Cam installation, however, is somewhat more complicated for these models as well as for the 1.6-liter 1988+ Hondas. Remember to inspect your timing belt during this procedure, and replace it if necessary. The same goes for the water pump.

To authenticate the manufacturer's horsepower claims, I took the car to Kirker Performance in Cleveland, Ohio, the guys who produce Supertrapps, one of my favorite exhausts. With the expert assistance of dyno guru Paul Langley, I was delighted to see an impressive increase of 11 horsepower

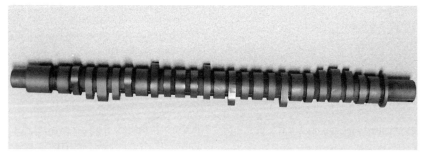

Cams are a popular way to add horsepower to your car. One word of caution, however. Sometimes, cams will only change the torque curve of your car's engine. In other cases, your car can actually lose horsepower, but often there will be a significant gain by adding a performance cam. It all depends on what else you have done to the engine. This very popular cam has been designed for 1992–1995 VTEC Civics by Gude Performance, and will idle like a stock cam. A properly modified fifth generation Civic Si, part of which is the addition of this cam, can net 20-plus horsepower over a stock engine. *Gude Performance*

Sprockets shown on a twin-cam, 1.8-liter Integra engine, which has been modified by J. G Engine Dynamics. With the help of some precise cam and ignition timing, the addition of a hot cam and an adjustable sprocket can net between 5 and 15 percent increase in horsepower. *J. G. Engine Dynamics*

(average) at the wheels! The high end was the major recipient of the power, but there was a significant increase at 3,000 rpm as well. At $200, that's cheap horsepower. But put down the phone. This engine had been dying for a cam.

Before adding the J. G. Engine Dynamics cam, I already had some decent modifications in place: header, hot ignition, performance air velocity intake, bigger injectors, Monster RC Engineering throttle body, wide open exhaust, etc. The addition of a hot cam (with its modified cam lobe geometry) provided a higher and more sustained lift, which opened the intake and exhaust valves a little more, and kept

them open a little longer. This cam seemed to complete the exhaust cycle for our engine, which if you think about it is just a fancy air pump.

By keeping the exhaust valves open longer, there was an increase in the effect in which escaping exhaust gasses create a suction to more efficiently draw fuel into the cylinder. The project CRX seemed to like this condition, as do many of its car friends.

But that is not always the case, as with some Honda engineers who were modifying a 1.6-liter VTEC engine for racing. One of the first changes they attempted on a basically stock engine was adding a performance cam, similar

in grind to ours. They, however, actually experienced a decrease in performance. How could that be?

Give Honda engine designers some credit. The newer engines are engineered so well, that sometimes changing the balance will disrupt the efficiency of the entire system. Consult an expert performance shop, like J. G Engine Dynamics, before emptying your wallet, because cams can't be returned.

Cam Timing

This is a component of engine timing that in the past was rarely adjusted, except by builders of race prepared or modified vehicles. In general, cam timing is much more precise than ignition timing (see

Installing an aftermarket cam is something that most readers can successfully accomplish. If you know how to adjust valves, or have ever changed a timing belt, then this task is no sweat. Pictured is the very simple 12-valve 1985–1987 Si head with a new JG cam in place. Note that the timing belt has simply been slipped off. As long as you keep everything lined up to TDC (mark the distributor's position before removing it), even a novice weekend mechanic can perform this swap. Of course, never even pick up a wrench without first reading your shop manual.

previous chapter). For instance, you can move your distributor from one end of the spectrum to the other, and most engines will usually still run. But move the cam just a few millimeters in any direction, and your engine will get real angry in a hurry.   That's because the camshaft controls when the valves of the cylinder head open and close—when to let air and fuel in, and when to let exhaust gasses out. Hondas and Acuras have tight clearances between the top of the piston and the bottom of the valve. Adjusting cam timing too much could result in bent valves, which will lead to your being asked to open your wallet.

Most Japanese cars manufactured since the 1980s have a single or double overhead cam setup, such as the 1991 SOHC, 1.6-liter CRX Si, or the 1991 DOHC, 1.6-liter ZC that was found in the Japanese version of the same car. With this type of engine configuration, the cam timing gear is at the opposite end of the camshaft from the distributor. Both are directly connected to the cam, so any adjustment to the cam timing will change the position of the distributor, affecting ignition timing. Since the cam timing gear is usually connected to the crankshaft by means of a timing belt or chain, an adjustment in the cam timing will also

change the relationship between the cam and crank.

If you are getting confused, you're not alone. The number of variables that can come into play here can be mind-boggling. For now, let's concentrate on the relationship between the cam timing gear and the distributor. Normally, this relationship is constant, but all that changes when you substitute an adjustable cam timing gear for the stock unit.

This is an easy change to make, as removal of the timing belt is not always necessary. But before rushing out to buy an adjustable gear, be aware that you will likely not gain much horsepower if you are running a stock cylinder head. If, however, your head has been cut to increase compression, then you will probably be able to find some extra power by adjusting cam timing.

The reason for this is simple to understand. The cylinder head on my 1985 CRX project car had been shaved (as are many competition heads), a condition that naturally retards cam timing. This is because the distance between the cam and the crank has decreased due to material that was shaved from the bottom of the head. An adjustable cam timing gear will allow you to advance the cam back to the factory setting (or any other spec). Further advancement of the cam will also advance the distributor, allowing *it* to be rotated deeper into the advanced range. Some of the hot drag racing four-cylinder Japanese cars thrive on -25 or more degrees of ignition advance. That's nearly impossible to get with a shaved head unless you can adjust the cam.

To begin the installation, first loosen the old timing belt with a 10-millimeter socket. Be careful not to lose the keyway that needs to be used when you install the new adjustable gear. Once the old gear is loose, you can easily sneak the timing belt off. Before you install the new gear, compare it with the old gear.

With the keyway as a reference, make sure that the new gear is adjusted so that the teeth line up with the stock gear. This way your car should run exactly as it did prior to the swap. Mark this "stock" position of the new adjustable gear right on both the inner and outer surface of the gear (a permanent black marker works great). This will serve as a good reference point in case you get into trouble later and lose perspective.

Now is a good time to inspect the belt, as it is one of the most important parts of your engine. A

It is recommended that you install an adjustable cam timing gear (like this one from J.G Engine Dynamics) if you plan to change your cam.
Robert Choo

worn or cracked belt can do a lot of damage (bent valves—open your wallet) if it breaks while the engine is running. That is why Honda recommends replacing the timing belt every 60,000 miles. If you decide to install a new timing belt, replace the water pump as well. If the water pump seizes, it will snap the belt, which will, in turn, bend the valves in the head.

Back to the adjustable cam timing gear. The new gear will replace the old one exactly (don't forget about the keyway). You can't put it in upside down, but remember that the adjustable bolts face away from the cam so you can get access to them.

Tighten it up, following torque specs in the shop manual, and slip the timing belt over it. Try to avoid using lubricant, as this could deteriorate the timing belt over time. Don't worry if the teeth of the belt don't line up exactly with the new gear. You can carefully rotate the cam gear slightly one way or another to facilitate slipping the belt over the gear. Just don't move the gear more than one tooth in any direction. The adjustability of the new cam gear will

If you are planning to put in a new cam, you may want to consider having some work done on your cylinder head. But don't *ever* trust your head to anyone except a machine shop specializing in Honda/Acura performance. Using state-of-the-art machinery, shops like J. G. Engine Dynamics can mill, polish, port, and generally improve flow and efficiency of any Honda or Acura head. *Javier Gutierrez*

make it possible to change the cam timing to maximize the performance of your particular engine.

The original numbers for my 1985 CRX project car were somewhat disappointing: 95 horsepower at the wheels. This is with some nifty trick parts already in place: header, ignition, performance intake, bigger injectors, Monster throttle body, exhaust, etc. With the car perched on the chassis dyno, I went to work on the cam timing. This can get complicated, and a chassis dyno is extremely helpful in trying to sort out these

The finished project (camshaft and sprocket installed), with an early version of a JG cam timing gear in place (1985 12-valve Si head).

No matter what engine you may have, the addition of an adjustable cam timing gear, such as this slick AEM sprocket, can help you fine tune your torque curve, usually without causing the onboard computer to have a seizure. No one we have ever talked to has been disappointed with this modification, but often chassis dyno time is needed in order to find just the right adjustment, that results in the desired torque curve. *Diamond Star Creative Group*

components to match the strengths of your car's engine. You will soon discover that even a tiny adjustment of the cam will screw up your ignition timing.

First adjust the cam, then put the ignition timing back to normal. Much trial and error is necessary, and it is not a good idea to undertake this without a chassis dyno.

At one point, the CRX was running with over -30 degrees of advance on the distributor—not running well, but running. This type of distributor advancement cannot be achieved without an adjustable cam gear. Some highly modified engines like this much ignition advance, but mine didn't. The best gain was achieved by slightly advancing the cam timing and dialing in 15 degrees of ignition timing, which captured an additional four horsepower consistently across the rpm band. J. G. Engine Dynamics sells adjustable cam timing gears for many applications for around $200, with exchange.

So what have you learned? Ignition timing can be complicated enough, but if you throw in a way to adjust cam timing, you will need a computer to figure out all the possibilities. Many high performance cars do just that. The rest of us have to rely on what works with our own particular cars.

One word of warning. Don't rush out and buy a cam for your car and expect instant horsepower. Often, you will have zero gain, and in some cases, even lose power!

When it comes to cams, some of the most knowledgeable tuners will say, "Give a Honda/Acura nut $500 and they will likely *cause* their car to lose performance." Usually, only a highly modified engine will benefit from a hot cam.

Chapter 10

Full-Blown Performance: Carburetion Versus Fuel Injection

Do you want to crank your car's performance level up a notch? Many experts today feel that the only way to go is with aftermarket programmable fuel injection, but there are also folks who feel that computers are for the office, not for racing. That real cars have a heart, and that heart is made of metal, not circuits. It's the old argument: What's better, carburetion or fuel injection?

One common viewpoint is: "Fuel-injected cars start easier, idle consistently, and you can easily control the fuel mixture to optimize performance." A counterpoint endorses a more classic view of the automobile: "Carbs are what give a car its personality. They're a simpler concept reminiscent of simpler times. You feel more connected to the car because you get more hands-on involvement." You can hear discussions similar to this one in garages all over the country, and the participants often become passionate about their views.

Let's take a long hard look at the pros and cons of both systems. For comparison, I needed vehicles that were popular with racers, easy to work on, cheap to buy and modify, were fun to drive, and had "personality." The 1984–1987 Honda Civic met these standards. There are tons of aftermarket performance parts available for these

The full-blown performance fourth generation Civic project cars: (left) dual Mikuni carbs, (right) aftermarket Simple Digital Systems EFI.

cars, as well as the later-model Hondas. Actually, the 1.6-liter 1988+ models would also have been a great choice for this project, but they are more costly to obtain, while the 1984–1987 Civic and CRX are plentiful and dirt cheap. The engines needed to be identically prepared. The 1.5-liter Honda blocks were overbored by 0.040 inches (known as "40 over"), and 1.6-liter Acura Integra pistons were slipped into the larger cylinders. Next, for advice on a hot cam, we went to J. G. Engine Dynamics in California. Trying to choose an aftermarket cam can be overwhelming. For Hondas, you can shell out $600 for a Mugen unit, or go cheap ($125) for a mild regrind. J. G. Engine

Dynamics offered a good compromise for under $300 that gave us good low-end torque, along with some nice gains above 5,000 rpm. And these guys are the experts when it comes to squeezing horsepower out of four-cylinder engines. They have built several 10-second Hondas, hard as that is to imagine. But that's another project.

POINT: Traditional Power

For the conversion to dual carburetors, everything had to be just right for it to be competitive with aftermarket fuel injection. Most readers are familiar with the problems that can be encountered when dealing with high performance carburetion, but this poor reputation dates back to a time when carbs

The twin carb project was the easiest to undertake, both in time and money spent. With all of the proper tools and parts on hand, most weekend mechanics can complete a

dual carburetion conversion on Saturday, and then go racing on Sunday.

were generally unreliable and difficult to adjust properly.

There is a new generation of carbs, much more user friendly, which can always be set up more quickly and easily than an aftermarket EFI system can be installed. TWM, one of the leaders in intake technology, sent us the latest in manifolds and linkage to take full advantage of the dual carb setup. Advanced Engine Management in Gardena, California, the largest West Coast distributor of Weber and Mikuni, provided carburetors. Steve Trinkaus at AEM knows both carbs and aftermarket fuel injection systems, and can assist with any intake or ignition need. AEM can also rebuild old carbs for around $125 each. Mikunis were chosen over Webers, because they are externally adjustable and Webers are not.

The next step was to deliver a consistent fuel flow of at least 3 psi to the carbs. That meant getting rid of the stock Honda fuel pump, a sickly looking item that sits between the distributor and the camshaft. Some folks advocate retaining the stock unit, although it is better to "push" fuel from the rear of the car than to "pull" it from the front, as the stock pump does. A new electric fuel pump was installed next to the fuel tank in the rear of the vehicle, and an inexpensive Purolator fuel pressure regulator was installed along the fuel line just before the carbs. Once the above steps were completed, all that was necessary was to remove the old manifold, carb, and pollution control equipment. This took about an hour and turned out to be the most time-consuming part of the project. Then the new manifold, carbs, and linkage were secured into place—done. Everything just bolts right on. All of the ports were matched, both on the head side as well as the carb side, to further optimize intake flow. At this point, the conversion was way ahead of the aftermarket EFI project in ease of installation and time commitment.

The heart of the dual carburetion conversion project are these twin Mikunis with a TWM 1.5L intake manifold. The stock manifold must be replaced since it was designed for a single carb.

The SDS EFI project car originally had a single carb, which was converted to dual carbs to improve racing performance. It now serves as the shell for the EFI conversion.

COUNTERPOINT:
Electronic Fuel Injection, by Dennis Witt

Technology has a subtle way of changing our daily lives. The amazing advances in microchip development have revolutionized the century-old process of mixing a fuel and air mixture in the modern automobile engine. In a very short time span, the manner in which competitors have attempted to maximize horsepower and torque curves has been dramatically altered by the combination of computer power and fuel injection.

Historically, fuel-injected cars were a rarity, primarily due to the cost of the system and its mechanical complexity. Today what was once impossible is now feasible at a very reasonable cost in both time and money.

Aftermarket systems now available allow for the conversion of old and outdated carburetted vehicles to take advantage of the powerful new electronically controlled fuel injection systems. Our comparison should validate the theory that a carburetor conversion "sucks" when compared to an electronic fuel delivery system that "injects."

The heart of our fuel-injected system is composed of an intake manifold and throttle bodies supplied by TWM, maker of components that are compatible with both carb and EFI systems. Injectors and technical advice were provided by RC Engineering, which has just about any size injector in stock and can tailor a "wet" system for any vehicle.

The brains of our conversion were handled by a compact computer developed by Racetech. The name "Simple Digital Systems" says it all. No more having to rely on a laptop to set individual air/fuel parameters. The SDS computer is a small, self-contained unit that can be programmed with ease. To summarize: Hardware = TWM; Wet system = RC Engineering; Electrical = SDS

Now a bit of advice for anyone attempting an EFI conversion: start with a fuel-injected car!

For the carbed project, the fuel pressure regulator is set for 3 psi and just to be sure a fuel pressure gauge is also installed to help with troubleshooting (if necessary).

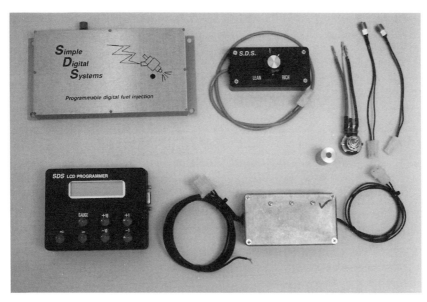

The electronic heart of the EFI project is this kit from Simple Digital Systems. *Racetech*

Converting a car that was not initially designed for fuel injection is a difficult process. Carbs only need 3 to 4 pounds of pressure, but it takes 40 to 50 pounds to run fuel injectors. If you start with a carburetted car, you will find that none of the existing fuel lines or hoses are capable of handling these higher pressures. So the first modification you face is how to get the fuel from the gas tank to the injectors without causing your fuel lines to burst. The solution requires the installation of a larger-diameter stainless steel fuel line from the tank to the engine compartment lines (a difficult and dirty task). That having been accomplished, if you haven't taken a

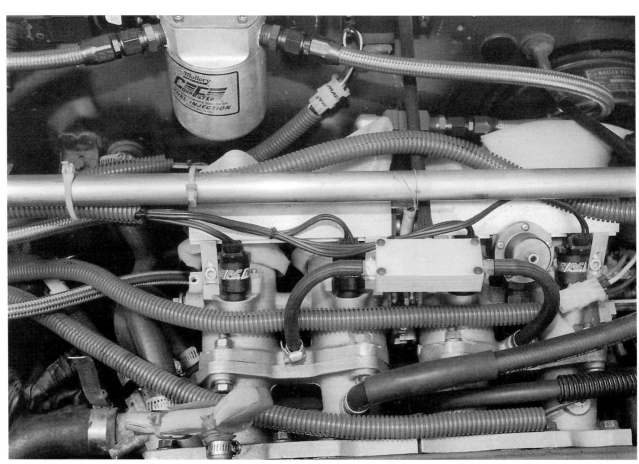

RC Engineering injectors, steel braided fuel lines, and a high pressure fuel filter (top) are all essential components in the EFI conversion project.

sledge hammer to the car in frustration yet and still want to move on, you will now need to get a high pressure fuel pump to keep the hungry injectors happy. I chose a pump manufactured by N.O.S and distributed by RC Engineering. This pump puts out over 100 pounds of pressure at the outlet. Next, AN fittings need to be attached to the fuel pump and plumbed into a new stainless steel line. Not using the highest quality components could cause a rupture of raw gas spraying over both electrical and hot engine parts, resulting in a fuel-fed fire that will render all of your hard work into a glob of melted metal and rubber.

A 3/8-inch-diameter steel line was chosen to handle the additional fuel flow, connected to a high pressure fuel filter to ensure that no contaminants clog the expensive system. The stainless steel line conversion was one of the most difficult parts of the project.

Another frustration was that the individual parts used to install an aftermarket EFI system come from different manufacturers, hence the project is not an "insert part A in tab B" process. A significant amount of time was expended trying to figure out how the entire system would be tied together. If your header is not fitted to contain an oxygen sensor, then a hole must be drilled so that a 22-millimeter nut can be welded in position. Your EFI system won't know what to do unless it gets feedback from an oxygen sensor.

Additional problems encountered were that the chosen Lucas injectors were not compatible with the SDS system, and there was a grounding problem that occurred when a wire inside the throttle position sensor was broken. When you choose which EFI system to use, make sure that you

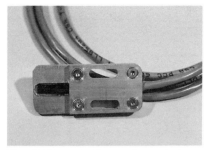

The SDS crank trigger. A bracket needed to be fabricated that could attach to the engine block on which this trigger could be mounted, so it could monitor movement of the crank pulley. *Racetech*

provide all necessary information to the injector supplier.

The moral of the story is that there are many things that can and will go wrong when you tackle a conversion like this. If you mentally prepare yourself to face these problems before you start, it could help preserve your sanity.

Time Commitment

The carburetion conversion is much simpler to undertake, period. With all components on hand, it can be done in one day. In summary, if you are starting with a carburetted car, you should add a more powerful fuel pump that can deliver 2 to 4 psi of fuel pressure.

A trip to the local auto parts store can give you several to choose from for under $75. Switching fuel pumps can often be a dirty job, and some improvising may be necessary, but an average mechanic will have no trouble with any part of this carb conversion project.

Removal of the stock intake system and replacement with a TWM intake is a no-brainer. You will need to add some fuel hose in the engine compartment, and splice in an adjustable (1–5 psi) fuel pressure regulator (a fuel pressure gauge is also recommended). Then, some fiddling with the throt-

This SDS programming keypad allows the driver to control a myriad of variables, right from the cockpit. It also eliminates the need for a laptop computer, which many other EFI systems require in order to facilitate changing parameters. *Racetech*

tle and choke cables should complete your labor of love.

The EFI conversion, on the other hand, will take a tad longer. I recommend starting with a fuel-injected car in the first place. That will save hours of labor converting a fuel delivery system that is used to providing fuel at 1–2 psi, to one that can handle 60 psi. If you don't change the fuel hoses, the new 60 psi fuel pump will cause the weaker hoses to explode fuel into every nook and cranny of your nice little car. If you have never replaced all of the fuel hoses in your car, you haven't lived. There is a great sense of satisfaction that comes with completing the task, similar to the feeling you get when you have been beating your head against a wall, and then suddenly stop.

Installing the new intake manifold is no big deal, but there is more fiddling required than with the carb conversion. The intake manifolds designed for most aftermarket EFI systems utilize a throttle cable system that operates from *below* the intake manifold. Our intake for the EFI car was provided by TWM, and it is a work of art, but changing around your throttle linkage can be a real

Rick Tinsley of Racer Wholesale owns possibly the fastest Solo I/Solo II Honda in the country. It is powered by dual carbs, and incorporates many of Rick's engine building secrets. Dyno results indicate that this (normally aspirated) 1.5-liter engine cranks out 170-plus horsepower with 190-plus lb-ft of torque.

pain. Much finesse is required when rerouting the throttle cable to below the manifold.

Another problem with some EFI intake manifolds is that they require more spring strength to keep the butterflies closed, and many stock throttle cables can't withstand this tension. A day at the track can be ruined when your throttle cable gives way under the pressure. (Don't ask how I know.)

Fine Tuning

Carburetion systems have been given a bad rap when it comes to fine tuning. Playing around with jetting can drive you a little crazy. But it is, at worst, a trial and error ordeal, something that any moron can endure. The shop that sells you the carbs should be able to give you a good starting point, and you can take it from there. Plan to spend anywhere from a few weeks to a

few months to get the setup that best fits your application.

On the other hand, the EFI systems are not easy to set up either. The problem is there are so many parameters, you don't know where to start. Even when you get some initial guidelines, the amount of variables you need to manipulate can be mind-boggling.

It takes a great deal of experience, again, mostly through trial and error, to get the hang of it. And in the end, you will find that you are speaking a different language than your friends. When you tell them your car is running a little rich today because your water temperature and manifold pressure seem to be affecting the duty cycle of your injectors (which is dependent on the MAP sensor and degree of dialed-in knock/retard), they will look at you as if *you* are retarded. If that happens, just scratch your head, declaring that you figured out that your closed loop high parameter needs to be 14:1 in order to obtain stoichiometric balance. That will shut them up.

The Bottom Line: Horsepower and Torque

Dual carburetion on a 1.5- or 1.6-liter Honda engine, if done correctly, can net 170-plus horsepower and a 160-plus lb-ft of torque. Some dual-carbed Hondas are putting out over 200 horsepower, although dyno tests show that much of that power isn't achieved until after the tach goes above 6,000 rpm. On the other hand, a fully sorted-out aftermarket EFI conversion will usually add about 5 to 10 percent to that number. So when it comes to raw power, the SDS system will almost always beat a dual Mikunis conversion.

And although the best built carburetted Hondas get good torque, there is more to be had

This roadracing dual-carbed 1.5-liter engine is capable of over 200 horsepower, but sacrifices torque to achieve power at high rpm.

with an EFI system. Well-known Honda engine builder Chuck Noonan of CRE Performance points out that, over the years his observations of dual carburetted cars versus *stock* fuel-injected Hondas reveal that the nonmodified Si models are actually *quicker* out of low-speed turns than the higher horsepowered dual carb vehicles. That's because even a stock fuel injection system can deliver better low-end torque than a carbed car. And when it comes to aftermarket EFI systems, your torque curve can be customized to deliver power wherever you need it. When it comes to torque, the EFI systems really stand out.

The bottom line is that the EFI systems can deliver slightly more horsepower, and even a stock EFI system inherently will provide better low-end torque. Add to that the adjustability of a system like the SDS unit, and the torque can be placed right where you need it most.

But you need to consider what type of racing you want to do with your car before deciding which system to buy. The Solo II street prepared class is infested with aftermarket EFI cars, but to run an aftermarket EFI system in a prepared class will cost a weight penalty of 150-plus pounds, and most drivers feel that this is too much weight to spot the carburetted cars. That's why dual carbs remain the hot setup for the prepared classes.

Drag racers, however, have a difficult time being competitive without some type of aftermarket EFI system on board. The most popular units are manufactured by MoTeC and DFI, and they are much more sophisticated than the SDS computer. The MoTeC M4 seems to be the best application for Hondas and Acuras. Most of the top drag racers have this system, but it isn't cheap–J.G.

Engine Dynamics can install one for around $4,500. That may seem expensive, but consider the fact that it took two years to tune the SDS system on the Honda project car, and it still isn't right. A performance shop specializing in this conversion is your best bet. That way it is done quickly and done right. The performance of these systems is outstanding, and coupled with today's technology, the possibilities are scary. Javier Gutierrez told us that his shop is now able to adjust the performance of an EFI system without even being at the track. Using satellite communications, and special telemetry equipment, he can monitor the parameters of a driver's EFI system from across the world as the driver is actually running laps. He can view these parameters *in real time* on his laptop computer. Adjustments can be made to the system from thousands of miles away via satellite, and feedback is nearly instantaneous. Let's see you do that with carburetors!

Tunability

Due to the multitude of parameters to consider, which in turn give way to an infinite number of programming combinations, initially setting up an aftermarket EFI system is a long, tedious undertaking. On the other hand, dual carbs (although no walk in the park) are much simpler to set up. But that's where the advantage ends. Once you get the knack of an EFI system, you can get it to do just about anything you want.

So you get to the track, and it is a hot humid day. No problem. Once you have a program stored for this scenario, you will be crossing the finish line ahead of the carbed cars.

If you have ever seen the Pike's Peak Hillclimb, you may

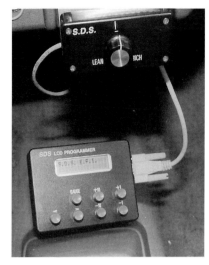

The SDS programming pad and fuel mix controller mount within easy reach of both the driver and passenger, so that tuning can be done on the fly.

have heard that most of the fastest vehicles have EFI computer systems on board that can adjust the air/fuel mixture dozens of times per second! They get to the top first because the atmospheric conditions at the starting line are vastly different than at the top. With an altitude change of over 7,000 feet, you could start out with a hot, sunny day and end up in the sleet and snow. And don't forget what 15,000 feet does to the air pressure. If you have a hard time breathing at that altitude, it is a sure bet that your car does too. The computer in these aftermarket EFI systems can adjust for this variable, and carburetors can't.

Reliability

With today's modern carburetors, reliability is not as much a problem as in the past. I had a pair of Mikunis that ran great for years, but eventually the throttle bodies began to wear and very small vacuum leaks appeared around the shafts. This is the same kind of problem that many British cars develop.

But throttle bodies on the EFI engines can also wear, and often they are under more stress. This is because an EFI system can be more sensitive to the loss of vacuum that will occur if your throttle doesn't completely close. For this reason, larger throttle return springs are often used. These put more tension on the entire linkage assembly, thus increasing wear to the components.

The former Lampkin/Leithauser Honda, now piloted by the team of Mieritz/Despelder. It utilizes an aftermarket EFI system similar to the one in our project. Nearly all of the top street prepared Solo II cars have converted from dual carbs to an EFI system to get the added combination of low-end torque plus precise fuel and ignition adjustment.

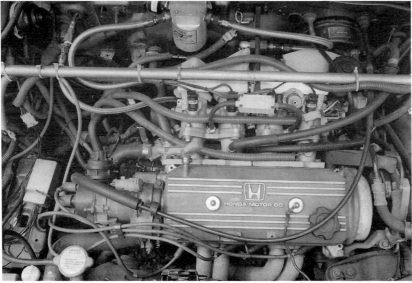

It's much easier to transplant an engine than it is to do an aftermarket EFI conversion. The end result, however, is almost (but not quite) worth the labor.

And injectors don't last forever, either. They can clog, wear, and once the spray pattern and flow rate has been altered, you must have them cleaned. Professional cleaning will cost over $100 per set, and sometimes cleaning won't help. Replacing an injector adds additional expense. Remember to replace your fuel filter (also more expensive on an EFI car) every year or two. Your injectors will be grateful.

Then there's the higher pressure fuel pump, which works harder and is more expensive than the low-psi unit on the carbed cars. If one of those wears out, the EFI pump will put a bigger dent in your wallet. Of course, these are about the only parts of an EFI system that wear.

So when it comes to reliability, it's probably a draw. But if something goes wrong, it will typically cost more money to replace components in an EFI system.

Conclusions

Actually, the choice to go with dual carburetors or an aftermarket EFI system is a simple one. You should base it on what you are planning to do with your car, and how high the credit limit is on your MasterCard. If you have some bucks, need low-end torque and tunability, and have plenty of time on your hands, then the choice is simple. Get yourself injected.

If, however, you are in more of a hurry and only want to spend hundreds instead of thousands of dollars, then dual carbs may be your best choice. Either way, you will have a killer car when you are finished and experience the thrill of full-blown performance.

Chapter 11

Radical Performance: Turbo and Supercharging

If you don't want to go to the trouble of increasing your performance through major head work, bigger pistons, dual carbs or aftermarket EFI, then you should consider adding a turbocharger or supercharger. In fact, a bone stock Honda engine is all you need to begin your blower project. As long as the engine is healthy, you are ready to go. (A turbo won't cure the problems associated with a weak engine.) And you can get about the same boost in horsepower as you would by religiously completing the projects outlined in the six previous chapters. Also, the cost in dollars may actually be less than your other performance options. And there is one big advantage: Your car will be more streetworthy than a car that has been bored out, fitted with a hot cam, and is running aftermarket fuel injection or dual carbs.

A discouraging word for all you 1.5-liter guys: Sorry. There are probably a few used turbo kits out there, but no one makes one anymore for the 1984–1987 CRX and Civic models. Years ago, HKS did have a real hot setup, but it just wasn't cost effective for them to

This sixth generation Civic coupe is one of the many J. G. Engine Dynamics-sponsored drag cars. *Turbo Magazine*

When you see the Jackson Racing decal on the windshield, it's a sign to back down because there is likely a supercharger on board. This Integra GSR cranks out 240 horsepower! *Moss Motors/Jackson Racing*

continue production, due to the increasing popularity of the 1.6-liter 1988+ Hondas. The problem isn't buying the turbo itself, it's finding the special manifold needed to power the turbo, as well as the other adaptive pieces that were included in the kits. A custom-made manifold found on the internet for

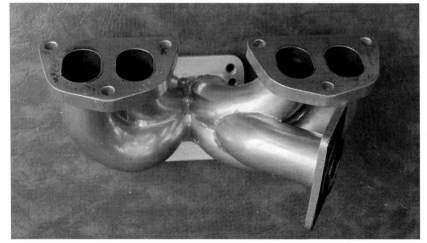

A rare 1.5-liter turbo manifold. That extra exhaust port branching out of the bottom of the unit powers the turbo with hot exhaust gasses.

$250 was used to successfully build a 1.5-liter turbo project, but it is both easier and cheaper to start with a late-model engine design.

However, if you are lucky enough to own a 1988+ model Honda, there are a few things you need to know before you get out that MasterCard. First, your stock

clutch may not be able to handle the 50- to 100-horsepower increase your engine will generate after installing a turbo. Be prepared for this additional expense. My SDS EFI Civic's Centerforce clutch has lasted for over 10 years of hard autocrossing miles. And "Fred" had a fresh heavy-duty OEM Honda clutch installed when the LSD went in five years ago, and both are still going strong.

Honda and Acura trannies, on the other hand, are extremely strong. Many of the 11-second Hondas are successfully using the stock transmission with no problems.

A word about OEM Honda parts. Quality! From oil filters to rings, clutches to batteries, the Honda stuff never fails to amaze us. They are obviously more expensive than at the parts store, but you will notice the difference in workmanship. A new heavy-duty Honda clutch will probably hold out through your car's turbo transformation, but if your present clutch is getting tired, switching to a new high performance clutch would be a prudent decision. Better to spend a little more money in order to be safe, rather than sorry.

Now comes the big decision. Which way do you go: turbocharger or supercharger? They both accomplish the same objective in a different manner, but the decision can be made easier depending on how you will be using your car.

Theory: Turbocharging Versus Supercharging
by Dennis Witt

If you refer to chapters 5, 6, and 7 recalling that an engine is actually just a fancy air pump, you are on your way to understanding how turbos and supercharging work. First, in a standard intake system, air enters (or is drawn into) the engine through the intake manifold. If there is a cold air induction system in place, similar to the Iceman, or if your car has any type of "ram air" intake, the air entering the intake manifold will be cooler and will be moving slightly faster with less turbulence than a stock delivery system. The effect can be slightly increased horsepower. A forced induction system takes this theory a lot further.

Lesson one: turbo and supercharging involve the delivery of air into the intake manifold. It's as simple as that. It's what the turbo system does to the air before it gets mixed with gas that makes it unique.

What it does to the air is compress it. So, big deal, what advantage is there in having compressed air? Well, it's a big deal because when your injectors mix gas with highly compressed air, the greater number of oxygen molecules combined with the proper fuel mixture creates a big deal more power. Air is composed of 2 parts nitrogen and 1 part oxygen, so it just makes

A 1.6-liter supercharged engine. The belt that powers the supercharger is turned by the crankshaft pulley, directly under the engine mount. It winds its way around the alternator and turns the pulley on the Jackson unit. This uppermost pulley comes within an inch of the inner fender. *Moss Motors/Jackson Racing*

sense that the more air you can fit into a cylinder, the more power you can generate up to the point where the stock components of your engine fail.

So how does a turbocharger go about compressing air? It all starts with the exhaust manifold. A turbo exhaust manifold diverts some of the exhaust gasses to the turbocharger. The turbo unit contains a turbine, which these exhaust gasses spin at a very high rate of speed. The size of the turbine, combined with the speed of the turbine, generate *boost*.

But how much boost is too much? Well, that depends on your engine. The more boost, the more horsepower—period. To what point? The point where your engine explodes. The more your engine can take, the higher the horsepower. Reputable turbo manufacturers have tested their systems, and they are the best source of information on the maximum boost level your engine is capable of. So how do you control the amount of boost exiting the turbine? Simple. You install a small valve known as a "wastegate" or "pop off valve." The purpose of this device is to divert exhaust gasses, once the turbine has reached the desired boost. When the volume of forced air encounters a closed throttle plate (as happens between shifts) it must go somewhere other than into the engine. If there was no way of relieving this pressure, it would either back up in the system and damage the turbo or blow out through the weakest link in the turbo system. The wastegate allows the excess pressure to be vented from the system by opening at a preset level of boost, thus avoiding a pressure spike in the system.

The laws of physics dictate that as air is compressed, heat is generated and the density of the air is decreased. A heated charge of incoming air is not what you want in your cylinder. Increased temperature of the incoming charge increases the chance of unwanted detonation of the fuel-air mixture. Detonation occurs when the mixture of fuel and air ignites before the plug fires. This means that the piston is still coming up on the power stroke and collides with the explosion before it should. Depending on frequency and severity of detonation, an expensive rebuild might be in order.

Intercoolers are the answer to high incoming air temperatures. Intercoolers are nothing more than glorified radiators, but instead of cooling the water circulating through your engine, they cool the incoming air charge to the cylinders.

There are two basic types of intercoolers: air-to-air and air-to-liquid. A general rule that can be applied to the incoming air charge is that an 11 degree Fahrenheit decrease in the temperature approximately equals an increase in power of 1 percent. Obviously, to maximize your power output you want to chill the incoming air as much as possible. Air-to-air intercoolers can operate with an efficiency factor of up to 80 percent, whereas air-to-liquid intercoolers can easily operate at this level and higher. Air-to-liquid intercoolers are a little more complex than the air-to-air type, due to the need to add a pump and a tank for the liquid to be circulated through the system, but the payoff comes in more potential power from the engine. Inserting an intercooler between the turbo and the throttle body does cause somewhat of an obstruction, but this is more than offset by the denser charge the cylinders receive, due to the cooling impact of the unit. This compressed and cooled incoming air charge must be properly mixed with a precise amount of fuel to ensure the maximum horsepower and torque. Since a stock Honda ECU was never designed to compensate for increased air flow provided by a turbo, a method to provide increased fuel delivery at

Gude Performance offers a complete bolt-on turbo kit for most 1990+ Hondas that can add up to 60 horsepower on a properly modified engine. *Gude Performance*

J.G. Engine Dynamics is one of the best turbo shops in the country, and carries aftermarket turbo units, like this one. If you look closely, you can see the turbine inside this Garrett turbo. *Robert Choo*

A simple fuel pressure regulator designed to increase fuel flow as boost increases. This unit is mounted just above the motor mount.

boost must be spliced into the system. Depending on the amount of boost you plan to run, an additional computer can be piggy-backed onto the stock unit, or a separate aftermarket unit can be used in place of the existing factory computer. The replacement computers can be specifically tailored for your application and have an almost infinite number of variables, which can be modified for every imaginable combination of conditions you may run into. There are many other manufacturers who offer anything from a very basic unit to top of the line. Only your budget will dictate which system you choose.

Modern computer-controlled cars are tuned for minimum emissions and maximum fuel economy. The parameters that are set at the factory constitute a compromise that ensures that there is a safety margin built into the system. In general, your factory computer is always trying to achieve a stoichiometric ratio of 14.7 parts air to 1 part fuel. This is the point at which the least amount of emissions are generated and the car will still perform in an acceptable manner. This may be fine for running at a steady state down the interstate, but if you want real power, more fuel must

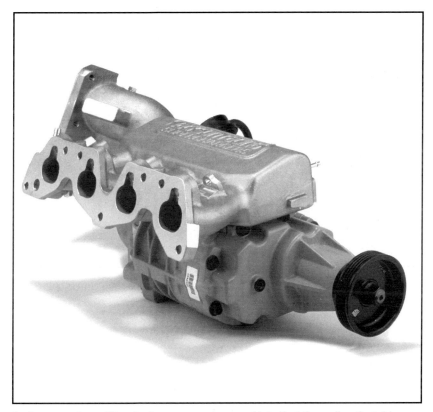

A close-up view of the Jackson supercharger. Note that the pulley that drives the unit requires the use of a three-groove belt, although 1988–1991 Hondas are only equipped to use a two-groove belt off of the crankshaft. A special belt is therefore provided in these applications. *Moss Motors/Jackson Racing*

be introduced into the system. A turbo system without a fuel enrichment program would result in a very lean mixture of about 30 parts air to 1 part fuel. Therefore, any turbo setup must have a way to enrich the fuel mixture as boost increases. This is accomplished either through the computer system or by utilizing a fuel pressure regulator to increase the fuel flow relative to increasing boost. Additional injectors may be added or larger injectors used to make sure enough fuel is added to the compressed air. Running a little rich at 12:1 or 13:1 may foul your plugs but will otherwise do no harm. If your fuel delivery system comes up short, creating a lean condition, major engine damage will occur. It is strongly recommended that an air/fuel ratio meter be installed, along with a boost gauge, and that your car spend some time on a dyno to ensure that your engine is getting a proper dose of fuel. Monitoring your boost and air/fuel ratios while on the dyno will allow you to make any changes on a chassis before you hit on the strip or the street.

As mentioned earlier, supercharging achieves the same effect as a turbo, but in a somewhat different manner. The energy required to turn a turbocharger is nothing but the spent exhaust gasses that would normally be lost to the atmosphere. By inserting a turbine in the exhaust stream, you are essentially getting a free source of power to compress the incoming air charge. A supercharger, on the other hand, requires the use of a belt running off the engine, much the same as a power steering unit or air conditioning. Since this belt can only turn by utilizing some of the power of the engine, a supercharger will result in an actual power drain on the engine. One other item to note is that if you run your car at higher altitudes, a supercharger will theoretically generate less horsepower as altitude increases. This is a result of the wastegate on a turbocharger being able to compensate to a certain level as altitude increases by the closing off of the wastegate. Since the wastegate does not open as soon as it would at sea level, it allows the supercharger to spin to a higher rpm level, increasing the compression effect.

Superchargers in general are a little more compact than turbochargers, due to the need for less plumbing, and superchargers can be a lot simpler to install. The

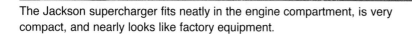

The Jackson supercharger fits neatly in the engine compartment, is very compact, and nearly looks like factory equipment.

A nitrous delivery system mounts easily in the engine compartment, taking up very little space.

number of vendors for Honda and Acura superchargers is very limited. Oscar Jackson comes to mind as a tuner with a long history and excellent reputation in modifying Honda products. Jackson Racing introduced the first supercharger for a Honda in late 1995, but it took three more years to develop a unit for the twin-cam, 1.6-liter and 1.8-liter VTEC engines. Comptech is developing new applications for Acuras, and the list is growing to include models other than the NSX (already available).

The Bottom Line

The list of new companies doing street and strip turbocharger conversions seems to grow bigger and bigger as each month goes by, but check the net or with your friends before you buy any kit. There needs to be proof that the kit will work for your application. Dyno numbers are not always enough. You need to speak first-hand with someone who has actually completed the project (magazines don't count either, since often these companies are also advertisers). A good place to start is with one of the popular web sites, such as the Honda Power Page. Even if you are building a hybrid, there is no law that says you can't also turbo or supercharge it, except maybe for the laws of economics.

The Jackson/Searing supercharger kit can work wonders for your late-model Honda or Acura. Two applications I observed included a 1988 CRX Si that put out 180 horsepower, and a 1997 Integra GS-R that spun the dyno wheels at 230 horsepower. And remember, a supercharger will actually add low-end torque to your high-reving, torque-challenged Japanese import. With Integra LS and GS kits available in mid-1999, there is no excuse. Price varies, but a kit can usually be had for under

The large NOS bottle full of nitrous gas is highly flammable and should be mounted away from ignition sources. This bottle in Rudy Zierden's 1988 CRX Si sits behind the passenger seat.

Rudy Zierden waiting to move out in his nitrous-powered second generation CRX.

$3,000. So go ahead and put a turbo or supercharger on your Honda. Then you will have the capability to show your rear end to those pesky 5.0-liter musclecars!

Nitrous: "Radical, Dude!"

If you don't want to go to the trouble of installing a turbo or supercharger, then you can still blow the doors off of those Mustangs and Camaros by installing a nitrous system. And even if your car is already "charged," you can still give it some gas (NOS), if your engine can take it. An NOS system is simple to install and is a cheaper way to get horsepower, but before

105

A trio of highly modified and lightened 10-second drag cars, all with engines built by J. G. Engine Dynamics. Pictured left to right are the rides of JoJo Callos, John Hoang, and Viet Lam. *photo by Jason Mulroney, courtesy of Turbo Magazine*

getting out that MasterCard, you had better be sure that your Honda or Acura can handle the extra strain. An older engine with worn bearings or rings may not hold together very well when exposed to either turbocharger, supercharger, or nitrous systems.

Nitrous oxide gas is mixed with the air as it is entering the combustion chamber. The result is an air/fuel mix that is supercombustible because, per molecule, nitrous oxide gas has more oxygen. The resulting explosion will force your pistons down harder than they ever have been pushed before. This will put a great deal of strain on your bearings and connecting rods. A newer Honda can usually take this abuse, but one with very high miles may not.

Since nitrous gas is very cold when it is discharged, a few drag racers have installed nitrous fogger systems aimed directly at the intercoolers. The purpose is to lower the temperature of the compressed air before it enters the intake manifold. Cooling of the air makes it denser, and results in better combustion. The most popular intercooler for 10-second Hondas, however, is one that utilizes cold water to cool the air. A final thought: Nitrous systems are not legal for any form of SCCA racing, but many of the fastest Honda and Acura drag cars don't leave home without them.

Chapter 12

Engines and EngineTransplants

Have some free time on your hands? Then why not yank out that old, tired 1.6-liter Civic engine and throw in a 1.8-liter Acura GSR powerplant? Sounds ridiculous? Only to someone who doesn't own a hopped-up Honda. In the past, this kind of mentality was reserved for the American Iron hot rodders. Replacing your small block with a big block, high horsepower V-8 was the realm of Chevy, Ford, and Mopar gearheads. But all of that has changed, and in a big way.

Did it start with the guys who figured out how to replace the unreliable and anemic inline six that lay under the interior of those beautiful early 1980s Jaguar sedans? Who was it who first said, "Yeah, I think I can fit a Chevy V-8 in there." And why was it that MGBs were manufactured with motor mounts that could also accommodate the Buick/Rover V-8? Let's face it, engine transplantation was not invented in Japan, even though one of the most popular transplants in the early 1990s involved Mazda rotary engines ending up in everything from Formula cars to Triumph Spitfires. The question really is, why did it take so long to catch on with Hondas and Acuras?

It all started in Japan. It's understandable that a Japanese-owned company would want to give its own people first shot at the

Transplanting a 1.8-liter Integra engine into a sixth generation Civic is a popular conversion for drag racers. Adding turbo, nitrous, and some other goodies can net mid 10-second quarter-mile times. This turbocharged 500 horsepower beast belongs to Jojo Callos, and has broken the 10 1/2-second barrier, reaching speeds approaching 140 miles per hour. *Jason Mulroney and Turbo Magazine*

best vehicles, and U.S. EPA guidelines don't make it easy for Japan to export the "hopped-up" versions of their cars to American soil. So when the auto magazines told us that the 1987 Civic Si could be ordered with an Integra twin-cam engine in Japan, it made us a little envious. The final straw may have been when the Del Sol was announced as the replacement for the much-loved CRX. But Americans initially received the lousy 1.6-liter SOHC engine, and the Japanese got the VTEC power-

plant. Since the Del Sol was already on the heavy side, compared to the much faster VTEC version, ours seemed like a boat anchor. The movement was already under way at that time, and it has steadily grown into a national revolution. If we can't get what they have, we'll make our own.

Since Honda wasn't about to make two different bodies for the 1987 Civic Si 1.5-liter and the Japanese 1.6-liter DOHC version, it made sense that if you could get an engine from one of those

This third generation Integra GSR motor (B18C1) has gotten a boost from Jackson Racing, and is capable of over 240 horsepower. *Moss Motors/Jackson Racing*

Japanese models, it should fit right into your Civic body. And it did. Better yet, you really didn't have to go to Japan to get the engine. You just had to go to your nearest junkyard and find a wrecked 1986–1989 Acura Integra. People started doing it more and more, to the point that it became somewhat common.

If you already own a late-model Acura, this section may be a little boring, but for the Honda owners, it holds the secrets to greater performance while retaining the look that many Honda

owners prefer. When the Honda body styles changed in 1988, the movement settled down briefly, thanks to the newly designed and extremely competent 1.6-liter, SOHC Si engine. Suddenly aftermarket hop-up parts became common, and this engine responded well to even low-cost modifications. Why spend big bucks to tear apart your Honda, when by just adding a cam, intake, and exhaust you could reach 130 horsepower? Then, Jackson Racing came out with a final reason not to do an engine swap: the supercharger. Now you could get 180 bolt-on horsepower, without even touching an engine mount.

Then three things happened that shifted the focus back to engine transplantation. First there was the death of the CRX and Civic Si. (How could Honda do this to us!) Second, Acura technology hit new heights with the 1.8-liter VTEC Integra GSR. And third, the internet became the preferred way to communicate. So when one gearhead figured that the GSR engine was a fairly uncomplicated direct bolt-in conversion for the 1992–1995 Civic, and hit the internet with how to do it, the hybrid movement began to grow at an astonishing rate. Soon, access to information regarding transplantation was available to everyone with a computer. You could find detailed instructions on how to do a swap, then you could go online to locate the exact engine model you needed. Since there are so many possible combinations, this book can't go into that kind of detail.

Two of the best resources for hybrid conversions can be found on the internet. The Hybrid page (www.hybrid.honda-perf.org) is run by Adrian Teo, and offers tech advice, as well as some detailed step-by-step instructions for completing an engine swap project. If

The engine compartment of Gary Graf's 1984 Civic CRX. The unreliable three-barrel carburetor has been upgraded to a Weber, and the car has been prepared to SCCA IT specifications. Properly adjusted, the car even starts in cold weather.

you want to try it, chances are someone else has already made the attempt and written about it on the Hybrid page. It's an excellent list of what works and what doesn't, and the transplant movement owes a big debt to all of the folks who have tried, failed, tried again, and then succeeded—and then tried to help other gearheads avoid the same mistakes.

When it comes to buying an engine, it's hard to beat the Gillespie boys at HASport (www.hasport.com). H stands for Honda; A for Acura; and sport for motorsports. They stock all of the hot engines, as well as many aftermarket hop-up items.

There are two ways to approach a hybrid project. First, pick the body style of the car that you most desire, then see what you can stuff into it. Or second, pick the engine and horsepower you want to have, then see what body is a good recipient. Since most people start with the car they already have, and then look to see what will fit, this massive amount of data is organized by year and body style. Keep in mind that with a lot of motivation and very hard work, you can shoehorn just about anything into a Honda or Acura. But this book has been designed for sane car owners who have varied interests, and don't want to spend the next year of their life alone in their garage. The projects listed below work. Some are easier to tackle than others; the decision is up to you.

Engine Chronology: The Modern Four-Cylinder Powerplants

The traditional four-cylinder engines were fitted into nearly every Honda model (except the early N-600 and Z-600). The first motorcycle engines in the 1960s S-500, 600, and 800 were no excep-

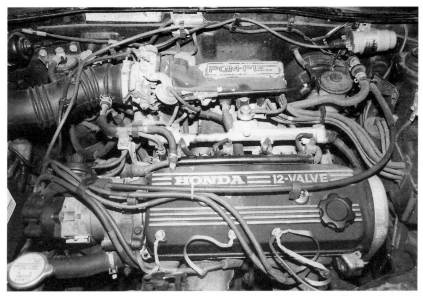

The stock engine compartment of autocrosser John Holzer's 1986 Honda Civic Si (note NOLOGY coil and wires). With some cleaver tweaking (timing adjustments), along with a K&N filter plus the NOLOGY wires and coil, John (a professional mechanic) manages to eke out a few more ponies than the stock numbers.

tion. All Civic, CRX, Prelude, and Acura Integras were strictly four-cylinder cars. Over the years, Honda has been able to squeeze over 200 horsepower from a stock VTEC engine. The new Integra Type R and the revolutionary S2000 really push the limits of four-cylinder technology. But every engineering advance has a basic starting point, and the early 1,498-cc was the first sign that things would soon get better. Listed below is an engine chronology of the Honda four-cylinder powerplants. These are the most popular engines used for transplantation, along with the Honda and Acura models in which they appeared.

EW1
1.5-liter SOHC Carburetted
76 horsepower
1984–1987 Honda CRX
1984–1987 Civic
1984–1985 Civic S

Not often sought after for transplantation, these engine blocks easily mate with the 1985–1987 Si heads. Entire running engines (head, alternator, carb, etc.) can be bought for under $600 from reputable dealers such as Midwest Engine Sales in Cleveland, Ohio (1-800-234-1423).

EW3, EW4, D15A2, D15A3
1.5-liter SOHC PGM-FI
91 horsepower
1985–1987 Honda CRX Si
1986–1987 Civic Si

The first good Honda pocket rocket engine was introduced in 1985. Using the same 1.5-liter block as their carbed brothers, the Si engines utilized multiport fuel injection feeding a head with only 12 valves instead of the anemic 12-plus 4 auxiliary valve design that tended to run hot on the carburetted cars. This 12-valve design turned out to be great for generating low-end torque, and is still a very popular engine for autocross. The Si head also responds well to being cut. For drag applications, up to 60 thousandths of an inch can be lopped off (about 1.5 millimeters or the height

D16A1—1.6-liter engine from a 1989 Integra, which is very popular with fourth generation Civic and first generation CRX Si owners who want to transplant a little more power. The 1986–1987 version is an easier swap, since the wiring between the two models (Integra-Civic) is nearly identical. The 1988–1989 Integra engine had a crank sensor, which the Hondas didn't have.

Rudy Zierden's 1988 Honda CRX DX has a heavily modified D15B6 throttle body engine. In stock trim it would be blown away by an Si, but extra horsepower is just a flick of the wrist away thanks to the on-board nitrous system.

of 1 1/2 dimes). Often, the 1.5-liter racing engines are bored by "40 over" (that's 40 thousandths of an inch, or about 1 millimeter) to accommodate the bigger 1.6-liter pistons from the 1986–1989 Acura Integras, which slip right into place. They are not typically used for transplantation except to replace a blown motor. Sometimes they are put into a 1985–1987 CRX HF, since this body style is so light (just over 1,700 pounds). These complete engines also cost around $600, so if you are looking for an Si head, you may as well buy the whole powerplant for that low price.

D16A1
1.6-liter DOHC PGM-FI
113-plus horsepower
1986–1989 Acura Integra LS and DS
CRX 1.6i-16 (Japanese model)

With a powerful, twin-cam 1.6-liter powerplant, this is the engine that could be ordered for the 1985–1987 CRX/Civic Si, assuming you were living in Japan at the time. In the United States, however, it came standard in the first generation Acura Integras. These engines respond extremely well to bolt-on hop-ups, and are capable of 130 to 140 horsepower with just simple modifications (air velocity intake, header, exhaust, cams). One of the most popular engines for transplant, it is a straightforward bolt-in application for the Honda CRX and Civic 1985–1987 Si.

A20
2.0-liter 12-valve SOHC
110 horsepower
1987–1989 Honda Accord
1985–1987 Prelude

The third generation Accord was clearly the most street-worthy Honda built to date, but it was longer and heavier. To make up for the weight gain, it was fitted with a slightly larger 12-valve

2.0-liter engine that was rated at 110 horsepower. Following the second generation Prelude's first year of production, this engine replaced the 1.8-liter CVCC carburetted powerplant in all Accords and most Preludes through the rest of the 1980s. Not a very popular engine for swapping.

D16A6
1.6-liter SOHC PGM-FI
108 horsepower
1988–1991 Honda CRX Si
and Civic Si

The introduction of this competent 1.6-liter powerplant was a good sign that Honda remained serious about continuing to build pocket rockets. This D16A6 was fitted with a new SOHC 16-valve head, which, when slightly cut, ported, and polished can boost power by 10 horsepower. The engine itself also responds well to modifications, but doesn't transplant well into the earlier generation cars. In stock trim, it will crank out 108 horsepower at 6,000 rpm with a redline of 7,100, but a rating of 120-plus horsepower can be had by spending as little as $800 (air velocity intake, header, exhaust, cam).

D15B6
1.5-liter SOHC Dual port
throttle body FI
62/70 horsepower
1988–1991 CRX and Civic HF

Using a slightly redesigned 1.5-liter block, the HF gave up on carburetion in favor of dual port fuel injection with a SOHC eight-valve head. Performance, however, was still poor, at only 62 horsepower. In 1990, two more ports were added, and performance was boosted by 8 horsepower. Reliability was much improved over the previous generation HF, and as always, these cars weighed substantially less than the other versions for this generation.

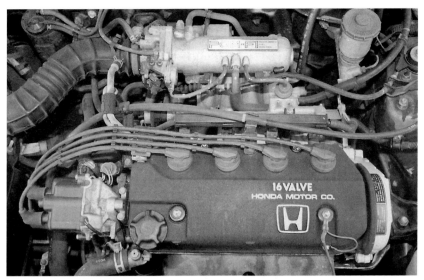

Andy Helgeson's 1991 Civic Si is bone stock except for an HKS air velocity intake. This D16A6 1.6-liter SOHC multiport EFI engine was vastly superior to the 1.5-liter throttle body powerplant found in the DX.

The 1988 CRX in both HF and Si trim was particularly attractive due to a low weight.

D15B2
1.5-liter SOHC PGM-FI
92 horsepower
1988–1991 Honda Civic LX

By adding a SOHC 16-valve head to the 1.5-liter block (above), horsepower was increased to 92. Neither engine is typically sought for transplantation due to lack of power.

D16A8, D16A9 or "ZC"
DOHC 1.6-liter 16-valve MPFI,
137 horsepower
1988–1991 Japanese Honda
Civic Si16-1.6i and CRX Si16-1.6i

Although never fitted into any Honda that was officially imported into the United States, the ZC engine came standard in the Japanese versions of the Civic Si and CRX Si. (They get all the good stuff.) Thankfully, engine importers like HASport bring them in from Japan and offer them for transplantation into our second generation CRX Si and fourth generation Civic Si. Although the 1986–1989 Integra D16A1 motor and the ZC look identical, the ZC Integra is a better choice for our 1988–1991 Civics because modifications to the mounting brackets are not necessary.

Internally, however, the ZC has more horsepower than the D16A1 due to a better compression ratio and higher performance cams. The Honda Si transmission also bolts right up to the ZC. What could be better? Obviously in high demand for the simplicity of transplantation and efficient design, the ZC doesn't come cheap. Call HASport for current pricing, but expect to pay around $1200. They will perform transplants for an extra $800–$2,000, depending on the specific swap.

B16A1 or "ZCG," B16A2, B16A3
DOHC 1.6-liter 16-valve VTEC
160 horsepower
1990–1991 Honda CRX and
Civic Si-R, 1992–1995 Civic Si-R
1993–1995 Del Sol VTEC

Japan got the first taste of these three nearly identical, revolutionary twin-cam VTEC engines when they were offered as a performance option for *their* version of the 1990 CRX Si (see above). Named the CRX Si-R, the car was never imported into the United States. In fact, none of the Si-R models listed ever officially reached our shores. However, many of these engines have made their way across the Pacific, winding up transplanted into our 1988–1991 Civics and CRXs. That's because Honda was kind enough to place it in the Del Sol VTEC (which was imported) in place of the disappointingly underpowered D16A6 that was standard for the Del Sol LX and DX. Boasting a 10.4:1 compression ratio and redline at 8,200 rpm (yeha), 160 horsepower was possible without modification. This is one of the most sought-after engines for transplantation, and engine importers, such as HASport, usually have them in stock. They run about $2,000.

B20A5
2.0-liter DOHC MPFI
135 to 140 horsepower
B21A1 - 2.1-liter SOHC MPFI
1988–1991 Prelude and
1991 Prelude Si

Although a lame carburetted 12-valve engine was offered on the base 1988 Prelude, the Si had a newly designed 16-valve, twin-cam 2.0-liter (1958cc) that produced 135 horsepower, and had excellent low-end torque (127 lb-ft at 4,500 rpm). A great engine, it did not find its way into the earlier Civics due to incompatibility problems affecting nearly all systems. This was the first year that Honda introduced the dual stage intake manifold, in which a second intake tract would open at high rpm. Sound familiar? This system was further refined, to be used again on the 1994 Integra GS-R. In the final year of the third generation Prelude, an extra 100 cc were added to the Si powerplant.

F22A
2.2-liter SOHC
125 to145 horsepower
1990–1997 Honda Accord
1992–1996 Prelude S

A 2.2-liter twin-cam engine capable of 125 horsepower was featured in the DX and LX models of the fourth generation Accords, but lucky EX, and later SE, buyers got a little more power. The same F22A engine offered in the DX and LX was given a trick exhaust manifold, boosting the horsepower to 140. Some of the 1992–1996 Preludes got the new and powerful VTEC motor, but other Preludes were not so lucky. The Prelude S used the F22A, and the Si was powered by a twin-cam 2.3-liter version of the same engine. Horsepower varied, depending on the model.

F23A1
2.3-liter SOHC VTEC
150 horsepower
1996+ Acura CL
1998+ Honda Accord

Sharing not only the same engine, but the same platform, both cars (in non–V-6 trim) are powered by a reworked version of the F22A design, except that this motor utilizes VTEC technology. For that reason, the F23A1 revs higher, and produces five more horsepower than the non-VTEC design.

D15B8
1.5-liter SOHC 8-valve MPFI
70 horsepower
1992–1995 Civic CX

This was the engine that allowed Honda to claim that it had one of the top three best gas mileage vehicles for any compact car from 1993 to 1995. Hybrid guys use them for paperweights.

This fine example of a 160-horsepower B16A ZCG engine graces the hood of Gaithersburg Maryland's Reaya Reuss' 1995 Del Sol VTEC. It is the "son of ZC," and has been dubbed the ZCG engine. *Reaya Reuss*

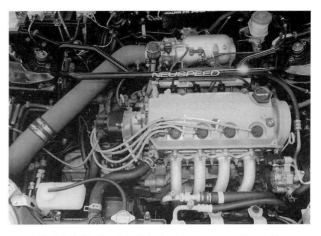

An example of one of the better powerplants Honda used in the mid-1990s. Left is a photo of the stock D16Z6 SOHC VTEC engine under the hood of Ralph Weaver's

1995 Del Sol Si. On the right is the same engine with a different valve cover that was used in the 1992–1995 Civic Si.

D15Z1
1.5-liter SOHC 16-valve VTEC-E
92 horsepower
1992–1995 Civic VX

Besides the gas-saving SOHC, 8-valve 1.5-liter D15B8, the 1992 model year also saw the production of this 16-valve VTEC-E (economy) engine which was fitted in the Civic VX. Rated at 92 horsepower, it had a redline of 7,000 rpm.

D16Z6
1.6-liter SOHC 16-valve VTEC
125 horsepower
1992–1995 Civic EX, 1992–1995
Civic Si, 1993–1995 Del Sol Si

Among the hybrid crowd, this is the only fifth generation Civic engine that stands any chance of remaining under the hood where Honda originally put it. This energetic little 16-valve, 1.6-liter, twin-cam VTEC came stock on the Civic Si and EX, as well as the midlevel Del Sol. You can replace your 1992 DX engine perfectly with one of these for about $2,500. On the other hand, if you already have one in your car, you can get an upgrade to the twin-cam head for around $900, which should net over 10 horsepower.

This four-cylinder, 2.3-liter VTEC engine was used in both the 1998+ Accord as well as the 1996+ Acura CL. The Mid-Ohio Drivers School uses a fleet of 40 Accords; students come from all over the United States to test the limits of this powerplant. The V-6 option for the Accord and CL has much more low-end torque than VTEC, but once you get the 2.3-liter cranked, it will really perform.

D15B7
1.5-liter SOHC 8-valve MPFI
102 horsepower
1992–1995 Civic DX and LX

Part of the variety of motors available for the fifth generation Civics, the LX/DX package included this 1.5-liter eight-valve motor capable of only 102 horsepower, with a redline of 6,800 rpm. These engines are easy to find because they are often discarded to make way for an Integra RS, LS, GS, or GS-R transplant.

B18A, B18B
1.8-liter DOHC 16-valve MPFI
130 to 142 horsepower
1990–1993 Acura Integra
LS, RS, & GS
1994+ Acura Integra LS, RS, & GS

The second and third generation Integra B18A engines are one of the most popular choices for transplantation. The B18's great torque, coupled with the way it enthusiastically responds to even the slightest amount of tweaking, makes all of your hard work seem worth it in the end. This engine lowers right into place on the motor mounts of the fifth generation Civics. They are readily available through most engine distribution companies, and cost less than the harder to find ZCG engines. These powerplants had a lower redline than the Integra GS-R motor (6,800 rpm), but the B18 block carries more torque, especially down low (120+ lb-ft at 5,200 rpm). As the engine developed over the years, the redline gradually increased from 6,500 to 6,800 rpm, as did the horsepower (130 to 142).

This nicely modified D15B7 engine sits under the hood of Woody Donnell's 1992 Honda Civic DX. With a header, intake, wires, coil, and performance exhaust, the engine's stock 102 horsepower has been boosted to about 115.

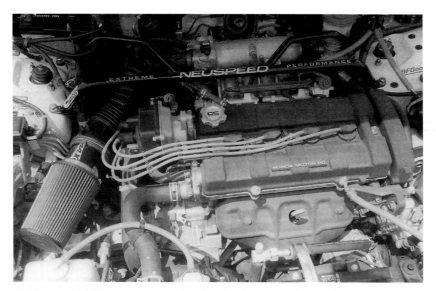

1994+ non-VTEC Integras were fitted with this extremely popular powerplant: the B18B. They seem to end up in many 1992–1995 Civics. Here, however, is a rare photo of one still in an Integra—come and get it!

B17A1
1.7-liter DOHC 16-valve VTEC
160 horsepower
1992–1993 Integra GS-R

Although the second generation Integra's B18 powerplant scored a big hit, the Integra GS-R's introduction in 1992 caused a ripple that continues throughout the Honda/Integra community. In place of the 1.8-liter engine, the GS-R came equipped with a smaller, but much more powerful 1.7-liter, twin-cam VTEC powerplant that cranked out a whopping 160 horsepower. It had a 10.0:1 compression ratio and screamed through the gears up to an 8,000-rpm redline. Overall, 1992 was a good year for engines, as Honda went on to produce several versions of the VTEC, fitting them into everything from the Del Sol (VTEC and Si), Civic Si and EX, Prelude VTEC, and even an economy edition of the VTEC, which appeared in the Civic VX. As usual, the Japanese got to play with this revolutionary new engine design a couple of years before we Americans, when the VTEC first appeared under the hood of the now-infamous 1990 Civic and CRX Si-R (never imported to the United States).

B18C1
1.8-liter DOHC 16-valve VTEC
170 horsepower
1994+ Second generation
Integra GS-R

By far the most popular engine for transplantation, the second generation GS-R engine is very similar to the B17A1 engine used in the first generation Integra GS-R. It has the same compression ratio and redline as the 1993, but due to the slightly bigger block there is much more torque available. This motor is hard to find, and when you do, expect to pay a premium price (usually over $3,000). The B18C1 is also perfect for supercharging or turbocharging applications, and will net 230 horsepower when done correctly!

This B18C1 engine lies under the hood of the 1995 Integra GSR that belongs to autocrosser Darren Mass, who races in SCCA's Street Touring class. With 170 horsepower on tap, this GSR engine is extremely popular with hybrid fans.

This example of non-VTEC power can be found in the 1996+ Civic LX, DX, and CX. A little low on power (106 horsepower), it does respond well to modification. The 1996–1998 Civics (including the slightly more powerful HX and EX) were not blessed with the kind of performance for which Honda is known. Specifically, there is no "sport" version available for these years, so it is likely that some of these engines will become victims of transplantation, once their warranties run out.

D15B
1.5-liter SOHC 16-valve
106 horsepower
1996+ Civic LX, DX, and CX

The 1996 Civic DX and LX were fitted with a slightly tweaked version of the D15B7 powerplant that appeared in the previous generation Civic LX and DX. This time, with a 16-valve head replacing the 8-valve, it was rated at 106 horsepower. The least powerful motor in the sixth generation Civic line, one of these can often be found in the corner of a hop-up mechanic's garage.

D15Z
1.5-liter SOHC 16-valve VTEC-E
115 horsepower
1996+ Civic HX

The 1996 Civic HX was powered by this VTEC-E engine (economy version). Although not very powerful, and not popular among the hybrid groups, it did, however, have some valuable low-end torque and excellent gas mileage.

D16Z7
1.6-liter SOHC 16-valve VTEC-II
127 horsepower
1996+ Civic EX

The new 1996 Civic EX was fitted with a redesigned version of the SOHC, 1.6-liter VTEC motor (D16Z) called the VTEC-II. Very similar to the powerplant in the 1992–1995 Civic Si, this new VTEC had only 5 more cubic centimeters and 2 more horsepower (127). It also was blessed with low-end torque. The EX carried the Civic Si torch until 1999.

B16A4
1.6-liter DOHC 16-valve VTEC
170 horsepower
1996+ Civic Si-RII
(Japanese market only)
1999+ Civic Si
U.S. version, 160 horsepower)

Although the Civic Si was retired from the U.S. market at the end of the 1995 model year, it remained alive and well in Japan, powered by this 170-horsepower, twin-cam VTEC engine, which will rev up to 8,200 rpm. Named the Civic Si-RII in Japan, this motor is nearly identical to the B16A3 unit that powered the Del Sol VTEC. Although promised to the U.S. market since 1996, the Civic Si finally appeared on U.S. shores in February 1999. Our version contained a slightly detuned B16A4 engine (get out the hop-up parts catalogs) capable of 160 horsepower. It will carry on the tradition that began in 1985 when the CRX Si launched Honda's pocket rocket movement. These engines can already be found in the United States, thanks to engine importers, but they are expensive.

H22A1
2.2-liter DOHC VTEC
180 to 195 horsepower
1992–1996 Prelude VTEC, 1997+
Prelude Si, 1997 Prelude Type SH

When the new body style Prelude was introduced in 1992, not everyone was impressed. The rear end was somewhat controversial, but then again, so was the H22A1 engine. Many were hoping that the Prelude would get a new V-6 powerplant, but Honda surprised everyone. The VTEC engine (variable valve timing and lift electronic control) had been around in Japan for a couple of years already (NSX, Civic, and CRX Si-R), but in the form of a smaller block. Honda, always using the Prelude to showcase new technology, applied this revolutionary engine design to a larger 2.2-liter powerplant, and behold: 180 to 195 horsepower (depending on the year) out of a lousy four-cylinder engine. This kind of normally aspirated power had previously been achieved in four-cylinder race cars, and only after considerable modifications. This engine was being offered to the public in stock (reliable) trim.

Honda fans didn't have too long to wait for the return of the Civic Si. After three model years of lackluster Civic performance (1996–1998), an Si version was finally released in spring of 1999. Its twin-cam, 1.6-liter VTEC engine (similar to the Del Sol VTEC) cranks out 160 horsepower.

Over the life of this fourth generation Prelude, the engine was slightly tweaked each year to deliver a little more horsepower. When the body style changed in 1997, the engine remained but the tweaking continued. With such a wonderful engine, you would think that it would be in high demand for transplantation, but much fabrication is required to get the H22A engine to work in any Civic, CRX, or Integra. Even if you insist on taking on this project, the result will likely be disappointing. The weight of the engine, coupled with the need to relocate many of the motor mounts, will leave you with a car that is extremely front-end heavy. Driving the car will provide the owner with a new definition of the term *understeer*. For this reason, an A22 engine into any Civic, CRX, or Integra is not recommended. The engine alone costs more than $4,000.

B16B
1.6-liter DOHC 16-valve VTEC approximately185 horsepower 1998+ Civic Type-R

Further advancement of the B16 powerplant has resulted in a 1.6-liter, normally aspirated, twin-cam VTEC engine that can produce 185 horsepower in stock trim, and has a redline of over 8,000 rpm. Leave it to Honda to achieve V-6 performance in a four banger. In 1998, Honda introduced this powerplant fitted onto a new rice-burning hot rod which they dubbed the Civic Type-R. As usual, it was only available in the Japanese home market, although the United States will hopefully soon be able to begin importing this pocket rocket in the new millennium. Rumors again say we should be able to test drive one by the end of 1999. So far, not many of these engines have turned up on U.S. shores, but you can bet

This C27A4 V-6 from a 1995–1997 Accord produces 170 horsepower, and is basically the same engine that was in the 1986–1990 Legend, with some tweaking over the years.

that they will be the new preferred object of transplantation for the 1992–1996 Civics.

B18C
1.8-liter 16-valve DOHC VTEC approximately 210 horsepower 1997+ Integra Type-R (Japanese)

When the Integra Type-R was introduced in 1997, it contained a reworked version of the GS-R's B18C1 twin-cam VTEC. With 195 horsepower on tap, the Type-R easily burns up the quarter-mile in under 15 seconds, and has set the standard by which all future four-cylinder engines will be judged. The Japanese version of the B18C engine is nearly identical to U.S. design, but since the car itself is 200 pounds lighter (the United States requires more emission and safety equipment), it is faster. Without all of the emission equipment, the Asian version can squeeze out 210 horsepower from this 1.8-liter block! For those who didn't believe that Honda's commitment to racing would directly benefit the

average car buyer, this engine certainly was indisputable proof.

The B18C has a 200-cc larger block, slightly lower compression ratio, and the same redline as the B16B. This will likely become a popular choice for both second and third generation Integra hybrids.

The Six-Cylinder Powerplants

Traditionally a four-cylinder company, Honda indicated its interest in making a high performance six-cylinder when the NSX was introduced in 1991. Prior to that, Acura Legends were the only Honda products to go with the V-6. In reality, it was the V-6 that spawned Acura, as Honda was concerned that loyal Accord and Prelude owners may feel slighted if all of a sudden they put a V-6 into a more luxurious Honda. So the Acura division was created to meet this need, as well as others, of the luxury car buyer.

The first V-6, however, eventually made it into an Accord in the mid-1990s, although the Prelude remained loyal to the four. When the VTEC engine first hit the U.S. shores packaged in a newly redesigned 1993 Prelude, most Honda fans stopped pining for a six. Acura, on the other hand, continued to develop the V-6 engine, hoping that the same buyers who drove CRXs in the mid-1980s would show interest in the Acura coupes and sedans as their tastes matured. Although there is truth to this principle, most automobile experts couldn't have guessed that *first time* car buyers would be attracted to these same luxury sedans. Late-model Accords and newer Acura TLs have become favorite hop-up instruments of generation X.

Officially dubbed the G25A4, this 2.5L 5-cylinder engine is the odd-ball of all Honda/Acura powerplants. Originally fitted in the 1991-94 Vigor, it also turned up in the 1995 TL (pretty much a repackaged Vigor), and remained the TL's standard engine until it finally was put out to pasture in 1998. Prudent TL buyers chose the optional 3.2L V6 powerplant for their 1996-97 models.

The C32A1 V-6 engine of this 1996 Acura 3.2-liter TL was meticulously modified by Star Performance Accessories. *Neil Tjin photo*

C27A, C27A1, C27A4
2.7-liter DOHC V-6
151 to 170 horsepower
1986–1990 Acura Legend
1995–1997 Honda Accord LX and EX V-6

The first Honda V-6 engine ever produced (outside of racing applications) was a 2.5-liter, 151-horsepower V-6 used to launch the first Acura. Afraid the "Honda" name would not be easily associated with a top-of-the-line luxury class vehicle, the Acura division was created. Even though Acura's engineering focus was on styling and luxury, there were still some significant technological changes to this C27A powerplant through its nearly 15-year history.

In 1988 the 2.5-liter block gave way to a 2.7-liter V-6 capable of 161 horsepower. This engine went on to find happiness in the 1995 Accord V-6. With further tweaking, the new powerplants are capable of 170 horsepower.

J30A1
3.0-liter SOHC VTEC
200 horsepower
1998+ Honda Accord LX & EX V-6
1996+ Acura CL

Honda introduced the first mass-produced VTEC V-6 (other than the NSX) when the Acura CL made its debut. A few years later, the 1998 Accord finally abandoned the ancient Legend V-6 platform from the mid-1980s, switching to this newer, more interesting VTEC V-6. Across the ocean, however, the 1998 Japanese-only Accord Si-R was powered by a DOHC VTEC V-6, which, surprisingly, is also rated at 200 horsepower.

C30A1
3.0-liter VTEC V-6
270 to 300 horsepower
1991+ Acura NSX

Right out of Formula 1 racing, the first NSX was powered by a

3.0-liter Acura V-6 VTEC engine (variable valve timing and lift electronic control) that was capable of producing 270 horsepower. The same V-6 continues in today's NSX, but it has been slightly tweaked from year to year, and is now capable of nearly 300 horsepower! Imagine going 0 to 60 in less than five seconds driving a stock Honda! Although a wonderful engine, it is not a good candidate for transplantation in any of the four- or six-cylinder Hondas or Acuras. Comptech has had much success hopping it up further, adding close to another 100 horsepower. This extra power, however, does not come cheap.

C32A1
3.2-liter V-6
200 to 230 horsepower
1991–1995 Acura Legend
1996 Acura TL

The C27A1 2.7-liter V-6 was replaced with a much more competent 24-valve, DOHC 3.2-liter in 1991 that could crank out 200 horsepower. In 1993 it was tweaked further to deliver 230 horsepower, and even housed in the very heavy Legend chassis, was capable of going 0–60 in 8 seconds. With a top speed of 150 miles per hour, this 2G Legend could cover the quarter-mile in 16 seconds. This nifty 3.2-liter V-6 engine would eventually go on to a new life under the hood of the Acura TL sport coupe.

C35A
3.5-liter V-6
225 horsepower
1996+ Acura RL
1999+ Acura TL

Although the Legend name was retired in the United States and Canada after the 1995 model year, it continued on to have a prosperous life throughout the rest of the world. Renamed the RL

One of the most common engine transplants is pictured here. Eric Bauer has a 1989 CRX DX that can blow the doors off of any Si. That's because, under the hood, there is a rare Japanese ZCG B16A1 from a Civic Si-R (160-plus horsepower) replacing the anemic stock unit. *Adrian Teo*

(road luxury) for the U.S. market, it was refitted with a 3.5-liter, 24-valve V-6 that had more torque, but less horsepower than the original 3.2-liter Legend configuration. In 1999, the TL sport coupe also adopted this powerplant.

Popular Engine Swaps

Obviously, if you drive an Integra Type-R, you don't need to be reading this chapter. These popular swaps are targeted for those people who have horsepower-challenged Civics and CRXs, and feel that they are not getting treatment from Honda equal to the manufacturer's home market.

1984–1987 Hondas:
Third Generation Civic and
First Generation CRX

There aren't too many good choices for these earlier Hondas. As previously suggested, don't start with a carburetted car (see chapter 10). The only really good choice for an engine transplant with the 1G Si chassis is the 1.6-liter twin-cam engine from a 1G Acura Integra. The 1986–1987 DOHC powerplant even shares the same electronics as the Honda Si. Of course, the 1988–1989 will also fit, but its ignition system monitors a crank sensor, which will confuse the Honda computer. The 1988–1989 Integra computer can be used, but the Honda wiring will then need to be modified to incorporate a lead to the crank sensor. The twin cam engine is a rather straightforward bolt-in procedure, as discussed earlier. One motor mount needs to be modified in order to make this swap, but most weekend mechanics will have no real trouble with it. If your Honda's body is not in good enough shape, Si donor cars with bad engines and good bodies can easily be found for between $500 and $800. It is very important to start with a good body, and pay particular attention to the unibody. Are there holes in the floor, around the torsion tubes, or around the rocker panels? Inspect the hatchback, rear fenders, and

Even though many of the hybrid experts refer to a particular engine transplant as being a "bolt-in" procedure, most cases require modifications to your car's existing engine mounts. One of the most popular and cost-effective (bang for the buck) engine swaps is the B16A1 engine (DOHC VTEC, 160 horsepower) into a

1988–1991 Civic or CRX. Engine mount kits, however, are needed to make this transformation go more smoothly. These mounts are from Place Racing, and will save you a great deal of time and energy. If you buy your B16A1 through a company like HASport, they will provide the mounts. *Adrian Teo*

Panhard rod for signs of cracking. No matter how much you love your car, don't start off with trouble. Find one with a good body in need of an engine, then you can sell yours once the swap is completed.

Integra engines are usually available at your local import junkyard in the same price range, but you won't be guaranteed that the engine is sound if you buy it there. It would be a shame to do all of that work and find that the boneyard engine's head is warped, or that the block is cracked. The best approach is to call an engine broker. Your guaranteed Integra engine will be shipped to you in less than a week ready for transplantation. Then for around $2,200 (not including shipping) you can have a great car, and you will be paying insurance for a Civic as opposed to the more powerful Integra.

As discussed in chapter 5, you may use either the Honda or Integra computer without even triggering your PGM light. With some simple mods to the Integra engine (air velocity intake, cams, header, exhaust, coil, wires) you

can boost the horsepower up to over 140, while retaining low-end torque. Using the Honda computer will also maximize torque under 4,000 rpm.

Remember, don't install a trick throttle body unless you also upgrade to bigger injectors. Dyno tests indicate a bigger throttle body will cause a loss of horsepower all through the range, especially down low. If you decide to do the Monster throttle body plus higher flow injectors, then the Integra computer will be your best performance bet. Potential horsepower can reach 150-plus with proper tuning, and drivability is excellent.

The other two engine choices for the 1984–1987 Hondas are the 1.6-liter, SOHC VTEC and the 1.8-liter, DOHC Integra LS powerplant. These are both much harder to transplant, and also cost between $300 and $1,300 more to buy.

Many have converted their 1984–1987 carburetted car to fuel injection by putting in an Si engine. Actually, you won't need the whole engine, just the Si head. This type of swap is not worth the time

and effort, but if you love your older non-Si, then be our guest. The only way this swap makes sense is if you start with an incredibly clean CRX HF. These cars weighed considerably less than the other 1984–1987 models. You will then need to replace the entire powerplant with the 1.5-liter Si engine (tranny as well). Everything will bolt in, but the wiring is a nightmare. For pure race cars, your time would be better spent by converting to aftermarket fuel injection (see chapter 10).

1988–1991 Hondas: Fourth Generation Civic and Second Generation CRX

There is no doubt which is the most desired engine for transplantation into these Hondas. One of the most popular swaps among the hybrid crowd is to use the 1.6-liter, DOHC ZC engine from Japan. After all, it's the engine that should have been in these cars in the first place. Just because we don't live in Japan shouldn't mean that we are to be deprived. With a net gain of over 30 horsepower, you will have a car that can out-perform most vehicles on the road. The swap is a rather simple, low cost bolt-in procedure, and except for the extra power, you won't even notice that you are driving a hybrid. The problem is that the engine is expensive.

Other choices for these Hondas include the D16Z6 SOHC VTEC engine from the 1992–1995 Civic EX and Si. It will bolt right up to your stock transmission, and results in a smooth ride that can reliably be used for a daily driver. To avoid wiring headaches, use your stock intake system, which will bolt right to the D16Z6 block, replacing the VTEC unit. You can retain your ECU, but you will need to get a VTEC controller.

If you can find it, the B16A1 1.6-liter Japanese Si-R engine is also a good fit. Dynamic Autosports has an installation kit that can make this swap a bolt-in procedure. Modification will be required in order to properly attach your shift linkage, and you will have to do some wiring.

A slightly more difficult transplant is the non-VTEC B18A from the early 1990s Acura Integra, but it is still rather popular. This will give you about the same horsepower as the ZC, and the engine is cheaper and easier to find, has more torque, and can be modified to go really fast. Now, with the help of HCP Power Innovations, a kit can be purchased that includes motor mount brackets and shift linkage, which is adjustable, making this swap a much easier task. The HCP kit can be used for the B16 swap as well. Hybrid enthusiasts have also used the B16A engine out of a Del Sol VTEC, but additional fabrication is needed. Unfortunately, the list of nonrecommended swaps includes the wonderful B18C Integra GS-R, which requires relocation of

On the surface Adrian Teo's 1992 Civic looks like many other nicely modified 5G Civics. But one look under the hood reveals that it is a hybrid. The Civic is now powered by an Integra GSR engine (B18C1), giving the car a boost of 45 horsepower over the engine it replaced. Of course, Adrian has made further modifications to the GSR engine (header, intake, etc.), resulting in even more power. For more information, check out the Hybrid web page: www.hybrid.honda-perf.org. *Adrian Teo*

three engine mounts and will compromise overall chassis balance as well as structural integrity.

1992–1995 Hondas: Fifth Generation Civics

The first guy who attempted a swap using a 1994 Integra GS-R B18C engine discovered that the motor mounts on the 1992–1995 Civic and second generation Integras are the same. In fact, these Civics seem to have been built with engine swapping in mind. The chassis is strong and rigid, and even the ECU requires little modification for the following projects.

The GS-R engine, as already discussed, is an excellent choice for transplantation because of its great torque and enthusiastic response to even low-buck modifications. The

For sustained high rpm driving, an oil cooler will help keep oil temperatures down, avoiding viscosity breakdown and engine damage.

Many Honda and Acura owners choose either one of these synthetic oils, or one of the better conventional oils like Castrol GTX or Kendall. You can't really go wrong with any SAE-approved oil.

1992–1995 Civic transmission, however, will not work with the B18s, so you will have to get the tranny, shift linkage, ECU, axles, and wiring harness. You should not get the impression that this is an easy swap, but you won't have to do much fabrication, and most Honda performance shops know how to do it properly.

Another popular swap for these Hondas is the Del Sol VTEC B16A3 or ZCG motor, which also bolts right in. The smaller engine block produces less torque than the Integra powerplant, but is still a potent performer. The other swap that seems to work well is the non-VTEC B18 Integra motor, but it is worth the money to find a true GS-R engine to transplant. If you are going to do all that work, and spend hours of your time in the garage, then you may as well go for the best. HASport usually has the B18C in stock, and they tell us that they have done a GS-R/92 Civic swap in less than four hours,

with only two to three workers getting their hands dirty.

1996+ Hondas:
Sixth Generation Civics

So far, the most transplantation success for the sixth generation Civics has been achieved with the same engines that work well in the fifth generation cars: the B18C Integra GS-R and the B16A Del Sol VTEC. The motor mounts between these Civic generations are the same. As above, you will need to get the axles, shift linkage, ECU, wiring harness, etc. Good luck.

Where to Turn

If you decide to attempt one of these transplants, you would be foolish not to visit the Hybrid web page at www.wgn.net/~joe_r/. They are the masters of transplants, and can provide information on emission concerns (a hot topic in California), ECU adaptations, as well as step-by-step instructions for doing many of the

swaps mentioned above, plus others. Details involving some of these more complicated transplant projects are a bit too complicated for the average weekend mechanic (I don't even understand a lot of it), so you will need to do a great deal of homework before attempting any of these projects.

Engine Care and Lubrication

Whether you tackle an engine swap or decide to hop up your present engine, you should ensure that you are properly caring for the engine. Always refer to your owners manual or factory workshop handbook for routine engine maintenance, such as changing the oil every 3,000 miles. But is there anything else out there that can help keep your car's engine running like new?

It would be nice if the answer were yes, but that would be a lie. How can that be, given all of the claims made by the lubrication industry? They drain the oil from the engine, heat it with a flame thrower, throw sand in the cylinder head, and spray water on the valves, and the engine keeps running. Give me a break. If you did that to your engine, no matter

There is no substitute for research and engineering when it comes to figuring out ways to increase horsepower. It's no coincidence that the company doing the most research on 1.6-liter and 1.8-liter Honda/Acura engines is the same company responsible for the most 10-second front-wheel-drive drag cars in the country. Pictured is a 1.8-liter, DOHC Integra engine being tweaked on a J.G. Engine Dynamics dyno. Imagine getting over 600 horsepower from a 1.6-liter or 1.8-liter engine. *Javier Gutierrez*

what product you were using, your motor would be toast in two minutes. You would never treat a Honda engine like that anyway.

It all started with STP. Remember its claims of reducing oil consumption. Well, STP was right, technically. By adding a can of STP, you can't fit as much oil in the crankcase, so you are burning less, because you are burning some of the STP instead. Believe it or not, this author is a psychotherapist turned Honda nut, and the

claims made by these commercials are easy pickin' for analysis. Here's another one. One manufacturer claims that no other lubricant is *more* effective at preventing wear. I'm confident this statement is correct. In fact, no other product is *less* effective either, because all these gimmick lubricants are the same! It would be great if products like Slick 50 prevented wear, but now the statistics are known, and Slick 50 has been asked to tone down its claims.

But there is one consensus that has been reached by many top racing teams, as well as the guy on the street, and that is that synthetic oil keeps friction under control better than any other product. That's why it is *not* recommended to use it after an engine rebuild.

Specifically, oil should be judged based on two main properties: the viscosity index and flash point. The viscosity index refers to how engine temperature affects the rate at which a particular oil

123

resists changes in its ability to flow. In other words, under high temperatures, a cheap oil will experience rapid change, while a good oil will resist changes in viscosity. Flash point is easier to understand, as it simply refers to the temperature at which an oil will give off vapors when heated. You've seen the commercials where a guy pours oil into a frying pan. A low flash point indicates that the film of protection coating the cylinder walls will burn off sooner than an oil with a higher flash point. When oil burns off the cylinder wall, you lose protection.

So which synthetic oils seems to be better for Hondas and Acuras? Test results indicate that Mobil 1 and Havoline have similar viscosity indexes, but Mobil 1 has a higher flash point. On the other hand, Castrol Synthetic has a higher viscosity index, but a lower flash point than the other two. All three well exceed the SG/CD ratings, and any would be a good choice. They also beat 95 percent of all of the other conventional and synthetic oils on the market. That is not to say that standard motor oil is no good. Many mechanics swear off synthetic and will only use a multigrade conventional lubricant.

Let's end this chapter with a little controversy. Many resources strongly believe that if you use synthetic oil, you can forget the "change your oil every 3,000 miles" rule. According to most owners manuals, the recommended oil change interval is 7,500 miles, but if you read the fine print, they indicate that the oil should be changed more frequently when you operate your vehicle under extreme conditions. That doesn't mean driving your mother-in-law to Bingo on Fridays. It refers to city driving, autocross, drag racing, off-road racing, or even operating your car in an environment where the air contains particles that can get past your air cleaner. So in L.A., you should probably change your oil weekly.

The controversy is whether or not a synthetic oil is exempt from this 3,000 mile rule. Synthetics do resist foaming, oxidation, and do not contain additives that conventional oils need in order to function properly. These additives tend to break down and can further contaminate the oil. Therefore, many believe that, as a rule of thumb, with synthetics, you can go two or even two-and-a-half times as long without an oil change.

But synthetics are even more efficient at removing particles from your engine and holding them in suspension until you open the oil drain plug. But once the oil contains too many contaminants, synthetic or not, it will no longer be able to suspend them and they will be redeposited inside your engine. So to change or not to change? To be completely safe, the 3,000-mile rule certainly won't hurt your engine, but if you are using synthetics, it could hurt your wallet. Whatever interval you choose, change your oil on a regular schedule if you want to keep your car happy.

Engine transplantation is often the only way to go if you want to campaign a successful drag car, like this sixth generation Civic. However, thanks to J. G. Engine Dynamics, some 1.6-liter engines are now breaking the 11-second barrier. *Turbo Magazine*

Chapter 13

Transmissions and Traction

Honda—On the Cutting Edge

Before the 1997 Honda Prelude was introduced to the public, I had the opportunity to put it to the test at a Detroit race track. It also had was one of the first four-speed automatic sequential sportshifts listed as an option for an affordable car. Since then, however, many auto companies have followed suit.

Honda always seems to be on the cutting edge of automobile technology, and it often uses the Prelude to showcase new technology, much as GM uses the Corvette. Antilock brakes, four-wheel steering, and the VTEC engine (variable valve timing and lift electronic control) are some good examples of Honda setting the standard for other companies to follow. The 1997 Prelude Type SH introduced another new piece of technology: ATTS (Active Torque Transfer System). Hopefully, this will catch on better than four-wheel steering.

ATTS is a differential that adjusts power to the front wheels, in essence increasing the speed of the outside wheel when the car is negotiating a turn. To picture how this system works, think about how the nondrive wheels of most cars behave in a turn. In a perfect world, the outside drive wheel would rotate faster than the inside wheel since more distance needs

Formula One driver, Adrian Fernandez is testing the traction limits of this 1997 Prelude Type SH at a race track north of Detroit, prior to the release of the fifth generation Prelude to the general public.

to be covered at the outer circumference of the turning circle.

But in the real world, the transaxle and drive wheels on conventional vehicles fight this simple concept of geometry. Since weight transfer is greater to the outside wheel, it tends to generate greater friction with the road, resulting in more grip to that tire.

This, however, forces the inside wheel to try to maintain the same revolutions per minute as the outside, even though it doesn't need to cover as much distance around the inside of the circle. Add to that a difference in friction due to weight transfer, with the

much lighter inside wheel being forced to do what it cannot avoid, and you experience a very common FWD problem: lost traction and inside-wheel spin.

For years, the solution to this problem has been one of the greatest automotive inventions of all time: the limited-slip differential. An LSD limits the speed of the inside wheel, allowing it to create its own pulling force, resulting in much-improved traction in a turn. The problem with LSDs is that they tend to create push, or understeer, in a turn. Under hard cornering, this requires some adjustment for someone who is not used to an

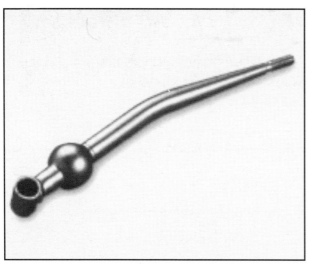

Many racing cars, as well as those for the street, choose to convert to a short shifter. The conversion is simple, and shifting becomes smoother and quicker as the shift pattern is shortened. *Lightspeed*

A clutching-type, limited-slip differential is often necessary to avoid inside wheel slippage and can get the power to the ground.

LSD. The 1997 Prelude with its ATTS system, however, requires no such adjustment.

Everyone is familiar with the fact that you can easily burn rubber (giving the impression that your car is more powerful than it

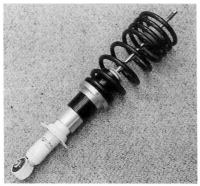

An adjustable spring perch setup will allow precise adjustment of a suspension. If traction seems better on one side of the car than the other, then your car may be too light in that corner. A system like this will allow experimentation with corner weighting. The first thing to try is to slightly raise up (1/2 inch at a time) the corner that is losing traction. Remember: lower is lighter.

actually is) by pulling out from a stop sign and going directly into a turn. Even a Chevette can burn rubber with this trick. With ATTS, however, the Prelude does not give in despite a heavy right foot. I'm talkin' dumping the clutch at 5,000 rpm with the steering wheel cranked at 45 degrees. I could hear Darth Vader's voice echo in my head as the Prelude shot around the turn with no tire screeching. (Impressive!) Hopefully, we will all have ATTS in our race cars someday, but until then, we must use the technology available to us.

The Limited-Slip Differential

With all of the suspension and engine tweaks discussed in the previous chapters, the problem many Honda and Acura drivers will encounter when accelerating out of a turn is loss of traction. On especially tight turns, thanks to the great low-end torque, most Hondas will have a difficult time controlling wheel spin without a limited-slip differential.

A cheap solution that many 1984–1987 IT racers use to solve the

problem is a sway bar transplant from another model Civic. For that generation Honda, front sway bars are interchangeable. The CRX bar is wimpy (16-millimeter), but the Civic Sedan bar is much thicker, and a Civic Wagon bar is huge (19-millimeter). Honda salvage yards will usually sell them for around $50. To test this theory, I decided to install it myself.

Big mistake. The stock Honda sway bar has so many little twists and turns, it looks as if Godzilla had used it for a toothpick. Nearly the entire front suspension needs to be unbolted from under the car, including at least one torsion tube, in order to make the swap. Without a lift, the process took four hours; I could probably do it now in three hours. It is well worth the money to invest in an aftermarket front sway bar, which installs without having to remove the stock front bar.

Newer Hondas don't really need to consider the addition of an aftermarket front bar, as their suspension geometry is considerably different—meaning better. As a matter of fact, many racers feel that both the new and old Hondas are too stiff in the front to begin with, and advocate loosening the stock front sway bar. So how do you know what to do? Simple. It all comes down to what type of racing you plan to do. For the street, you should probably do nothing to the front end.

If you are going to install a limited-slip differential, hold off on increasing front end stiffness until after doing some testing and tuning with the posi in place. But without an LSD, you may benefit from the bigger bar, especially if you have the 1984–1987 torsion bar front end.

Open Your Wallet and Say Good-Bye

If racing is your goal, you will find very few inexpensive shortcuts. The front sway bar transplant may work for you, but chances are you'll find that there is only one way to play with the big boys: You will need to put money into the car that you won't be able to get back when the car is sold.

This may also result in less street driving, since if the car is stolen your insurance will not reimburse you for performance improvements. And because these parts are expensive and street driving could wear them out more quickly, the car will probably sit in the garage much more, except for races and the occasional Sunday drive.

So what's the point? To experience the rush of pushing your driving abilities to the limit in a truly competitive car . . . to explore new boundaries . . . to go where no Honda has . . . (never mind). Is it worth it? Maybe not, but if you have ever had a chance to sit behind the wheel of a car that has the capability of winning its class at a national event, you understand.

A Mid-Ohio Drivers School instructor leads his students through an exercise that teaches them how to deal with loss of traction. The inside front wheel nearly lifts off the ground around these two turns. Aggressive attempts to apply power too early before reaching the exit apex will result in big-time wheel spin.

But one word of caution: Taking your car to this level of performance may force you to face the ultimate test of your driving ability, because there will be no more blaming the car.

Time for LSD

The best performance improvement per dollar that you can make to improve traction is installing a limited-slip differential. Unless you know what you are doing or enjoy tearing a transaxle apart, here's our advice: Ship the entire transmission to the guys who are selling you the slip, and have them install it and ship it back to you when it's done.

In my own case, I picked up a spare CRX Si five-speed transaxle at a junkyard for $250 (that's cheap), and shipped it out. I also took another one, and tried to install the LSD in the tranny myself. Guess which way I will do it next time? Not that you can't do it yourself. It's just a major pain. You would be surprised as to how many little parts are packed into that small tranny.

With a good shop manual by your side you may actually survive the ordeal. If you want it done right, however, let the experts do it.

And here's some advice on shipping: Go to a U-Haul or Ryder rental center and buy two large boxes. Completely drain the fluid out of the gearbox (this will take some time) to ensure that there is no discharge during shipping, as the box could get wet and tear open. Put one box inside the other, pack it well with cardboard and Styrofoam peanuts, fold the excess top of the box inside itself, then take it to UPS. They will ship it for less than $20!

If you try to ship it by truck, it could cost as much as $120. The total cost for the limited-slip, including shipping and new bearings but minus the money spent on the extra transaxle is right around $800. Since CRX "Si" transaxles are in demand, you should be able to easily sell your spare if you choose to.

For newer Hondas and Acuras, the more standard horsepower they have, the more wheel slippage you will experience. LSDs are available for most models, but it is not very cost effective to buy a spare 1.6-liter VTEC tranny to do this project. 1988–1991 CRX and Civic Si trannies are plentiful, but will cost $200 to $400 or more. You should be able to work out a core charge arrangement with an LSD distributor.

Don't remove your only tranny and send it to them. Remember, they could have it for a while. A long while. Months, possibly. Never trust a parts distributor unless he can promise you up front how long it will take to ship your part. Ship the distributor a spare tranny, and wait for it to come back with the new LSD installed.

Don't You Just Love Seeing the UPS Truck Stop in Front of Your House?

Let's face it. This is something all car lovers have in common. When the transaxle with the new LSD arrives at your front door, don't be too intimidated by the process of removing your old transaxle and putting in the new one. I watched a couple of race mechanics do it at the track in two hours, and that included a lunch break.

Why did I do this swap at the track? To see exactly what difference an LSD would make in autocross times. Using the stock tranny, I took 15 runs *without* the LSD, until I knew I could not get the car through the course any faster, and then 5 more runs were taken, and these times were recorded. They did not vary by more than 0.20 second. Then the tranny with the LSD was put in, and I took several laps to warm up the tires, in this case, 225/45/13 Hoosier Autocrossers.

The next five runs were recorded, and on a 30-second course, the LSD was 0.60 second faster than the runs with the stock tranny. And this course only had two places where there was noticeable tire spin before the LSD was in, so depending on the conditions, the difference is likely to be greater.

Many auto repair shops can install Honda transaxles (it's a fairly easy procedure), but if you choose to try it yourself, here are some pointers. In addition to following the steps in your shop manual, there are a few tricks that

A tranny change doesn't have to be an overwhelming job. We changed trannys right at the track in order to compare the stock differential to an LSD!

The best way to determine the difference that a limited-slip differential can make is to run a course with sharp turns that allow for power to be applied before actually reaching the exit point of the turn.

can make the tranny swap easier. You will need access to an air compressor to get the axle nuts loose, or if your car is older and has spent time outside, a breaker bar as long as your garage. The axle nuts must be loosened while the car is on the ground. Then put the car up on stable jack stands, disconnect the battery, and drain the transaxle fluid.

The front suspension needs to be disassembled next. Loosen the strut receiving sleeve and wrestle the strut out of the sleeve so that the brake assembly is free to move. Then pull the axle out from behind the wheel hub and also from the tranny. If you want to replace the outer boots, now is a good time. Honda dealers rarely stock the inner boots, since they seem to last forever, but you may want to check to see that the boot clamp is tight, as it may loosen when the axle is pulled out of the tranny.

Crawling under the vehicle (always use a spotter) you will need to locate the shift linkage and, using a hammer and hole punch, try to remove the pin that connects the linkage to the tranny. This pin usually does not want to come out, so you will likely have to unbolt the entire linkage assembly from the bottom of the shift lever and worry about the pin later, once the transaxle is out and you can get better leverage or a bigger hammer. Before unbolting the tranny, you will need to support the engine with a jack.

This jack will come in handy later, as it can be used to move the engine up and down to assist with lining up the bolts when installing the new transaxle. Support the tranny with another floor jack before removing the last few engine bolts. You can then lower the transaxle and slide it out.

Next, you will need to remove that pesky dowel pin securing the shift linkage to the old tranny and put the linkage onto the new tranny. You should use antiseize when putting the pin back in, and on anything else that you may want to remove again in the near future.

Please forgive this shop manual cliché, but just reverse the above steps to install the new LSD tranny. The biggest headache will likely be trying to line up the bolts from the engine to the tranny. Using a two-jack setup should make this part of the job much easier.

Turn, Turn, Turn!

I found myself yelling this phrase to Fred (my project CRX) the first time the car was raced with the LSD. Be prepared for plowing, especially if you have experimented with ride height. The combination of an LSD, increased negative camber up front, and insufficient toe-out can cause you to take the scenic route through the first hairpin turn you approach. Keep the windows rolled up so that your friends don't think you're crazy if they hear you yelling at your car to turn.

With the LSD installed, you may need less negative camber and more toe-out. The reason is that, as you enter a turn, the posi will tend to drive the front wheels further into the turn, especially if you are moving a little too fast. Entering a turn too fast is a common "preposi" habit that can be hard to break. Drivers without LSDs expect the front wheels to slide a little, which they often compensated for by left foot breaking. When done with skill, this will cause the rear end to get slightly loose and result in a nice four-wheel drift.

But with an LSD in place, the front wheels will maintain traction as you turn the wheel, which is what you pay a posi to do. If you go in too hot, the result will be oversteer. With a posi front end, you may need to slow down a little entering the turn. This will pay off big time on the way out, since power can be applied earlier and with more gusto, resulting in a faster exit speed. Fine tuning the front suspension to match your individual driving style can be accomplished by experimenting with negative camber, toe, sway bars and sway bar bushing material, shock and strut stiffness, and the easiest adjustment of all, tire pressures.

Honda Transmissions

In general, late-model Acura and Honda trannies are very strong and reliable. Drag racers with turbocharged engines cranking out well over 400 horsepower rarely develop tranny problems. Axles will snap, clutches will break, but the trannies have a reputation for holding together under extreme conditions. The same goes for roadracing and autocrossing, but as strong as they are, wheel slippage will occur, especially when exiting turns. An LSD is the only real fix for this problem. A good LSD will usually cost between $650 and $800, with exchange—not installed, depending on the model and manufacturer. A Mugen, Quaife, or Torsen unit, however, will set you back a great deal more cash (between $1,000 and $2,000). Our Mugen LSD has worked flawlessly for the past 10 years without having to be rebuilt once, but so has our cheaper no-name "clutching-type" design, which is what most performance parts distributors sell for under $800. Always install a new clutch when replacing the differential.

Early Honda trannies also have a reputation for holding up well. The only weak design that Honda ever manufactured was the 1984–1987 automatic transmission. The 1988–1991 automatic didn't win any awards, either. Other than

In 1972, looking at this silly Z600 gearshift, it was hard to imagine that Honda would someday build stock trannies that could handle 300-plus horsepower.

that, you will likely not experience any difficulty.

One big question that many racers face is which standard tranny to choose: five-speed, four-speed, Si or not? There were three different gear ratios offered on 1984–1987 Hondas, but in the 1990s the four-speed was retired. Gear ratios also vary in the newer Hondas and Acuras, but there is one rule of thumb to follow: The Honda Si transmissions are usually geared lower.

As for the Acura division cars, the "sport" versions (GS-R, Type-R) also have a gear ratio that allows for better low-end torque. When in doubt, consult the engine distributors about what transmission would be best for your application.

When the first "Si" was introduced, I made a close examination of the different transmissions offered, and the way they affected performance. The first one of these cars to hit our shores was the CRX Si, which came with a 4.40 final drive ratio. On the autocross course in second gear, this tranny will get you out of a pivot turn with excellent torque. This transaxle is slightly shorter than the tranny in Civic or carburetted CRX. The Civic 1500S and Civic Si have a 4.20 ratio, which provides a longer first and second gear. From an autocrossing standpoint, when racing on a more wide open course, you may be able to avoid that shift into third gear. The Civic carburetted tranny has a

4.00 ratio, which should be avoided for Solo II, but not necessarily for roadracing. From my testing, it seems that there are pros and cons to both the 4.40 and 4.20. If your club tends to set up tighter courses with occasional 180 degree pivots, then the 4.40 is likely the best choice.

Gear Oil

It seems like everyone is using synthetic fluids nowadays: Mobil 1 in the engine, Castrol in the brake lines, and Redline in the tranny. But is there really anything to putting a synthetic gear oil in your transaxle? For the most part, if your car is only a few years old, you do not need to stray from the owners manual.

There are several exceptions to this rule. First, if you have installed a limited-slip differential, then a good synthetic gear oil, such as Redline, will help enable the differential to "hook up" more smoothly. Overall wear will be reduced, as is the case with most synthetics, so your diff should last longer.

Another good reason to go synthetic is if there are a lot of miles on your car. Once a tranny gets a little worn, synthetic oil will make a difference in smoother shifting. I have tested Redline in the 1984–1987 Hondas and 1986–1989 Integras, and they respond well. Multi-grade synthetic oil will also perform well in your transaxle.

Last, if you are racing, a good synthetic will help ease some of that extra strain that is put on your gearbox. Roadracers especially will see benefit, as downshifts can be less troublesome. As for the cost, the price is worth the benefit if you fall into one of the three categories above. Synthetic gear oil is about five times more expensive than regular motor oil, but it's not as if you change it every 3,000 miles, or that your tranny will hold five quarts. In this case, cost is very low and the gain can be moderate.

Traction Control Systems

Many of the best new vehicles can be purchased with an optional traction control system. Examples include the 1997 Prelude's ATTS, as well as Subaru's AWD system that "transfers the power from the wheels that slip to the wheels that grip." Although different, both systems work to avoid wheel slippage, thus maximizing control. For various types of racing, however, these systems are frequently "turned off" so that the driver can regain full control, allowing them, for example, to put the car into a four-wheel drift,

if necessary. For street driving, however, the traction control devices work very well.

In the past, unless your car had a traction control system installed at the factory, you were out of luck. But now, there are alternatives. Some companies have introduced devices that monitor and compare revolutions made by rear wheels to the front wheels. Then, by activating a rev limiter, spark is alternately removed from the spark plugs, limiting power to the drive wheels and decreasing wheel slippage. Aftermarket EFI systems, such as MoTeC, come with this type of traction control system incorporated into the fuel delivery system. They cut fuel to injectors similar to how a Formula

1 engine avoids slippage and/or dangerously high RPMs.

As you are aware, the higher the horsepower, the harder it can be to control launch. The Honda and Acura drag racing crowd knows this problem all too well. Front-wheel-drive cars have an additional disadvantage that RWD cars don't need to worry about. In drag racing, or when leaving the line in Solo I or Solo II, weight is shifted to the rear of the car, causing FWD cars to experience even more loss of traction. The MoTeC unit compensates for this by controlling the fuel delivery system. Even RW drivers can benefit from this technology. In roadracing or autocrossing applications, RW drivers can dial in the amount of

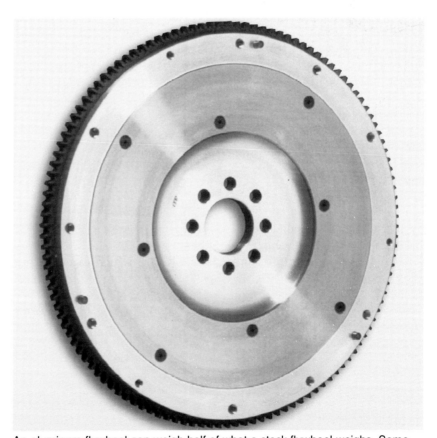

An aluminum flywheel can weigh half of what a stock flywheel weighs. Some low-end torque may be lost, but the rate at which the car will accelerate more than makes up for it. Most competitive FWD drag cars don't leave home without one. *Stillen*

oversteer they want to carry into a turn. Countersteering will still be necessary, but they will be able to keep their right foot floored without having to feather the throttle. Sounds like fun.

As with any new experience, it takes practice and several trial runs before you can decide where to set your launch limit, and how to take full advantage of a traction control unit. To the spectators, it may sound slower and be less exciting to watch, but the bottom line is that you spend more time going forward and less time spinning your wheels. I, however, prefer lower quarter-mile times.

Conclusions

No matter how much horsepower you have at your disposal, it will do you no good unless you can get the power down to the ground. It is very satisfying when you can embarrass the RWD musclecars at an autocross with a less powerful Honda or Acura. The tables are turned, though, at a drag race or hill climb. Obviously the horsepower differential will come into play more here than at an autocross, but the other striking point is that when a RWD car accelerates, the weight shifts to the rear, improving the traction at the drive wheels. Therefore, the RWD car can put down that power better than the FWD car. The importance of maintaining good traction is clearly illustrated in this setting.

Traction can be improved for all Hondas and Acuras by following the examples in this chapter, as well as in chapters 3 and 4. But one must often choose between maximum handling and streetability. Too many good street or dual-duty projects become race-only vehicles because they sacrifice ride comfort for enhanced and precise control. On the other hand, once you experience the handling that your Honda or Acura can achieve by incorporating the modifications in these chapters, you may not want to drive your car on the street. The purpose of street driving is to conveniently get from one point to another. Driving your car to its full potential will put yourself and others at risk. Even on an open country road, the challenges are not worth the danger of self injury. Autocross and drag racing, for example, are excellent ways to legally race your car at its full potential without putting yourself at increased risk.

As good as the OEM Honda/Acura clutch components are, high performance engines (especially when fitted with nitrous, turbo or superchargers) may require a race clutch setup to ensure precise engagement. These Exedy parts will do the trick, even when your transmission is asked to operate under extreme conditions, such as drag racing, or inching your way home from work during rush hour. *Diamond Star Creative Group*

Chapter 14

Brakes

The aftermarket brake market is filled with marvelous items that will not only look great on your car, but will stop it even faster. But before getting into the many options available, there is a point that needs to be made. If you own a Honda or Acura, you probably don't need to upgrade your brakes. This may seem like a controversial statement, since there are so many brake products on the market that claim to increase the efficiency of your braking system. But just because there are fancy brake parts available, doesn't mean that you have to buy them.

It's no coincidence that a chapter on brakes is near the end of the book. If you have a budget for your project, then the modifications mentioned in previous chapters should take precedence in terms of both your time and money. Next to Porsche, the Honda Motor Company has engineered some of the best braking systems on the market. My 1985 project CRX Si is one of the fastest autocross cars in the country, and has benefited from technology courtesy of the biggest names in aftermarket performance parts. The braking system, however, is pure Honda. Containing all original components, it still utilizes the standard rear drum setup. The front calipers are two decades old, and the pads (which are also OEM

Performance brake components, like these AEM CoolTech calipers, will surely help stop your Honda quicker than the stock brakes, and can add a great look to your car. Brake modifications, however, should only be a top priority for roadracers, Solo I drivers, and frequent visitors to driver's schools and track events. *Diamond Star Creative Group*

Honda) haven't been changed for 5 years.

This is not a suggestion that the brake system should be ignored. On the contrary, fluid level should be checked often, and your entire system should be flushed every two to three years to avoid moisture build-up. Moisture in you brake lines can slow stopping distance, and also lead to corrosion from the inside of your brake components and lines. Calipers and pads need to be checked yearly, and rotors should be cut whenever new pads are installed, or replaced if they are too worn or warped. Beyond this routine maintenance schedule, you should consider sticking with the original braking system. There are, however, two instances in which brake upgrades are either recommended, or required.

Engine Transplantation

Hondas and Acuras are precisely balanced, finely tuned instruments. The stock braking system has been designed to perform under extreme conditions, helping to slow your car without loss of control. ABS or not, the original brakes can do the job. The desire for more power, however, can often throw off this balance.

Let's look at an example to illustrate this point. You have a late-model Civic or CRX, and want to transplant a bigger, more powerful engine. Often, one or more of the motor mounts do not completely match up, therefore requiring fabrication and/or relocation. If any engine mounts need to be moved in order to refit a new powerplant, the engine will clearly not end up in exactly the same place as the former stock unit. Sometimes this bigger engine will lean slightly in one direction or another as opposed to the original engine. And then there is the issue of the increased weight, not only due to having installed a larger engine, but also because upgrading to a different transmission is necessary. In these cases, clearly the balance of a Civic or CRX can be changed in either subtle, or obvious ways.

Aside from making changes to the suspension to compensate for additional oversteer (larger rear sway bar, stiffer springs), the front brakes may be called upon to do more work because of the now-heavier front end. In this case, a brake upgrade is *recommended*. If you obtain the engine from a junkyard, sometimes the tranny, axles, and brakes can all be used for the transplant. Often, however, it is easier to buy larger and more efficient calipers, along with a bigger rotor. Be careful, since anytime you change the size of your brake rotors or calipers, you jeopardize ever being able to use your stock rims due to clearance problems.

Roadracing

Any time you abuse your brakes, such as in roadracing,

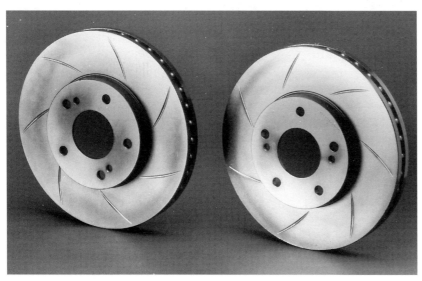

A Stillen slotted brake rotor can offer enhanced cooling over the stock unit, since it is able to capture cool air in its slotted channel as the rotor turns. As this air is brought back to the brake pads, they are cooled.

Cross-drilled rotors for Acura/Prelude offer even more cooling than slotted rotors, but reduce the contact patch of the brake pad. These should only be used when cooling is a high priority.

track events, or driver's schools, an upgrade is *required*. The heat that can be generated from constant high speed racing has been known to melt a wheel's center cap, warp a rotor, boil brake fluid, or even turn a brake pad into dust. As stated before, Hondas and Acuras have excellent stock braking systems, so you may need nothing more than to change to a performance brake pad.

Autocrossers usually do not need, or want, to use a harder pad. The reason is that the performance pads are designed to disperse heat better than stock pads, and they do not heat up as easily. In Solo II, you want pads that will heat up quickly, so that they will stop more efficiently. For roadracing, a stock pad will heat up and stay hot, causing the brake fluid to boil, making it impossible to stop. Heat is so much a factor, it is common to see a roadracer come in to the pits with their rotors glowing bright red. Stock rotors, pads, and fluid were not designed to withstand this amount of heat, and will fail.

Turbocharging and Supercharging

For those who stray from the normally aspirated crowd, there is some logic to upgrading your brakes. Given the fact that you will likely be going faster, it follows that you may use your brakes more than what you were doing before the blower was installed. Probably the soundest approach to a brake upgrade involves stealing a braking system from another Honda or Acura model. For example, replacing the rear drums from your 1984–1987 Civic/CRX with the rear disc brake setup from a first generation (1986–1989) Acura Integra. If you ventured into the junkyard to buy the engine, you may as well grab the rear brakes while you are there. This is a straightforward

Roadracers use a serious brake rotor/hub setup. This is an example of what you can find under the skin of a third generation GT-4 Acura Integra.

swap, and will give you all of the benefit of a factory-type brake upgrade without having to go through the trouble of sorting out performance brake parts.

Another quick brake conversion involves 3G Preludes. The rotors from a 4G Prelude VTEC are larger than the 3G rotors, and they can be interchanged. Some racers who go to the trouble of swapping rotors also replace the stock calipers with those from an Acura NSX. Even though the NSX calipers are meant to fit a rotor that is 4 mm thicker than the VTEC counterpart, shims have been used successfully to make this conversion worth the effort. The cost of NSX calipers, however, may make this project cost prohibitive.

Aftermarket Brake Pads and Rotors

What harm could possibly be done by investing in a trick set of brake pads? You would expect these high quality, expensive pads to stop your car quicker, and with less brake fade. Often, this is the case, but there is a hidden price to pay.

Even these cheap pads (under $15) will stop your car quickly, and will not warp expensive rotors. That is why we recommend retaining the stock Honda/Acura system unless you plan on roadracing. Stock pads and rotors will overheat, as will conventional fluid, when subjected to the extreme conditions of a road course.

Everyone knows that friction is required to make brakes operate properly. Friction, however, causes wear. A Honda stock braking system is designed to wear the pads, but if you upgrade to performance

Three popular brake fluids: Valvoline synthetic (500 degrees Fahrenheit), Castrol GTX (440 degrees Fahrenheit), and Motul (300 degrees Celsius, or 570 degrees Fahrenheit). These brands will retain less moisture than a conventional fluid, and under hard, repeated braking, will not vaporize like fluids with lower boiling points. For average street driving, however, any fluid listed in your owners manual is adequate.

pads, you may be wearing your rotors. The last time I looked, pads were cheaper and easier to replace than rotors.

Another common problem with using competition brake pads on the street is that your rotors may tend to warp. One solution to this problem is to buy performance rotors, then send them off for cryogenic treatment, which is proven to resist warping. Another solution is to simply stick with the stock pads, avoiding the need to undertake this elaborate and expensive endeavor. So does this mean that performance pads won't decrease your stopping distance? On the contrary, by spending big bucks, you will likely experience a drop in your 60-to-0 times. It's all a matter or priorities. Racers have no choice, but nonracers do. It's probably wiser to spend your

money on a better set of tires. But if you choose to spend it on performance pads and rotors, you may quickly discover that your tires have become the weak link in your braking system.

There have been many different brake pads on the market, composed of everything from asbestos (old type) to carbon fiber. As a general rule, the lower the cost of the pad, the more the pad tends to wear.

What about the advantages of cross-drilled rotors? Why do small holes drilled in the rotors improve performance? The main reason for using a cross-drilled rotor is that as the wheel turns the rotor, those drilled holes pick up pockets of air, which tend to cool the pads as well as the rotor itself. A cooler pad and rotor combination should then be expected to stop the car better. That, however, is not always the case. Holy rotor, Batman, how can that be? The answer is simple. A rotor containing holes has less contact surface for the pads to grip. As long as your stock pad is not overheating and causing brake fade (vapor lock), then you should be able to stop quicker than the guy who has installed drilled rotors. If heat is an issue, however, cross-drilled rotors may be the way to go.

Brake Fluids

What harm could possibly be done by changing over to a better brake fluid? It is likely that no harm will come. In fact, there are definite advantages to replacing your stock fluid with synthetic, or high performance fluids. Brake fluids are graded based on their boiling point. Regular over-the-counter fluids are fine for regular driving, but when you add either more weight or

power to your car, there will likely be more demand placed on your brakes. Also, if you live in a part of the country that is particularly hilly, such as San Francisco or Pittsburgh, you could also benefit from a fluid that resists boiling.

Regular brake fluid will barely make it to 300 degrees Fahrenheit before boiling, but the popular high performance brands, such as Castrol, will go to about 440 degrees Fahrenheit. The best fluid I tested, however, was Motul synthetic, which resists boiling up to 570 degrees Fahrenheit. Compare the boiling point of the synthetic fluids in your local parts store to see which is best for your application before you buy.

The condition that results when brake fluid boils is called "vapor lock." The fluid heats, gives off a gas, and that gas becomes trapped in air pockets within your brake lines. When you then push on the pedal, the fluid does not compress uniformly, and your calipers may only respond partially, if at all. This is another reason to select a fluid with a high boiling point.

All brake fluids are rated by the Department of Transportation (DOT), and have been assigned grades based on standards for that particular year or period. In other words, a DOT 5 fluid has passed all of the latest standards set by the U.S. Department of Transportation regarding brake fluids. That does not mean that a DOT 3 fluid is not safe. All it means is that it met standards set by the DOT several years ago. Don't choose your fluid by the DOT rating; choose it by the boiling point and whether you want synthetic or standard. Anything less than DOT 3, however, should be avoided.

Chapter 15

Interior and Exterior Modifications

Exterior Modifications

Is it vain to want a good-looking car? Maybe so, but often you may find that people judge *you* based on how *your car* looks. Have you ever had anyone write "wash me" on your car by scraping off dirt? How about when you see a car you wish you had, but there is a dent on the fender, and you say to yourself: "If that was my car, I wouldn't be riding around with a dent in the fender. I'd fix it immediately." And finally, have you ever seen a nicely detailed older car, even one that you have no interest in, but you notice it because the owner has taken a lot of time to restore it to original condition? Then, you find yourself thinking: "I respect a guy who takes good care of his car." Let's face it, *we* judge other people based on how *their* cars look.

On the other hand, if racing is your thing, the look of your car has nothing to do with speed and handling. Wings and air dams may make a car look cool, but unless you are racing at very high speeds, the downforce created by these wings will make little difference in your car's performance.

There seems to be two basic types of automobile owners. Those concerned with form first and function second, and those who feel that function should be the priority, and what a device looks

Stillen body kits are available for most late-model Civics and Integras, and can make a striking difference in your car's appearance. Pictured is a kit for a sixth generation two-door Civic coupe. *Stillen*

like is irrelevant as long as it works. In the past, when it came to hopping up a Honda or Acura, a car owner was often forced to choose function over form. But due to the recent interest in import performance, manufacturers are now building functional parts that will also enhance the good looks of your car. And for enthusiasts who want their cars to be unique and also reflect their radical personalities, this is the chapter for you.

Body Kits

There are many aftermarket body kits currently available for the late-model Civics, Accords, and Integras, however if you have a pre-1988 model, you may have a difficult time locating the parts you want. When the first CRX hit the showrooms in 1984, Mugen had already designed a cool body kit that could help distinguish your CRX from all the others on the road. The kits were readily

Stillen also makes body kits for Honda Accords, like this front end spoiler. *Stillen*

Stillen can even make an Accord wagon look cool! *Stillen*

available in Japan, but distribution in the United States was less consistent. There was no internet then, and few Japanese hop-up magazines around, so access to the limited body kits was more difficult for Honda owners living further away from the larger urban cities. But now, even though these kits are scarce, a trip to the internet will usually locate what you are looking for, whether it's spoilers, or an entire Mugen kit.

For most late-model Hondas and Acuras, there are now body kits readily available. But be careful, because quality varies. Chris Pergl, the owner of a 1995 Integra GSR, had to spend big bucks just to install his "combat kit" from one manufacturer because it would not line up correctly. A Wings West three-piece spoiler, on the other hand, was an easier bolt-on procedure. This was also the case with the Touring Front Spoiler distributed by Stillen, which installed easily on T. J. Baker's 1996 Civic EX. So don't be fooled by the lower-priced body components, because the money you save on the parts will be balanced out by the cost in both time and money to compensate for the lack of quality. When it comes to aftermarket body components, you really do get what you pay for.

As for quality, I recommend turning to a company that has been there from the beginning. Just as Oscar Jackson of Jackson Racing helped start the import hop-up movement back in the early 1980s, Rod Millen's company, Stillen, has been helping make Japanese cars go faster, stop quicker, and look better for the past two decades. A Stillen part is guaranteed to fit properly, and is designed to work with your other performance components.

An example of this problem, which many people have faced, is

a new exhaust system failing to fit without banging against the rear sway bar. Worse yet, it might not exit precisely at the port that was precut in their newly installed rear ground effect. Components purchased through a single company that produces all of these parts, like Stillen, can help avoid this type of headache. Always ask questions before you buy.

Functional Body Modifications

A race car driver will add a part to his or her car only if it performs some type of valuable function, or if it saves weight by replacing a heavier part. Race cars can often reach speeds high enough so that lift becomes a factor, causing the car to lose traction, resulting in a decline in handling, or worse. This is the only condition in which air dams actually perform a function on a typical sedan or coupe.

Just as Formula cars benefit from negative lift technology, so do Hondas and Acuras, especially when traveling at high speeds. A front end air dam, or spoiler will serve to keep air from getting under the car, thus defeating lift. Most racing sedan bodies utilize air dams that nearly scrape the ground and completely surround the car to keep air from getting underneath, even when cornering. There are many functional applications available for Honda and Acura vehicles, but do not buy

This homemade fiberglass hood for a 1985 CRX saves 22 pounds. It has very little form, but it is a very functional body modification due to the reduction of front end weight.

racing spoilers from a shop that specializes in form. Refer to a trusted name in racing design, such as Stillen or Mugen.

Interior Modifications

We all spend a great deal of time in our cars. Whether you're driving to work, or just cruising around, it's nice to be able to be comfortable in the cockpit. And keep in mind that no matter how nice your car looks on the outside, you can't admire it when you're behind the wheel. While others are doing double takes as you drive by, you may not be able to stop noticing that tear in the dashboard above the speedometer.

From a racer's point of view, a dent in the side of the car is a battle scar that tells a story of how you overcame adversity to eventually win the race against the evil, non-Honda driving competitors. In other words, many racers don't care as much how their car looks from the outside, as long as everything is still in place, but the interior of a race car is another

thing. Just like a fighter pilot, the race car driver relies on gauges to help him or her determine how the car is running. And in this case, comfort *is* important. Roadracers and IT drivers who remain behind the wheel of their cars for lap after lap will tell you how much of a workout it is. Some of our heroes, like Alex Zanardi, are athletes through and through. F1 and Indy car drivers can stand head to head with any baseball or basketball star when it comes to being in shape. The constant g-forces they are exposed to wear down even the best athlete. Even Solo I, II, and drag racing can take a lot out of you during the course of the day. It is important that your cockpit be comfortable.

Most of us spend a great deal of time and money on performance enhancements, not to mention engine modifications. Even though Honda and Acura have well-equipped dashboards, you will often need more information about how your car is performing than what the factory has decided

you need. Let's face it, the majority of people who buy Honda products are not gearheads. Most don't even read their owners manual and wouldn't know an oil warning light from a temperature gauge. We've all heard the story about the spouse (I'll leave it to you to determine the sex) who heard a funny noise coming from the engine compartment, and dealt with it by turning the stereo up louder. Sometimes it's hard to understand the opposite sex. Spouses can remember exactly what outfit they were wearing on your third date together, over 10 years ago, but can't recall just how long that red warning light on the dashboard of their car has been blinking.

In any event, the standard warning lights and gauges on most Hondas and Acuras are not adequate to meet the needs of most of us hop-up types. Depending on how you are using your car, there is certain information that you should have about how your engine is running.

Gauges

Most Honda products do not have one of the most important gauges needed to help avoid engine damage before it is too late: the oil pressure gauge. And for those of you who have driven other people's cars that are similar to yours have surely noticed that all temperature gauges are not created equal. Some register a normal operating temperature by moving the indicator halfway between *cold* and *danger*. While others, even though they are the same make, model, and year, record "normal" as being about one-quarter of the way to the top of the scale.

And then there's the tach. For whom has the average factory tach been designed? Certainly not any of us car guys. Even the larger

George Bowland was one of the first autocrossers to design and build a sucker-mobile. No wings needed here. A separate motor provides suction by removing air from under the sealed floor assembly, thereby creating downforce, even at slow speeds. In his victory at a skid pad g-force challenge, George pulled nearly 2Gs. When full downforce was induced by the sucker motor, the car barely had enough power to move under its own power from a standing start.

aftermarket tachs are only useful if you look at them. Drag racers, Solo I, IT, and roadracers don't always have time to watch the tach. One of the best inventions to date has been the shift light. When autocrossing my Solo I CRX, friends have mentioned that they can see my shift light come on even when I'm on course and they are in the pit area. Hillclimbers and drag racers have no room for error. If they make even the slightest mistake that results in lost time, it can't be made up. That run is ruined. They need to have a shift light that Mr. Magoo could see even if he was wearing sunglasses. Shift lights are also very beneficial to IT and roadracers, although they spend so much time behind the wheel, they can probably tell you exactly what tone corresponds to 6,500 rpm. That is, if they can hear the engine. Even unmuffled Hondas and Acuras are quiet compared to a Mazda RX-7 with a straight pipe. Not only can't you hear your own engine when passing an unmuffled rotary car, you're lucky you can even think. From a distance, it's a beautiful sound, but up close, it can nearly cause your ears to bleed. For those occasions, a shift light becomes invaluable.

Most turbo and supercharged cars require additional gauges, such as a boost indicator. It is prudent, however, to also install an exhaust temperature indicator. Since turbocharged cars use exhaust gasses to power the turbo unit, exhaust temperature is a very important thing to know, especially during cool down (before you shut off your engine). As you know, coolant stops flowing through an engine once the engine is shut down. Shutting off a turbocharged engine before it has properly cooled is a main cause of turbo

Two types of interiors: one having function as a priority (bottom), and the other with a little more emphasis on form (top).

and engine damage. There are systems that will continue to run your engine, even after you turn off the key, until proper cooling has been achieved. Only at that time is the ignition disengaged. An exhaust temperature gauge can tell you when it is safe to shut down, or whether you should take a few more quiet laps around the block. It will also tell you when it is time to back

off. Usually, as soon as you release the throttle, exhaust temperature is reduced significantly, since you are instantly decreasing the amount of combustions per minute that are occurring in the cylinders.

Cockpit Comforts

Aftermarket seats come in all shapes and sizes, depending on the purpose of your vehicle. You

This Personal Fittipaldi steering wheel can make the driver feel as if he/she is in the cockpit of an expensive supercar.

An array of Auto Meter gauges from a supercharged car: boost (middle), exhaust temperature (top), and large face tach with an adjustable shift light (bottom). The shift light (not pictured) is also available separately, and uses rpm chips to tell the driver when the engine has reached maximum torque and horsepower. Proper adjustment of a shift light can only be determined by taking a few dyno runs and analyzing the torque/horsepower curve. Then set your shift light to come on a few rpms before the torque curve begins to flatten out.

can even buy brand name racing seats mounted on casters for your office, for those weekend racers who experience withdrawal and have a hard time making it through the work week. Since Hondas and Acuras come standard with excellent seats, installing an aftermarket seat should be near the bottom of the list in overall priorities. That is unless you plan on pulling some serious G's, or you are looking to reduce weight at all costs.

Racing seats are both lighter and more restraining than factory units. Depending on the model, you can save between 15 (1984–1991 models) to 40 pounds (late-model Accord/Prelude). If dropping pounds is a priority, check with the manufacturer to find out the exact weight of the seat before ordering it. Don't assume that a "racing" seat is lighter than the factory unit. That is not always the case. They range from a low of about 10 pounds to as much as 40 pounds, depending on features such as a reclining back, head rests, etc. Some aftermarket seats will bolt right on to your pre-

This Sparco seat weighs only 11 pounds, costs under $250, and will restrict lateral movement during high g-forces.

sent rails, although others won't, and fabrication will be necessary.

Another problem that people run into is that some aftermarket seats will reduce head room. Others who have limited head room with their factory seats, especially on cars with power sunroofs, purchase an aftermarket seat to increase their head room. Seats can be as personal a choice as wheels. That's why it is important to sit in a seat before purchasing it, because ride height may vary. And don't assume that since a seat fits in your friend's Honda it will fit in yours. Even back in the mid-1980s, when Honda was trying to keep things very simple, just about every non-body part could be swapped between a Civic and CRX, *except* for some suspension pieces and the front seats.

Fun Stuff

Although very important to many racers, an aftermarket steering wheel is mostly a luxury item. For models equipped with air bags, it can be cost prohibitive to replace the steering wheel. But for the guys who are thrilled they finally own a car that has a third brake light, a custom steering wheel can be a fun addition to their Honda/Acura. Prices range from under $75 (Grant GT-type wheels) to more expensive items, like a Mugen or Personal Fittipaldi. Racers who need to turn the wheel during the course of racing can benefit from a steering wheel that

Right
What can we say? What better way to play Grand Turismo than from behind the wheel of your own (parked) Integra. All the sounds from this particular Playstation game are piped through the car's high-watt stereo system.

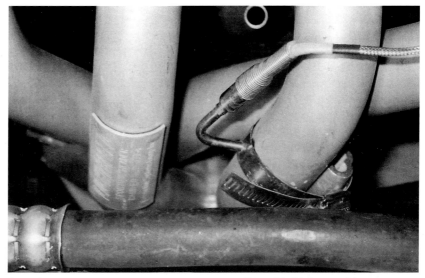

An exhaust temperature sensor connects easily to this Lightspeed header.

Tenzo high watt driving lights add some distinction to the grille of this 1998 Civic DX.

is not a perfect circle, or has some flat spots to help determine which way is up.

Last but not least, high-power stereos, shift knobs, and drilled aluminum pedals can really personalize your vehicle, but all fall into the category of "fun," nonessential items. Of all the fun interior modifications that have been made over the years, none can hold a candle to the onboard Sony Playstation that some car owners have installed. Think about it. What better place to play Grand Turismo than the cockpit of your (parked) Integra GSR?

Chapter 16

Modifications on a Budget

Now that you have had a chance to review the modifications that can help your car go faster and handle better, you are faced with a choice. Which do you do first? Chapter 1 advises that you set a budget, and make decisions based on these priorities. To illustrate this point, here are clusters of modifications that should be done, given the amount of money you have to spend.

This will vary based on how you want to use your car, so two different areas have been identified: *Dual Duty* (street during the week—mild autocross/drag on the weekend) and *Full Race* (Solo I, II, roadracing, drag). Under each category, several budget amounts will be listed: Low Buck (under $500); Moderate (under $2,000), and Serious Project (under $3,500). Labor costs have not been considered, since they vary greatly. Most of these changes require only a moderate amount of mechanical expertise. Those who plan to go all out, or do not need to consider a financial budget, may benefit from reviewing the modifications listed in the Serious Project category to help set priorities.

Dual Duty

Do you need your car to get you back and forth to work during the week, but also want to play with it a little on the weekend?

When it comes to priorities, suspension modifications belong at the top of the list. As nicely as Honda and Acuras handle, there is significant room for improvement, especially in correcting understeer. Performance springs, like these Eibach units, should therefore be a primary consideration when planning out a hop-up project. *Diamond Star Creative Group*

Then you need a dual-duty project car. Often, serious racing modifications will render your car a pain in the @$$ to drive on the street. This section is dedicated to providing hop-up alternatives that will work on the track, without compromising comfort on the street. In other words, there needs to be a healthy balance between form and function.

You will not end up with a championship race car by following these guidelines, but you will be able to preserve your car's street integrity. There are many possible scenarios; these modifications will add to the overall fun in both street driving and weekend amateur racing, even though the modifications you choose prohibit you from competing in the "stock" classes.

Internal engine modifications or rebuilds are not addressed in these sections, as they can completely eat up your budget. I have

145

been extremely competitive with a 1985 CRX that shows over 100,000 miles on the odometer. The original bearings were checked and tolerances were measured during a ring job, and they were still within factory specs. Don't fix the block unless it is broken. If you are starting with an engine that has poor compression, then new rings need to be fitted, which will seriously affect your budget.

Hence the importance in starting with the right car.

The Low Buck Hop-Up ($500)

Your goal is to improve both handling and straight-line performance with a budget of $500. Without access to used performance parts, this can be a difficult assignment. Assuming you purchase all the parts new, there are two that should be given first priority. Low-cost performance springs can usually be found for under $300 per set. Remember to get stiffer springs in the rear. For the torsion bar 1984–1987 Hondas and the 1986–1989 Integras, all you really need are rear springs and a rear sway bar, which can be had for the same money. The rear springs will lower the car, and you can crank down the torsion bars by hand (see chapter 3).

With $200 left, an air velocity intake is the best bang for the buck when it comes to increasing horsepower (average gain is five

Newer Hondas and Integras, like this third generation Integra (top), make excellent dual-duty cars. They provide comfort and reliability during the week, and can be competitive in autocross/drag on the weekend. On the other hand, full-blown race cars are usually stripped, have very stiff suspensions, and are not very comfortable to drive on the street. Therefore, older Hondas and Integras, like this first generation CRX (bottom), make great full-blown race cars. It's not financially practical to strip a late-model Honda or Acura, but the older cars have depreciated to the point where you will not incur as much of a financial loss by rendering the vehicle useless for the street.

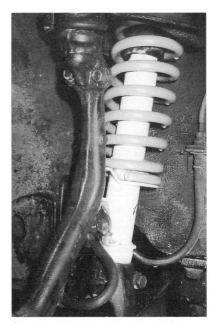

Springs, like these distributed by Progress, are a good choice for a budget hop-up.

horsepower). Fuel-injected cars should review chapter 5 for additional tips. A K&N reusable powerfilter will add between one and three horsepower and costs only about $50, allowing for additional suspension mods. Road racers with carburetted cars should consider an aftermarket Weber and high flow air cleaner to improve horsepower. That will likely put you over the budget by $100, so instead of competition rear springs, you may want to consider cutting the stock springs. If you want to spend all $500 on handling, then cutting the springs should still leave enough money to buy a rear sway bar. If you do this, then you may be able to afford a set of stiffer nonadjustable struts/shocks. This is a good complement to suspensions utilizing cut springs. KYB, Tokico, and Koni all offer a less expensive alternative to the high priced, fully adjustable systems.

Weekend drag racers should consider these combinations, as they emphasize speed over handling. Buying a cam (SOHC non-VTEC engines) plus an air velocity intake ($200) and a rear sway bar is one possibility. Cutting one or two coils off of the springs will both lower and stiffen the car, but is only recommended if you can't wait to buy competition springs. Polyurethane bushings may be too rough for the street, but they are a cheap way to improve handling responsiveness instantly.

If you have access to used parts (junkyards, internet), then you can get much more bang for the buck. Since many drivers are switching to the new cold air induction systems, they may be selling their first air velocity intake for less than $100. Rear sway bars can also be found in junkyards on Acura models that will fit the Honda cars that were denied this feature by the factory. The same

Dennis Witt blasting up the opening quarter-mile straightaway on his way up to the top of Giant's Despair. Hillclimbing has some of the strangest classes encountered in amateur racing. "Smod" refers to "street modified," street legal cars that are allowed major engine and suspension modifications. This 1985 CRX (Fred) has over 100,000 miles on the engine block, the last 10,000 of which was pure racing mileage. The car still has its original bearings. (That statement will surely jinx the future life of this engine block.)

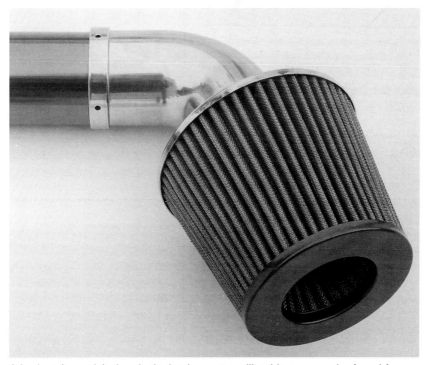

A budget (generic) air velocity intake system, like this one, can be found for under $100. Call your favorite parts distributor (NOPI, etc.) and ask if they have an alternative to the more expensive parts.

goes for springs. On 1984–1987 Hondas, rear springs from a station wagon are stiffer than the Civic/CRX setup. One of the best handling CRXs in the country contended for a National Autocross Championship using the cut rear springs from a Civic station wagon.

Depending on how you spend your money, you may want to consider getting the fuel injectors cleaned and/or balanced (see chapter 5). This can really benefit cars with high mileage, as well as older (1980s) Honda and Acura models. Marren Motorsports and

RC Engineering both offer this service. Often, you may need to replace an injector, so the cost can vary from around $125 to $400, depending on how inefficient your injectors are.

Moderate Hop-Up (Under $2,000)

With some extra money in the budget, the next priority for autocrossers should be to upgrade your struts/shocks. Tokico Illuminas and Konis, in addition to being externally adjustable, carry a lifetime guarantee. You can send back a pair of rusted worn out shocks, and they will send you a pair of new or refurbished replacements! Expect to pay around $500.

That leaves another $1,000 in the budget, assuming you spent the

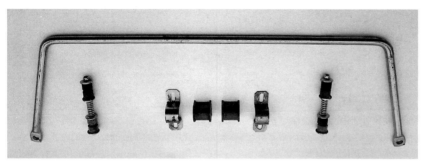

Even a cheap rear sway bar like this one (under $80 through J.C. Whitney) will reduce rear body roll as well as stiffen the rear, to help induce oversteer

Mike Louie's 1993 Civic is a good example of a moderate hop-up project car. Mike has struts, springs, wheels, and a ceramic-coated header. With the money he saved on a brand name air velocity intake (his is homemade, and works nicely), he could afford other modifications, such as the Neuspeed strut tower brace.

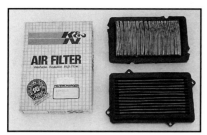

K&N makes high flow air filters for most fuel-injected Hondas and Acuras. They replace the stock filter perfectly, and add 1 to 3 horsepower without voiding the factory warranty. The stock filter is pictured above, and the higher flow, washable K&N unit is below.

A set of good race wheels and new race tires can run as high as $1,300. Pictured is a 13x7 Duralight with a Hoosier 20/8.0/13 cantilever slick. Buying used wheels can nearly cut that price in half.

For the Solo II Street Touring class, where "R" rated tires may not be allowed, larger-diameter wheels with low profile tires will improve handling by decreasing sidewall flex. These Konigs, however, will put you over the $2,000 budget.

first $500 as in the "low buck" hop-up. Depending upon your needs and priorities, and which expert you consult, there could be many recommendations presented to you. More power is often the choice of both car owners and part distributors. The problem with more power is that you will likely not be able to take advantage of it on the autocross course. So if your preference is street performance, a hotter cam with an adjustable cam timing gear is one way to go. A header can range from between $100 for an inexpensive unit (Pace Setter) to nearly $400 for the DC Sports unit. You save weight and make your car breath better at the same time. Certainly, replacing the exhaust system would be advised by this point in the project, and would also capture at least five horsepower.

None of these options, however, should be the next priority for the dual-driver car. In order to take full advantage of all of the modifications performed so far, the best way to spend the final $1,000 is to buy an extra set of wheels and race tires. Whether you are a weekend autocrosser, do time trials, or hang out at the drag strip, your times will improve substantially if you have

the capability to put on a set of race wheels and tires for your weekend fun. Absolutely nothing in racing feels better than getting the traction you need, when you need it. In autocrossing, it is worth an average of two seconds per lap on a one-minute course over your stock setup. The time drop is not

so dramatic in drag racing, but ETs will instantly respond to better grip off the line. Refer to chapter 4 for more details. It is important not to skimp on the wheels, since a good set can last a lifetime of autocrossing. Shortly after buying cheap steel wheels, you may begin to wish you had opted for the

This project C-Rex is a good example of a dual-duty car that can be driven to work during the week, and raced (autocross/drag) on weekends.

Full race vehicles stress form over function. The interior of Bob Redlack's Civic is designed to quickly give him the information he needs at a glance. Not much room for a passenger, as the ignition and coil block leg room. With no radio, a copilot would have to rely on oil, water, and exhaust temperature gauges for entertainment. With the g-force that this car is capable of, "hanging on for dear life" would likely be the only thing on a passenger's mind. Note the high-tech aftermarket fuel injection controller next to the tach. Even though there is way more than $20,000 invested in this nationally competitive Civic, it has been on the market for around $10,000.

lighter, wider aftermarket 1, 2, or 3 piece alloys.

Finally, soloists should spend any leftover funds on camber plates (torsion bar cars) or camber adjusters. If the wallet is empty you can always make your own camber plates. For late-model Hondas and Acuras, however, it is not a good idea to elongate the control arm anchor bolt holes. Wait until you can buy the appropriate aftermarket part (see chapter 3). On the other hand, front and rear stress bars do make great homemade projects.

Serious Project (Under $3,500)

When it comes to Hondas and Acuras, $3,500 is often enough to build yourself a nationally competitive autocross car. In the mid-1990s, driver extraordinaire Randy Pobst nearly piloted a second generation CRX to a national title in CSP, one of SCCA's most competitive classes. If not for a downed pylon, the title would have been his. Not bad for a car that had just been fitted with a junkyard engine.

An additional $1,500 seems like a lot of money, although as your car gets more and more competitive, performance seems to come at greater costs. In other words, the first $2,000 could get your car 7/10ths of the way, but to get the next 3/10ths may cost you a lot more money. The trick is to not go crazy. The goal of this section is to retain the use of your vehicle for the street. There are many performance parts that you could install that would compromise this plan.

There are several options available, and again they have to do with your priorities. For example, $1,500 is not enough money to buy a supercharger, nor will it allow for an aftermarket fuel injection conversion. (I wouldn't do that again, even if I were paid.) If you have a carburetted car, there is no good way to spend this money and keep your car as a daily driver, because your fuel delivery system will be on this next hit list. Dual carbs just don't cut it for the street.

But first it's time to go for that header and exhaust. Spend the money on a quality coated header, and you won't be disappointed. The Lightspeed or DC systems are great, but any of the top names can meet your needs, so shop around. At best, it will set you back $400, unless you opt for a cheaper system, like Pace Setter ($100). Next, the exhaust should be upgraded (see chapter 7). You will spend anywhere from $350 to $500 for a good exhaust system. These changes alone will net you 5 horsepower, depending on your car.

With around $600 left, and without sacrificing streetability, the following modifications should be considered. Bigger injectors will complete the circle you started in phase one when an air velocity intake was added. With the new header and exhaust in place, you have air entering and leaving much more efficiently, and your computer may not be able to take full advantage of these changes. Chapter 5 addresses this modification, and you will use up most of the remaining money in the process. There may be enough left for a Monster throttle body,

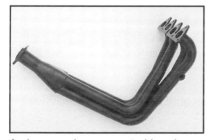

An inexpensive noncoated header, like this S&S unit (under $150) will do a good job at efficiently releasing exhaust gasses, and can save money in your hop-up budget.

but this step should never be taken until these other components are in place. Depending on what you may have left, an ignition system would be a good choice at this point in the project, as they can cost as little as $150. Make sure it has a rev limiter (and set it at 7,000 rpm or lower), so that your friends who ask to codrive your car don't blow the engine.

Weekend drag racers could easily install an NOS system for under $600. Horsepower would be on demand for the strip, without compromising streetability. The other option is to beg and borrow (don't steal) to buy a supercharger. You will need at least $2,500 for the complete kit (depending on your car), but for those that have one, there is no substitute. Look back over your budget to try and cut corners wherever you can, then call Jackson Racing. You may not have the nicest wheels on the road, but when you hit the throttle, that burst of low-end torque will make your day.

One last thing to consider for drag racers. The extra 40 ponies you get from adding a supercharger will end up costing you approximately $60 per horsepower. If you get lucky at a junkyard, and buy a group of your friends some pizza and beer, you may be able to improve on that power-to-wallet ratio by performing an engine transplant. For streetability purposes, however, don't get too radical. Stick to the straightforward bolt-in applications that don't end up making your car too nose heavy.

Full Race

Often, building a no-holds-barred, full race car need not be more expensive than a dual-duty project. Unlike the parameters described above, there are significantly greater differences in budget allocation, depending upon the

An adjustable spring perch suspension system like this one, which incorporates Carrera springs and Tokico shocks, will improve the handling of your car to the point where you can be regionally competitive. The best part about using Carrera springs is that you can select from dozens of spring rates. How do you know which are best for your car? Simply call a company like OPM, designer of this system, and ask. Be prepared to give weights for your particular Honda/Acura, and describe what you want to do with your car—racing, street, dual duty.

racing venues: autocross, roadracing, and drag. Since efforts need not be taken to ensure vehicle street worthiness, attention can be focused on all-out performance and handling without concern for comfort. In other words, function takes precedence over form.

The Low Buck Hop-Up ($500)

Many of the same priorities outlined in the "low buck" dual-duty section earlier in this chapter also apply here. Autocrossers need to spend their $500 on improving the car's handling before concentrating on speed. Stiffer springs

The interior of a full race car is pure no-nonsense practicality. At extremely high g-forces (many of these racing Hondas and Acuras can easily pull 1.5-plus Gs), it becomes hard to stay put in a conventional seat. This Sparco seat costs under $250, and weighs only 12 pounds.

and/or torsion bars plus a rear sway bar will likely eat up half of this low buck budget.

Roadracers, on the other hand, will find a $500 budget too restrictive to allow actual track competition. All of the spending needs to concentrate on safety, as SCCA rules require a full cage, legal harness, a fire bottle, etc. If just focusing on the vehicle itself, and ignoring for now the driver safety gear requirements, a full roll cage will wipe out your first $500. To be practical, a minimal roadracing budget needs to be at least $600 to $700, just to be able to pass the initial SCCA technical inspection. Conversely, one good thing about building a full roadrace project is that relative power can be increased simply by taking parts *off* of the car. So even if all you have left in your budget is $1.99, this task can easily be accomplished. Depending on the class in which you plan to compete, removing all nonfunctional items will decrease weight by over 200 pounds. This

also applies to an autocross car; however, you should read the SCCA competition rules before getting out the blow torch.

On the other hand, building a competent, low buck drag racer is possible even with a $500 spending limit. That's because your focus will be on speed as opposed to handling. As you have read in previous chapters, there are some inexpensive ways to boost power. However, with a $500 spending limit you will not be able to turn 13-second quarter-mile times in any Honda or Acura. You will also experience a law of decreasing returns as the amount of money you spend increases. In other words, the first $500 you put into the car will net you the most bang for the buck, but after that, the cost of speed will increase at a higher rate. So the faster your car is already, the more cash needs to be coughed up in order to see additional drops in ETs.

To get things started, a 5-horsepower improvement can be realized by adding an air velocity

intake. With the next $300, a performance camshaft with an adjustable cam timing gear (non-VTEC engines only) can net another 10-plus horsepower if your car is in generally good health. Remember, a hot cam will not help a sickly engine. Then, gather up your change and get down to the local muffler shop. Cut off the exhaust system from the engine side of the car and have a pipe welded on so that it exits out the side of the car in front of the passenger rear wheel, or run it straight out the back. Low-end torque may suffer, but when you get the rpm up, there will be a significant gain in power. A lot of weight will also be saved in this process. If you are not planning to go to phase two in the future, then you should get some type of cheap muffler installed so that some amount of back pressure can be maintained.

Moderate Hop-Up (Under $2,000)

Autocrossers will still primarily be following the formula for dual-duty cars, but they can save money by opting for a nonadjustable stiffer shock or strut ($200–$250), instead of Tokico Illuminas. A full race Solo II car traditionally competes in classes that don't require DOT-approved tires, so a set of lightly used slicks ($200) will make room in the budget for other goodies, such as a noncoated header ($150).

The next priority is to buy the right wheels for your class (about $500). Refer to chapter 4 for suggestions. There will be plenty of cash left over to fabricate a cheap exhaust system (as above) with a nice muffler at the end to provide the back pressure and low-end torque you need for autocross. A Supertrapp ($150) can be tuned right at the track to add a little torque where you need it, depending on

Although he had the pole, California native Steve Cook's 2G CRX ran into problems on the first lap of the 1998 SCCA Valvoline Runoffs and he wasn't able to repeat as national champ in GT-4. The budget on this race car is completely off any scale in this book.

the course. With the remaining $250, a hot cam will provide easy bolt-on power. If money is budgeted properly, $2,000 can get you most of the way to a regionally competitive Solo II car.

Roadracers will finally have some money to play with when moving from a low buck project (above) to this level of modification. Improved handling needs to be the first area on which to concentrate, as the goal is to make the chassis as tight as possible. The parts needed and their costs are similar to those used in Solo II (shocks/struts, springs, rear sway bar, bushings). This will consume much of the extra $1,500 that was added to the low buck modification budget. Four extra rims should be purchased from a local

boneyard, as they will come in handy when mounting a set of race tires. You will probably only be able to afford steel wheels at this time. A good set of roadrace compound race tires is the final expense you will be able to make in this level of modification (see chapter 4). At least with competitive tires you can get out on the race track and try out the new suspension. Power improvements will have to wait for later.

Drag racers, on the other hand, will again put power above all other considerations. Once you get going very fast, you'll need to pay more attention to keeping the car pointed in the right direction as it zips down the quarter-mile.

In the previous section, the goal was to make the car breathe

better, so now you should concentrate on giving it some extra fuel. Bigger injectors and a Monster throttle body will consume $500-plus dollars, and more for a six-banger.

Now it's decision time. If you plan on going all the way, then stop right here and save the rest of the $1,000 for the next section. However, if $2,000 is all you want to spend, and you want the lowest ETs possible, then a nitrous system is the answer. For most Hondas and Acuras, the cost is under $500 for a complete system (NOPI). A serious DOT-approved race tire is the next item on the list, and will eat up the rest of the $400–$500 left in the budget. DOT is the way to go with this level of budget because you will likely

153

need to be driving your car on the street to get to the event. If you can afford it, buy an extra set of wheels for either your street tires, or for the new race rubber, to cut down on wear when you are driving to the event. They aren't pretty, but steel wheels are cheap. Since this project car will not be used as a dual driver, you probably want to use your stock alloys for the track, since that's where you will be using your car the most. The alloys are lighter, and look better. The steel wheels can then be mounted with street tires for getting you to and from the track.

Serious Project (Under $3,500)

Autocrossers now will be going for serious power. Although some Solo II cars use turbo and superchargers, they are not very popular in the sport, since you are required to compete in the modified class. For street prepared, this extra $1,500 needs to go for aftermarket fuel injection (see chapter 10). With the way the rules are written, it is the only way to become seriously competitive.

If competition in the prepared class is the goal, then you will need dual carbs to be a contender, unless your car is already fuel-injected. In that case, additional modifications to the fuel system will cost you a weight penalty, so additional suspension modifications become the priority. In a fully prepared race car, taking weight off of your car can actually cost money. Replacing the stock hood with a much lighter fiberglass unit will cost $500 or more, and window glass should be replaced with Lexan.

The rest of the money should go to cylinder head modifications, and if not purchased during the moderate phase, a camshaft-sprocket combination (all legal for the prepared classes).

Stock class competition can also be expensive, as the price for an extra set of factory alloys plus DOT race tires can often cost more for the stock competitor than for the other classes. But check out the rules for your class before getting started with a $3,500 budget. You will likely have some money left over.

I will not address the SCCA national class cost preparation, as it is financially prohibitive for all of

A Jackson supercharger system costs between $2,300 and $2,800, depending on your model. Unlike a turbo system, it can boost horsepower by 40 to 50 percent without sacrificing low-end torque.

these budgets. As for the IT road-racer, in addition to what was purchased with the $2,000 budget, the next item to consider is the carburetor. Replacing that stock three-barrel carb with a Weber (about $400) will make a big difference in performance, and is allowed under IT rules. If your car is fuel-injected, then money can go to buying a racing seat, and to do some internal modifications to the cylinder head and intake system, such as porting, polishing, and port matching.

Drag racers who saved $1,000 from the previous section can add that to the extra $1,500 from this section to install a turbo or supercharging system. This is usually the most rewarding way to go drag racing, given a limited budget. The other possibility is to search the engine transplant section to see what may fit into your car. Some of the engines listed may fall in this budget amount.

The Last Word

Improving your car's performance while sticking to a budget can often be a difficult thing. There are many decisions to be made based on the priorities you have set. Once you choose how you will use your car (street, dual duty, or full race), these decisions become easier. Don't give in to pressure from friends who may influence you to buy parts that are either over your budget, or

"Eat My Rust" is a statement that is usually made by someone who cares more about function than form. Full time race vehicles often fall under this category, because your car's body will typically sustain damage either by making contact with those pesky orange pylons (Solo II), rocks and trees (Solo I), guardrails (drag), or another competitor's car (IT and roadracing). After pounding out the body damage all week sustained from the previous weekend of racing, it seems futile to get out the car wax on Friday.

that you simply don't need for your application. They may simply be trying to obtain validation to justify the fact that they just wasted their money on a new "cool" part that serves no function. And don't give in to easy credit. If a particular part is over the budget you set, instead of picking up your Mastercard, pick up your mouse and search the net for used performance parts. If

you have read this book and still have performance questions, feel free to visit *The Honda/Acura Performance Handbook* web page (www.hondabook.com) and ask. We will try to answer your questions and keep you from wasting valuable resources on parts that either don't work, or that you don't really need. Good luck, and save the racing for the track, not the street!

Appendix

Resources

Performance Parts and Services

Gude Performance (bullfrog cams, turbo kits, reprogramming ECUs, fiberglass hoods, etc.)
28780 Vacation Drive
Canyon Drive, CA 92587
(909) 244-3533
www.gude.com

J. G. Engine Dynamics
431 South Raymond Avenue, No. 102
Alhambra, CA 91803
(626) 281-5326

Jackson Racing (superchargers plus lots of Honda/Acura stuff)
440 Rutherford Street
Goleta, CA 93117
(888) 888-4079
www.jacksonracing.com

AEM (Advanced Engine Management)
200 Corporate Pointe
Culver City, CA 90230
(310) 258-0030
www.a-e-m.com

Stillen
3176 Airway Boulevard
Costa Mesa, CA 92626
(714) 755-6688
orders only: (800) 711-4128
www.stillen.com

Lightspeed Racing
6644 San Fernando Road
Glendale, CA 91201
(818) 956-7933

Comptech
4717 Golden Foothill Parkway
El Dorado Hills, CA 95762
(916) 939-9118
www.comptechusa.com

King Motorsports (MUGEN distributor)
105 East Main Street
Sullivan, WI 53178
(414) 593-2800
www.king-motorsports.com

NOPI (Number One Parts Inc.) (sponsor of the NOPI Nationals in September)
486 Main Street
Forest Park, GA 30050
(800) 277-6674
www.nopi.com

Strano Performance Parts
68 White Street
Brookville, PA 15825
Parts: (800) 729-1831
Tech Advice: (814) 849-3417
www.stranoparts.com

Magazines

Grassroots Motorsports Magazine
425 Parque Drive
Ormond Beach, FL 32174
(904) 673-4148
www.grmotorsports.com

Turbo Magazine
9887 Hamilton Avenue
Huntington Beach, CA 92646
(800) 94-TURBO
www.turbomagazine.com

Wheels and Tires

TSW Wheels
(800) 658-0765
www.tswnet.com

Taylor Wheels
(515) 276-0992
www.taylorcorporation.com

BBS Wheels
(800) 422-7972
e-mail: marketing@bbs-usa.com

Tire Rack
771 W. Chippewa Avenue
South Bend, IN 46614
(888) 981-3952
www.tirerack.com

John Berget Tire (used and new race tires)
(414) 740-0180

Mid-Atlantic Motorsports (race tires)
(248) 852-5006

Clutch and Transmission Components

Autotech Sport Tuning (Quaife differentials)
(800) 553-1055
www.autotech.com

Centerforce Performance Clutch
2266 Crosswind Drive
Prescott, AZ 86301
(800) 899-6439
www.centerforce.com

Safety Equipment
Racer Wholesale (helmets, suits
    plus lots of racing stuff)
(800) 886-RACE (7223)

Safe-Quip (racing seat belts and
    harnesses)
(800) 247-4260

Kirk Racing Products (roll cages
    and bars)
(205) 823-6025
e-mail: info@kirkracing.com

Autopower Industries (roll cages
    and bars)
3424 Pickett Street
San Diego, CA 92110
(619) 297-3300

Solotime (graphics, safety
    equipment, K&N filters)
(316) 683-3803
solotime@southwind.net

Ignition Systems
MSD ignitions
1490 Henry Brennan Drive
El Paso, TX 79936
(915) 857-5200
www.msdignition.com

Electromotive (ignitions)
9131 Centreville Road
Manassas, VA 20110
(703) 331-0100
www.electromotive-inc.com

Jacobs Electronics
500 North Baird Street
Midland, TX 79701
(800) 627-8800
www.jacobselectronics.com

NOLOGY
7360 Trade Street
San Diego, CA 92121
(619) 578-4688
www.nology.com

HKS USA, Inc.
2355 Mira Mar Avenue
Long Beach, CA 90815
(562) 494-8068
www.hksusa.com

Injection and Carburetion
RACETECH USA (Simple Digital
    Systems programmable EFI
    kits + turbo kits)
(403) 274-0154
www.sdsefi.com

TWM Induction (intake
    manifolds, throttle bodies,
    ITG filters, adjustable fuel
    pressure regulators)
(805) 967-9478
www.twminduction.com

Marren Motorsports
412 Roosevelt Drive
Derby, CT 06418
(203) 732-4565
www.injector.com

RC Engineering
1728 Border Avenue
Torrance, CA 90501
(310) 320-2277
www.rceng.com

K & N Engineering (air filters and
    intakes)
PO Box 1329
Riverside, CA 92502
(800) 858-3333

Overseas Distributing (Weber
    carbs)
(604) 879-6288

Suspension Components
Tokico
1330 Storm Parkway
Torrance, CA 90501
(310) 535-4934

Ingalls Engineering (camber
    correction kits)
(800) 641-9795
www.ingallseng.com

Carrera (shocks, struts, and springs)
(770) 451-8811
www.carrerashocks.com

Koni North America
1961A International Way
Hebron, KY 41048
(800) 994-KONI

OPM (Optimum Performance
    Machines)
Atlanta, GA
(770) 886-8199

Exhaust Systems
Kirker Performance
    (manufacturers of Supertrapp)
(216) 265-8400

GReddy Performance
9 Vanderbilt Avenue
Irvine, CA 92718
(800) GREDDY2

DC Sports
286 Winfield Circle
Corona, CA 91720
(909) 734-2030
www.dcsports.com

Thermal Research and
    Development (stainless steel
    exhaust systems)
(818) 998-4865

Pace Setter Performance Products
    (headers, quick shift kits)
(602)233-1818
www.pacesetterexhaust.com

Engines
HASport
Brian Gillespie
(602) 470-0065
www.hasport.com

New and Used Parts

Eartley's Motorworld (one of the largest distributors of new Honda/Acura OEM parts)
Wilkes-Barre, PA
(717) 820-6861

Matta Motors (new and used Honda/Acura parts)
Glassport, PA
(412) 672-6202

Miscellaneous

Auto Meter Products, Inc.
413 West Elm Street
Sycamore, IL 60178
(815) 895-8141

Diamond Star Creative Group (advertising agency specializing in representing companies in the import performance market)
Alan Paradise
(619) 463-5100

Personal (steering wheels)
(800) 826-2734

Carbotech Engineering (brake pads and shoes, cryogenically hardened rotors)
(954) 493-9669

John Wynn (motorsport and commercial photography)
(610) 692-8784
www.wynnphoto.com

Trenton Brakes Corp. (low cost Honda/Acura brakes and rotors)
1242 Princeton Avenue
Trenton, NJ 08638
(609) 989-8600
www.trentonbrakes.com

Places to Go and Things to Do

Sports Car Club of America (SCCA)
(303) 694-7222
www.scca.org

The Mid-Ohio School (drivers school and home of the Runoffs)
(614) 793-4615
www.midohio.com

Honda Power Page
www.hondapower.net

Honda Links Page
www.lycaeum.com/Honda.htm

Unofficial Honda Accord Page
www.li.net

Hybrid Page
www.hybrid.honda-perf.org

The Prelude Web Site
Ed Sawyer, owner
www.webcom.com/wv/prelude

CRX Performance Page
heart.engr.csulb.edu/~jmathews

CRX Resource Page
resource.crx.org

CRX Page
kumo.swcp.com/synth/crx

3G Prelude Page
dnai.com/~jnarvaez/prelude

Honda Civic Performance Page
www.uneaqdesigns.com/civic

Integra Registry
www.integra.vtec.net

Hybrid Civics
www.geocities.com/MotorCity/Speedway/9671/other.html

Great Automotive Page (including Honda/Acura) and online magazine
www.autofan.com

iCHiBAN Motorsports (East Coast drag club)
www.ichibanmotorsports.com

Index